MESSIER

HOCKEY'S DRAGONSLAYER

by

Rick Carpiniello

Foreword by
Brian Leetch

McGregor
PUBLISHING
TAMPA, FLORIDA

Library of Congress Cataloging-in-Publication Data
Carpiniello, Rick, 1956–
    Messier : hockey's dragonslayer / Rick Carpiniello : foreword by
Brian Leetch.
      p. cm.
    ISBN 0-9653846–9–1 (tradepaper)
    1. Messier, Mark, 1961–   . 2. Hockey players--Canada Biography.
I. Title.
GV848.5.M43C37   1999
796.962'092--dc21
[B]
                                          99-36864
                                             CIP

Photos by Bruce Bennett Studios

Interior design and typesetting by Sue Knopf, Graffolio

Essay entitled "What It Takes To Be No. 1" by Vince Lombardi
used with permission by Estate of Vince Lombardi
by CMG Worldwide, Indianapolis, IN.

Published by McGregor Publishing, Inc., Tampa, Florida.
Canadian edition simultaneously published by Stoddart Limited.

Printed and bound in the United States of America.

CONTENTS

For Maureen,
my inspiration

FOREWORD

by Brian Leetch

My introduction to Mark Messier wasn't exactly friendly or pleasant. The first time we met, well, it left a mark and it taught me a lesson.

It was 1988, my rookie season with the New York Rangers. I had played for Team USA in the 1988 Olympics and joined the Rangers with seventeen games left in the season. One of those games was at Madison Square Garden against the Edmonton Oilers, a team that was headed for its fourth Stanley Cup in five years.

I didn't know a lot about Mark. I knew about the Oilers and the way they played. I knew a lot more about Wayne Gretzky and, because I'm a defenseman, Paul Coffey. Being from the east, I wasn't as familiar with the other guys, and Mark wasn't as prominent in my mind.

So when we were getting ready to play the Oilers at the Garden, some of the older guys on our team were saying, "Messier will take bad penalties." They were saying, "Hit Messier. He'll retaliate and take bad penalties. Try to get him off of the ice."

I remember the puck coming up along the left boards. Mark was coming the other way. He didn't go for the puck. I was going for the puck. He just speared me right in the gut. Got me pretty good. He didn't knock the wind out of me, but I took a dive, went down in the corner, and waited and waited. I stayed down, trying to draw a penalty.

The referee finally blew the whistle, but he didn't call a penalty. I had a huge gash across my stomach. That was the first time I ever faked an injury and the last time I ever faked an injury. It was embarrassing lying there on the ice. But it was funny that it was Mark. It's funny when I look back that my first encounter with Mark wasn't off the ice, or shaking his hand or anything. It was getting speared by him. We still laugh about that today. The first time Mark really made an impression on me was in the 1990 playoffs, in Game Four against Chicago. I watched him when he took over that series. The way he skated right through people was unbelievable. Until that series, I had never realized how good, how dominant, he was. I had never watched a man with that type of strength take over finesse-wise, too, and have the impact he did. The way he skated through the middle with the puck, it was like he almost didn't make any moves. He bulled his way through. He willed his way through. Since then, I would always keep an eye on what was going on with him out there.

Until 1991, I still had never met him. We had just finished playing against Canada and Messier in the Canada Cup that fall, and there were strong rumors that he was coming to the Rangers. We traded for him before the second game of that season. Nothing would ever be the same.

My roommate on the road had been Brian Mullen, but Mullen was traded to San Jose during the off-season. I was still without a roommate, and I heard that the coaches and front office had decided that I would room with Mark.

I was kind of interested in seeing how that was going to turn out. Off the ice, it was really easy. My routine was pretty simple. When we were on the road, I'd get to the room, watch TV, order room service, and get ready for the game. I wasn't really into going out to eat. I'd be too tired. Mark came in and it was pretty much the same thing. He'd think I was going to go out for dinner, then I'd ask him, "What are you doing for dinner?" He'd say, "I don't care." We'd lie there for a little while watching TV, and he'd go, "I'm thinking of getting room service," and I'd say, "Yeah, I feel like room service too." It just made it easy.

He didn't really like going outside because of how well known he was. In a lot of cities, it was an ordeal for him to go out of the hotel, especially in Canada. Besides, he was usually too focused on the game. So it was good. It was never uncomfortable where anybody felt they had to initiate anything. Right from the start, it was pretty easy to have him as a roommate. Obviously, the more you get to know somebody, the more you talk about different things. Your talk goes from superficial to more serious: personal things, team, family. When Mark came in, I was the only one living in the city. He said, "I've got to check that place out." I said, "You'll love it." He moved to the city, too. That made it easy, because we commuted together all the time, from the city to our practice facility in Rye, New York.

We became close quickly and easily, too. We'd get up in the morning, and neither of us felt like talking much. We'd turn on Howard Stern on the radio, or flip on some music. If he was driving, I'd grab the paper, or if I was driving, he'd grab one, and we'd get a little update on what was going on. We'd get to practice, go to lunch afterwards. It was pretty easy.

People ask me all the time what I learned from Mark. Mostly, what Mark taught all of us was how to carry yourself off the ice, how to treat people with respect, how to include everybody on the team in everything. What helped me on the ice, more than any lesson, was that Mark was the best player I've ever played with. His speed opened up things for me.

He also taught me this: When you get to the NHL, your failures become magnified. I took the mistakes and the things I did wrong very personally. I felt like I was letting everybody down. I'd be really down, and he helped me to just forget it and be ready for the next shift or the next game.

What he told me a lot was that when you have a game you're not happy with, or you make a mistake that maybe cost you a goal or something, you feel bad for your team. He'd say over and over that most times the best plays are riding the border of being the worst plays. He said to try and be the type of player that tries to make the big play, the play that very often borders on being a big mistake. He said, "That's the type of player you are. You've got to keep doing that. We need you to keep doing that." He helped me remember that the goal was to win, and for me to try to be the guy who was trying to be the difference. There are plenty of guys to make the safe play. It's going to backfire, he said. There are times it's not going to always turn out. But keep doing it, and more often than not you're going to be helping. When you have somebody like that who you respect and who has been through everything, it's easy to listen.

Right off the bat, that helped me feel more comfortable around him. You're never trying to make a bad play. You feel bad when it does happen. But it helped me to keep moving forward.

The rest was just learning situations, learning through him: Off the ice, the way he dealt with his family, the way he dealt with situations in restaurants. The way he did things first class, being respectful and keeping a distance from certain situations. Then he'd say, "Let's go play and have fun."

But again, what helped me most was how good he was on the ice.

When Mark arrived in 1991, I don't think anyone had an idea what to expect. It was more, "Sit back and let's see." We couldn't believe he was on our team. Before that, everybody on our team sort of looked at each other as equals, and all of a sudden we had somebody on the next level. It wasn't like, "Let's get in line and follow." It was more like, "Let's watch and see what's going to happen. Let's see what this guy is all about."

He did the greatest thing. He tried to sit back and fit in and be quiet. He didn't try to say, "I'm the guy." He tried to get a read on all the players and personalities, right down to the equipment guys, and just see how the whole organization is set up. He looked at everything—even the team doctors—and how everybody was working together for the same thing.

Finally, at one point during the first season, he stood up and said, "I haven't said anything because I was new and I was trying to learn everything." Then he said, "This can't happen. We can't be doing this or that at certain stages." The way he spoke was great, the way he got his thoughts across so clearly. It was amazing for anybody. For a player to be able to express the thoughts he had was great. A lot of guys can figure out over the long course what's the right thing that needs to be done, but to be able to come out at the key time and say it is very unusual.

He came to the organization to change everything about losing. The Rangers had lost for fifty years before he came, and he said there's got to be a reason, and that was the big challenge he was looking at. In 1994, we won the Stanley Cup. The first Stanley Cup for the Rangers franchise since 1940.

Fifty-four years. That's a long time. There were Rangers fans who thought this was never going to happen. You'd see the reaction with each round that we got further into the playoffs. You'd feel the whole city tightening up the closer we got. It was something the way he did it. He was the main guy in the Eastern Conference championship series against the New Jersey Devils, a wild series we won in double over-time in Game Seven. It was amazing. Then, after we won the Cup, Mark finally took advantage of his celebrity status. He didn't miss any-thing after that—MTV, Letterman. He did all that stuff. That's when he did enjoy himself, for sure.

A lot of what Mark taught us had been taught to him by Glen Sather, the general manager and former coach of the Edmonton Oilers. Sather made a big impression on all of the Oilers. Mark said that over and over. Sather taught them a lot about how you carry yourself in a first-class manner, and about respect, and about all the hard work that goes into winning. He taught them as much off the ice as he did on the ice, and that all carried over.

Those guys—Mark, Wayne, Kevin Lowe, Coffey, Grant Fuhr, Jari Kurri—grew up together. They were just a bunch of young kids having fun, and they had to go through the tests of the NHL. They were tested by the Philadelphia Flyers and lost. They they got to the next level, challenging the New York Islanders for the top spot, thinking they were that good, and then realizing they hadn't taken the next step. For all those guys to come of age at the same time, to all become such dominant players, and to throw Sather into that mix, that was a unique combination.

The way the Oilers were back then with each other, that's how Mark was with us. You watch: When somebody scores a goal and he's on the ice, he's as excited as anyone in the whole arena. You really have to be a secure person, and a very team-oriented person, to be genuinely as happy as he is for other people's success, every time. There's no jealousy or feeling that, "I should have done this." He's excited for everybody, whether it's a rookie or anybody.

There was one thing he didn't like too much: Practical jokes. He didn't play jokes on guys. He never goofed around with guys' equipment or cut guys' shoelaces. He didn't believe in hazing. So when somebody did something to him, he was always taken aback. He just didn't believe in any of that stuff. He always thought it didn't keep people together. It actually singled people out. It didn't all of a sudden make you accepted because someone put shaving cream in your shoes. He said it made people feel more separated or made them stand out for a reason. He always stayed out of things, or if he heard the guys were planning something, he'd say, "No, no, you can't do that." I know if I didn't feel comfortable in a situation, the last thing I'd want is to be singled out even more and for everyone to laugh. I have no problem with laughing at myself, but I'd rather do it when I feel comfortable with everyone, not as a way to make myself feel comfortable.

When Mark left after the 1996-97 season, it was surprising and disappointing. He was a free agent, and all season long they weren't negotiating a new contract. We had talked about it throughout the year. You know, "What are they thinking?" and "It's going to end up costing them more down the road." It never surfaced that he wouldn't be back. It was always an automatic that he was going to be back. It was just a matter of how much the Rangers were going to end up having to pay him. When the season was over, I talked to Mike Richter one time. He said, "I just talked to Mark. Have you talked to him recently?"

I said I hadn't in about a week. Mike said, "I don't think he's coming back." I said, "What?" So I called him, and he told me he wasn't coming back. I thought, *This can't be true. It's one of those scare tactics,* but he said, "They don't want me around. I can't believe it."

When he left and signed with Vancouver, it all went down pretty quickly. I was just shocked. I couldn't believe it. The situation was bad. But even after he was gone, part of him remained.

I don't think there are too many people who have been around Mark and want to be successful that don't remember the things he did. Adam Graves and I still sit next to each other and talk about situations and things that happened. There's no way around it, because he's been such a big part of our careers. His name is bound to come up. Everything with the Rangers is the way it is because of Mark. We have two buses to take us to games and practices, and there's a snack set up before the game. Guys used to take cabs, and go get something quick to eat by themselves. He just got it all set up. He wanted us to do things as a team.

It was always like that with Mark. With Mark, everything is always about the team.

PREFACE

It has been the opportunity of a lifetime. Not writing this book, but rather having had the chance to work with, and to know, Mark Messier and the people who surrounded him. And to have been surrounded by those associated with the great Edmonton Oilers teams in the 1980s, and with the never dull, at times magnificent New York Rangers teams of the 1990s.

There was a night in Burlington, Vermont, where the Rangers held their training camps. I had just had dinner with my Uncle Dan and Aunt Myrna and was looking for a cup of cappuccino that would provide the caffeine needed for several hours of work that still had to be done.

Completely by accident, I strolled into a place where most of the Rangers' players were unwinding with some beers. The reporter-player relationship can be awkward at best in such a situation, where generally speaking, the reporter is not welcome. One player noticed the clumsiness of the moment. It was Messier. He jumped to his feet, greeted me, and invited me to sit at a table with himself, Brian Leetch, and Mike Richter, motioning for his two teammates to slide their chairs over to make room for me. Messier not only paid for the coffee, but he insisted I stay a while. It was a little thing, but it was typical of the way Messier cared about making everybody feel comfortable and accepted.

Virtually all of the guys who came to New York via Edmonton were that way. They all learned the lessons Messier learned. They were special people.

Many of those people crossed paths in both cities. It was an honor and a privilege to have known them—notably Kevin Lowe, Wayne Gretzky, Adam Graves, and Craig MacTavish, among others—each a warrior on the ice and a champion gentleman off of it.

Along those lines, I must thank all the players and coaches who contributed to this book simply by passing through Madison Square Garden and filling my notebook during the six years Messier spent on Broadway. There are too many names to mention, but their quotes and stories saturate the book.

There were also those who did me enormous favors by agreeing to be interviewed at length specifically for this book. Those included the amazing and gracious Gretzky; Graves, who is possibly the kindest man on earth; Leetch, who wrote the foreword and who, for two months in 1994, played at a level that perhaps a small handful of players have ever reached; and the intelligent and ruminative Richter.

They also included Rangers president/general manager Neil Smith; Rangers coaches and ex-coaches Mike Keenan, Colin Campbell, and John Muckler; players and former players including Jeff Beukeboom, MacTavish, Ken Daneyko, Tony Amonte, Esa Tikkanen, Kelly Buchberger, Tie Domi, Kris King, Steve Larmer, Geoff Smith, Andy Moog, Denis Potvin, Randy Moller, and especially Lee Fogolin, the leader of the Baby Oilers when they joined the NHL in 1979. Also coaches and former coaches Scotty Bowman, Harry Neale, and Terry Crisp.

This book would have been impossible without the help of Barry Watkins, the senior vice president of communications for Madison Square Garden, and Kevin McDonald, his former assistant and now a scout; Rangers VP of public relations John Rosasco and his staff, particularly Jeff Schwartzenberg, Rob Koch (now with the Atlanta Thrashers), and Frank Buonomo (now with the Nashville Predators).

Considerable contributions came from Glenn Adamo and Ken Rosen of the NHL's broadcasting department; Joe Whelan, John Davidson, and Michael McCarthy of MSG Network; Michael Berger of Fox Sports; Rick Minch of the New Jersey Devils; Devin Smith (formerly of the Vancouver Canucks) of the NHL Players Association; Mike Ulmer of the Hamilton *Spectator*; Barry Klarberg, Messier's accountant; Frank Brown of the NHL; Rick Resnick of *Blueshirt Bulletin*; columnist Barry Stanton of the *Journal News*; and John Dellapina of the *New York Daily News*.

I am forever grateful to Chuck Stogel, who hired me in 1976 and taught me about work ethic; the late Tom Whelan, a man completely without ego and my idol in this business; the great Al Mari, who taught me how to work a lockerroom; Dick Yerg, who helped push me toward hockey even at his expense; and Chris D'Amico and David Georgette, who pushed and shoved me to be better.

Gratitude goes to Lonnie Herman, publisher, who not only talked me into writing it, but also gave me necessary pep talks (and one helluva lunch at Malio's in Tampa) throughout the project; and to Dave Rosenbaum, an author in his own right, who edited the book and who, in fact, "found" me for this project.

Thanks to the Messier family, who could not have been nicer in their six years as "Rangers." They made sure we hit all the right restaurants whenever my wife, Maureen, and I visited Hilton Head. Maureen was the force behind this work. She sacrificed a lot of hours and dinners and shows and vacations together to allow me to do the work, and imparted strength and confidence that I wasn't sure I had. She also was inspired once by seeing "The Look" first-hand, when she bumped into Messier in a Montreal hotel lobby as he made his way to a decisive playoff game in 1996.

I must thank all my family members—my siblings, their spouses, and their kids—for their encouragement, and just for making me laugh. Laughter is something that has always come easily among us, a trait left to us by our grandfather, Leonard. Mostly, I want to thank my mom for always being there for me unconditionally, and my dad for becoming such a good friend as I got older. And a very special thanks to my great aunts, Clare and Tillie, who used to let this ten-year-old boy sleep over and stay up late on Saturday nights so I could watch hockey games.

1

The Look

"You should have seen his eyes."

A young, impressionable Adam Graves would never forget the night Mark Messier played his signature game. Most of those who saw it say they had never before, and have never since, seen a game so completely dominated by one player. Messier ruled the ice mentally, physically, and skillfully. He imposed his will on two teams, crushing one of them and carrying the other. He intimidated with his stick, his elbows, and his speed. And his look.

The Edmonton Oilers had won four Stanley Cup championships in five seasons, but had begun to disassemble the dynasty because owner Peter Pocklington could no longer afford his expensive, star-rich roster. Pocklington's most notable trade, or sale, sent Wayne Gretzky, hockey's greatest player, to the Los Angeles Kings in a stunning deal during the summer of 1988.

Gretzky not only was his sport's Babe Ruth, but he was also a close friend of Messier and many of the other Oilers greats. There were tears when he left, and his departure began the tearing-down of one of the greatest teams ever assembled. He had also been the Oilers' captain. Then Messier took over the "C," the little three-inch letter that weighs hundreds of pounds on those who aren't built for the burden of leadership. On Messier, the "C" fit like Superman's "S."

In 1989, the Oilers were beaten in the first round of the playoffs by Gretzky and the Kings in an emotional seven-game series. Many of the Oilers, and a lot of their fans, were as happy for Gretzky as they were sad for Edmonton. Gretzky won his ninth Hart Trophy as the NHL's MVP. In 1990, however, Messier won *his* first Hart Trophy, and the Oilers looked like a team with a chance for something few thought possible: a Stanley Cup in the post-Gretzky era.

To this day, Messier says winning without Gretzky wasn't his priority. He insists winning the Stanley Cup was his only motivation.

But the dream ride toward that 1990 Cup took a nearly disastrous turn in the first round, when Edmonton fell behind the Winnipeg Jets, three games to one, in the best-of-seven games series. The Oilers, however, stormed back to win three games in a row and advance to the next round. In the second round, the Oilers swept Gretzky's Kings. In the Conference final, Edmonton won Game One over Chicago, 5-2, for its eighth straight win.

Messier, however, was playing as if he was hurt. When the Oilers lost the next two games to the Blackhawks and fell behind two games to one, they faced a crossroads: Game Four on May 8, 1990, in Chicago Stadium, the most difficult place to play for a visiting team. The Oilers could not afford to lose and fall behind 3-1 again. Making the situation more daunting, the Oilers hadn't won in Chicago in their last seven visits.

So the task facing the Oilers in Game Four was clear: Win, or else. The Oilers' dynasty was facing an abrupt end.

Chicago Stadium was hot, as usual, during early May. The heat was also being turned up on Messier, who had only one assist in each of the two losses.

"We knew we got ourselves in a situation we didn't think we should be in, and after being down 3-1 to Winnipeg that year and coming back and winning in seven games, we knew it was going to be very difficult to climb that mountain again against a team that was playing pretty well," Messier recalled.

On the morning of Game Four, Messier sat in the stands and stared straight ahead while the Blackhawks went through their game-day skate. He had an animated private conversation with Edmonton coach John Muckler. Some thought Messier was dictating strategy. Some thought he was chewing out Muckler.

"You know what happened?" Muckler said years later. "That was a discussion about another player on our team. We must have been there a half an hour, and everybody thought we were talking about the gameplan. We weren't talking about the gameplan. It was an individual incident that happened in Chicago the day before, and we were discussing it. Everybody thought it was a great big powwow out there, but it wasn't. I'd like to say it was, but it wasn't."

Traditionally on game day, the visiting team has its morning skate, goes for lunch, takes a quick nap, then goes by bus or cab from the hotel to the rink. When the Oilers began arriving at Chicago Stadium for Game Four, Messier was already there. He had arrived early in the afternoon, hours before he would usually arrive.

"It was totally out of character for him to be there and be so quiet and so serious," recalled Oilers center Craig MacTavish. "He was dressed early. He didn't say anything. He didn't have to say anything. Everybody knew."

Adam Graves, who had been acquired earlier in the season from Detroit and had played a key role on the energetic "Kid Line" with young Joe Murphy and Martin Gelinas, remembered how quiet Messier was.

"He got there and got dressed real early and he was rocking back and forth in his stall," Graves said. "You should have seen his eyes."

One person who saw Messier's eyes that day was Mike Keenan, the Blackhawks' coach.

"I watched him skate in the morning," Keenan said. "I watched him sitting in the stands, and I watched him in the pregame warmup. You could see it in his face."

Messier's look had become legendary in the NHL, but on this night the look was even more intense. Messier's deep-set dark eyes and marble chin made for one of the great game faces in sports. The determination behind the face, though, made it all that much more impressive and effective.

Mark Messier lives to win championships. And Edmonton had to win this game if it were to win another championship, its fifth with Messier.

"Everybody on the team that year wanted to make a statement," said Muckler, who was an assistant coach on the first four Oilers championship teams before becoming the head coach. "Obviously, Gretz wasn't there any longer and everybody missed Gretz not being there, and it probably kind of put up the idea that we couldn't win another Stanley Cup. That was the challenge that year."

■ ■ ■

A Stanley Cup can't be won by a single man, not by Gretzky, not by Messier. But sometimes, a single game can be won by a single player, and only the biggest players can win a game like the game that night.

3

Old Chicago Stadium, which has since been torn down and replaced by the United Center, was the most intimidating place in pro sports. From the foghorn that could knock you off your seat after a Blackhawks goal, to the Barton pipe organ, which at full volume reached a decibel level equivalent to twenty-five brass bands and could shatter every window in the building, the Stadium at times was deafening. But most frightening for an opponent was the noise generated by the big crowd in the NHL's smallest building.

Fans had been roaring in Chicago Stadium since 1929. The little barn had steep seating and hanging balconies that squished people into the brick edifice. None of the outer walls was more than one hundred feet from the ice surface, which was nine feet shorter than regulation size and had tight, sloped corners.

This, combined with the Blackhawks' physical, hard-working style of play, made Chicago Stadium a terrible place for visitors.

Messier, interviewed on the *Hockey Night in Canada* broadcast prior to the game, stuck out his chin and said, "I know I have to play better. I have to get some offense for the team, along with some other people. But, for sure, it has to start from me. I have to go out in the first period and lead the way for our hockey club in order for it to be successful."

There was only one problem: Messier was playing hurt.

"You could see that Mark was playing hurt at the time," said Jeff Beukeboom, who was injured and out of the Oilers' lineup that night. "He wasn't his usual dominating force, even though he was still dominant. The newspapers were asking, 'Where is Messier in this series?' That was all he needed to hear."

From the opening faceoff, Messier inflicted damage on and instilled fear in the Blackhawks.

"Mark came out, and I knew after the first shift the game was over," Keenan recalled. "The series was over. The first two shifts he broke two sticks, one over Denis Savard, another over Doug Wilson, and he didn't get a penalty. That was the end of us. You could see it in his eyes: that steely stare. I didn't say it to my team, but I knew we were in deep trouble."

Savard, the Blackhawks' most dangerous offensive player, had scored six points in Chicago's victories in Games Two and Three. Wilson was their defensive leader. Steve Larmer had 21 points in 17 previous playoff games. Dirk Graham was Chicago's captain. He played on heart and a cracked kneecap. Messier took his toll on every one of them.

On the bench, Messier had a permanent scowl. He did very little talking. On the ice, Messier opened the game with a nasty elbow on Graham, which went unpenalized. On his first shift, he broke his stick over Wilson's neck. The tone had been set.

"He was vicious," said teammate Kevin Lowe. "It was a challenge: 'Let's play. Anyone who wants to play, here I am. Let's go.'"

During his first shift, Messier skated down the right side and got off one of his patented one-legged snap shots. The shot sailed just wide of the left goalpost and goalie Greg Millen. Following another close call, Messier skated behind the net and smacked mean Dave Manson with his stick.

"Messier has really got it cranked up these first six minutes," Hall of Fame coach Scotty Bowman said on the *Hockey Night in Canada* telecast.

Then Messier set up a powerplay goal, with a one-touch pass to Steve Smith, whose shot was neatly deflected by Glenn Anderson for a 1-0 Oilers lead. Later in the period, Smith and Joe Murphy sandwiched Savard with a huge hit in the Oilers' defensive zone, and Murphy fired the puck down the ice. Messier put his head down, pulled away from the field, and caught up with the loose puck near the left faceoff circle. Wilson had a chance to cut him off as Messier turned toward the net, but Wilson's heart wasn't in it. He had no interest in stepping in front of this human locomotive. Messier made a power move to the net, stuck his knee out, just in case Wilson wanted to challenge him, then shot a backhander between Millen's pads for a 2-0 advantage.

"Wilson bailed out," Lowe recalled. "He saw Mess coming and said, 'I don't know about this.'"

Moments later, Messier planted a vicious elbow onto Dirk Graham's chin, sending the Chicago captain to the ice. Messier, seated in the penalty box, motioned toward Graham three times, pushing up his chin with his finger, as if to warn him, "Keep your head up." Chicago scored on the power play to cut Edmonton's lead to 2-1.

Just eleven seconds into the second period, Messier beat Wilson to the puck in the right corner and cut toward the net. Messier threw a backhander that landed at the feet of goalie Millen. As Messier shoved his stick across Wilson's chest, Oilers winger Craig Simpson knocked the puck into the net. The Oilers had a 3-1 lead.

Keenan immediately pulled Millen and replaced him with backup Jacques Cloutier. On his next shift, Messier hammered Steve Larmer off the boards at center ice. Messier then caught young, rugged Jeremy Roenick circling out of the defensive zone without the puck and blasted him with an elbow to the head. At the very least, referee Bill McCreary should have whistled Messier for interference, but he chose to ignore the infraction. Even with the crowd roaring, fans could clearly hear Roenick, on the seat of his pants, yelling "Fuck off" at Messier.

Roenick, not one to be intimidated, went back at Messier, chased him behind the Oilers' net, and whacked him with his stick. The two exchanged cross-checks in front of the net. The puck went to the corner, and Roenick nailed Glenn Anderson. After the puck was iced and the whistle sounded, the brash and still angry Roenick chased Messier down behind the net and put his stick in Messier's midsection. Messier, knowing that all eyes were on them, refused to take the bait and risk drawing a penalty.

"Messier won't react," Bowman told the *Hockey Night in Canada* audience. "He's been a presence tonight."

For most of the game, Messier's large amount of ice time had forced Keenan to keep the inexperienced Roenick on the bench. Keenan didn't want the Roenick-Messier matchup. But Roenick would get more ice time later, and he'd get a measure of revenge, when he picked off a pass from Oilers defenseman Reijo Ruotsalainen and ripped a shot past goalie Bill Ranford, cutting the Oilers' lead to 3-2.

At that point, the Blackhawks were trying to eliminate Messier, trying to wear him down, beat him up, and do anything to slow this charging train. Steve Thomas took a run at Messier and went for his head. Messier saw him at the last moment and ducked under the hit. The game, which developed into full-scale war, got filthier. Steve Smith knocked Larmer into the goalpost. Messier got banged by Dirk Graham's high elbow at one end of the ice, then got lowbridged by Steve Konroyd at the other end. But he didn't slow down a bit. Indeed, he seemed to be fueled by the Blackhawks' strategy. If anything, he played faster and harder.

The Oilers' Kid Line gave Edmonton an enthusiastic boost with a series of hits. It also allowed Messier a breather. When Messier stepped back onto the ice, Simpson intercepted a pass and found Messier skating down the middle of the ice. Messier took the pass and gained top speed in a hurry. A desperate Wilson jabbed his stick at Messier in a hopeless attempt to knock him off balance. The blade of Wilson's stick stabbed Messier in the neck. Messier continued on, deked Cloutier to the ice, and scored on a backhander. The Oilers had a 4-2 lead. Then Messier winced. His head fell as he felt the pain in his neck.

"Right in the fuckin' throat," Messier exclaimed to the team trainer. "Right in the fuckin' throat."

Before the period ended, Messier got in a few more whacks. During a faceoff, Messier lined up against Greg Gilbert, who tried to hook him. Messier raked his stick across Gilbert's face. Gilbert responded with an elbow, and up came Messier's stick, again across Gilbert's face.

When the second period ended, the Oilers had only eleven shots on goal, but had a 4-2 lead. Messier had been in on every Oilers goal and had made an enormous impact.

"Is Mark Messier unstoppable here tonight?" Bowman asked.

Early in the third period, Messier roughed up Roenick in the corner. When Manson charged over to protect his teammate. Messier saw him out of the corner of his eye, and snapped Manson's head back with a surprise elbow. Manson then cross-checked Messier to the chest.

"He was on his own level that night, his own plane," Keenan said. "Of course, he was a specimen to begin with. But that particular night, there was no way the Chicago Blackhawks were going to beat the Edmonton Oilers in that game or series. And he let everyone know that."

"We had them on the ropes," Larmer said. "I don't think, if it wasn't for him, they could have won the series. He singlehandedly beat us that night. He was like a man possessed. I talked to Jeff Beukeboom about it later. He said Mess never said anything all day. The only thing he said, just before the game, was 'We can't take stupid penalties.' Then on his first shift he broke his stick over somebody's arm. Then he ran over somebody. Nobody wanted to go near him the rest of the game.

"Nobody else on their team believed they could win. But he set the tone and everybody else jumped on board."

In 1994, Messier came up with another classic performance when he rescued the New York Rangers from elimination in Game Six of the Eastern Conference finals. Messier not only guaranteed victory prior to the game, but went out and scored a hat trick in the third period to lead the Rangers in wiping out a 2-0 New Jersey Devils lead.

"The games were very similar," said Lowe, who played with Messier on both the Oilers and the Rangers. "But Game Four in Chicago there was more pressure on him particularly and less on the team. There had been a few questions raised by members of the media about him personally. That's what was amazing about Game Four."

Said MacTavish: "The 1990 game still ranks as the single most dominant individual performance I've ever seen in hockey; not only been a part of, but seen. I've never seen a guy have that big an impact on a hockey game. In '94 I felt there were similar circumstances and conditions at work, but I really believe in 1990, he made it happen. In '94 it happened and obviously he was a huge part of it, but in '90 he made it happen."

Having tied the series at two games apiece, the Oilers went home and beat the Blackhawks 4-3 in Game Five, then returned to Chicago Stadium and clinched the series with an 8-4 win. The Oilers faced the Bruins in the finals and won the series, four games to one, for their fifth Cup in seven years. When the game ended, Messier had his crowning moment.

The captain gets the Cup first, so this was a first for Messier, who had never before been the captain of a Cup-winning team. But when he found the microphones, cameras, and notebooks, he made sure to dedicate the Cup win to the guy who had handed it to him four previous times.

"This one's for you, Gretz," Messier said.

It would be the last Cup for this great team.

2

Glory Days in Edmonton

By the mid-1990s, Mark Messier and Wayne Gretzky made more than $12 million a year combined. In 1995, the Edmonton Oilers' entire payroll was about $9.6 million. That, more than anything else, explains why the Oilers' dynasty of the 1980s—arguably the greatest hockey team ever assembled—was no longer together.

Long after they were broken up by owner Peter Pocklington's inability to afford his star-loaded roster, the Oilers of the 1980s were helping other teams win Stanley Cups in Pittsburgh and in New York, or helping other teams get to the finals in Los Angeles, Philadelphia, Detroit, and Chicago. When *The Hockey News* celebrated its fiftieth anniversary by choosing the top fifty players of all time, the Oilers of the 1980s had four players on the list: Gretzky (No. 1), Messier (No. 12), defenseman Paul Coffey (No. 28), and winger Jari Kurri (No. 50). The Oilers scored 446 goals one season, and scored more than 400 goals for five straight seasons. No other team in history has ever scored 400 goals in a season.

"I think there's never going to be a team like that again in the NHL," said Esa Tikkanen, who was one of several key post-season performers for the Oilers, and later for several other teams.

It's hard to say it wasn't the best.

"We could have won six or seven Stanley Cups," Gretzky said. "Who knows? You can easily say that it had a great possibility to win more. You know, everybody's always going to argue about a lot of the Canadiens teams, the Islanders team that won four in a row, the Philadelphia team of the mid '70s, the Bruins with Orr and Esposito.

9

Everybody's going to always debate and argue. I don't know what's the best team. I'll leave all that up to everybody's opinion. But I'll guarantee you that, without question, it was the most exciting team ever.

"People in Edmonton left every game saying, 'That was phenomenal.' There'd be games where we'd be down 7-1 after the second period, and Glen Sather wouldn't even say anything. He'd just say, 'If you guys want to win tonight, you can win.' And we'd go out and win 8-7. Or we'd be winning games 6-1 and teams would tie us 6-6, and we'd win 9-6. Like I said, I don't know if that was the best team. That's debatable forever. But there's no question in my mind, it was the most exciting team ever put together, right from the goaltending of Grant Fuhr and Andy Moog, to Kevin Lowe blocking shots, to Dave Semenko's toughness, to our speed, to Mess, to our love of the game, and the talent we had on the team. I don't think there's any question it was the most exciting team ever."

Gretzky was simply the greatest player ever, the holder of 61 NHL scoring records, the man who not only scored more goals than any player in NHL history, but who also had more assists in his career than any other player has ever had goals and assists combined. Thirteen times, a player has amassed more than a hundred assists in a season; Gretzky had eleven of those 100-plus-assists seasons.

Gretzky was the star of the Oilers' high-octane show, but it would be incorrect to say he was the whole show, or that he was the only reason the Oilers were special. The young Oilers of the 1980s drew their character from their coach and general manager, Glen Sather, and molded what they learned into a team loaded with leadership, poise, and a tremendous will to win. They were confident. Although they never thought there was a game or a series they couldn't win, they respected their opponents. They also respected the game and enjoyed playing it. Their work ethic came naturally because they were having so much fun on the ice. Off it, too. The younger players—particularly Gretzky, Messier, and Lowe—learned from Sather, and from the original older Oilers, such as Lee Fogolin and Ron Chipperfield.

But there was more to the Oilers than talent. There was something unique about them.

"The whole team was inseparable," said Craig MacTavish, an extraordinary defensive center and, like most of the important Oilers, an intelligent man loaded with character. "Mark and Wayne lived in the same apartment and they were best of friends, as everyone else was on that team. I mean, the team had such a tremendous amount of success that the players controlled the locker room to the point where the players were so good, they would weed out the bad guys that would come in in a very short period of time. Glen had given them that luxury, that bad guys might come in, but they'd be quickly weeded out.

"Winning was everything, because everybody enjoyed winning and we wanted to keep it going, and Glen, rightfully so, would come down on the team after losses. He was a real results-oriented coach. I mean, no matter how well you played, if you lost you still lost. And vice versa—no matter how poorly you played, if you won then everybody was absolved from any responsibility. Never critique the wins. It was great in that respect."

It all started with Sather, who had the blessing of the owner, Pocklington, to have almost complete power over hockey decisions. Glen "Slats" Sather had been a rough, tough player for ten NHL seasons. In 1976, he signed with the Edmonton Oilers of the World Hockey Association. Later that season, he became the Oilers' coach.

The WHA had become a rival of the NHL. For seven seasons, it had signed as many of the NHL's players as possible, often by luring them with huge contracts. But there was a more subtle form of raiding going on. The NHL did not allow players under the age of 18 to be drafted. The WHA had no age limits.

Prior to the 1978-79 season, the Indianapolis Racers signed a scrawny, underage 17-year-old named Wayne Gretzky. But the cash-strapped Racers had to sell some of their assets. In November, Sather traded for Gretzky.

The Racers then went out and found another 17-year-old who had been born eight days earlier than Gretzky in 1961. He was a player the Racers hoped would take Gretzky's place. His name was Mark Messier.

Five games into Messier's WHA career, the Racers folded.

When the Racers folded, Messier signed with the Cincinnati Stingers. He wasn't an instant hit. He played in 47 games in the 1978-79 season and scored only one goal, which didn't even come on a shot. It was scored on a dump-in that bounced and eluded the goalie, Pat Riggin.

"It's a good thing they don't judge you on one season," quipped Messier.

That would be his only season in the WHA. The league folded after 1978-79, and four of its franchises—the Oilers, the Winnipeg Jets, the

Quebec Nordiques, and the Hartford Whalers—were invited into the NHL. Before they were allowed in, however, some of the WHA's talent was spread around the NHL. The existing NHL teams reclaimed lost players from the newcomers, who were each allowed to protect two skaters and two goalies. Gretzky was one of the four players protected by the Oilers. Then, the four new teams were allowed to fill their rosters with unprotected players from the existing NHL teams.

Sather struck gold in the entry draft. He picked Kevin Lowe in the first round, Mark Messier (with the 48th pick overall) in the third round, and Glenn Anderson in the fourth round. The next year, 1980, was another drafting bonanza for the Oilers. Sather selected Paul Coffey in the first round, Jari Kurri in the fourth, and Andy Moog in the seventh round. In 1981, Sather picked goalie Grant Fuhr in the first round.

Almost immediately, the Oilers' talent was obvious. Their speed was frightening. This team had everything but NHL experience, and it would get that quickly.

"We grew up together," Gretzky said. "I mean, we started playing together at 17, and we knew it all, like most 17-year-olds."

The group became a family, and the big three were Messier, Gretzky, and Lowe. Gretzky and Lowe shared an apartment. The threesome was almost inseparable. Coffey, Anderson, and some of the other players were also very close. From teenagers, they very quickly became young men.

"When we got there, meaning myself, Kevin, Mark, we were just young raw kids that had a dream of one day playing in the NHL," Gretzky recalled. "Our whole concept was survival. That's all we really thought of because we thought at any time we could be sent to the minors and, or worse, eliminated kind of out of the picture. So we were no different than any other kids who turned pro in that we were just thrilled to be there.

"What happened was, in putting together the organization, Glen put together some key people and some key ingredients. They knew the kind of team they wanted to build, and they knew the character of the people they were going to go after. I believe the first expansion draft pick was a guy named Cam Connor, who had scored the overtime winning goal for Montreal against Toronto the year before in the playoffs. He drafted Lee Fogolin. Without question, the two guys who at that time were the role models and leaders of our hockey team were Lee Fogolin and Ron Chipperfield, who was the first captain of the Oilers in the NHL. Those guys were really the people who Glen believed would be the right people to direct his young guys, because he was going to live and die with a young team. He didn't care if they were 18, 19, 20, he was going to let those guys mature and learn from these people. That was his whole philosophy."

Sather was more than a recruiter of talent and a motivator. He was a teacher, and he had a tremendous influence on Messier and the rest of the team.

"He tried to teach you an attitude, a way of carrying yourself, a way of being a professional on and off the ice that made you a stronger, confident, and better person and player overall," said defenseman Jeff Beukeboom. "That's why, if you look at those teams and the players who were on it, not necessarily just the stars but also the players who filled in, they're all strong character players that every team would love to have. If you really get down to it and look at Glen Sather and Mark Messier, there's a lot of similarities in their character and their qualities and their drive to succeed."

Like Messier, Sather had a softer, more emotional side.

"You see it, but it's not as obvious as with Mess," Jeff Beukeboom said. "You knew what his makeup was, from his family life and how much his family meant to him, to the game, to having fun between games, after games, and everything you could imagine. Slats was never like that. He was more business-like. He was on his toes around his players and trying to teach them that little bit extra, or always trying to test them in a good, positive way. He always tried to get the best out of his players. When you needed to be brought down a notch, he was always willing to do that, also. But his No. 1 goal was to make everyone better, and I always saw that in Mess, also."

Sather had a profound influence on everybody on the team, according to Craig MacTavish. He was a man who not only enjoyed hockey, but enjoyed life.

"I think he really brought those qualities to the locker room, where everybody became not only a much better hockey player, but a more well-rounded person and had other interests and enjoyed doing a lot of different things, like Slats and Mark," MacTavish said. "They loved to Ski-Doo and hunt and fish. They did all of that. And I think Slats really admired the way Mark played hockey. They had a real mutual admiration for one another. Mark really admired Glen's lifestyle, the way he had such a passion for life. Glen really admired the way Mark played hockey, and Glen always would have liked to have been a Mark Messier as a hockey player: a big, mean, tough, talented, no-nonsense guy. They had a great relationship in that respect, and they had a great respect for one another and they really helped one another."

Sather was wise and cagey. He, too, was learning on the job, although he'd had his headstart in the WHA. Sometimes, he was as gentle as a steamroller. Sometimes he was oh-so-subtle. Sather would chew out players, then turn around and try to build them up. He yelled at everybody, from his stars to his fourth-liners.

In one meeting after practice, Sather ripped into Messier. Messier was shaken and yelled back at Sather in front of the entire team. Afterward, Messier was teary-eyed and emotional. Sather took back everything he'd said. In front of the entire team, he admitted he was wrong. He made sure to point out to the team just how much he respected Messier. The next time the Oilers were together, all of the players talked about the Messier-Sather set-to and how important that moment might have been in the team's history.

"It was so strong. Everything that happened at that instance affected the team tenfold," said Beukeboom. "Slats is always proud and con-fident, and it's the only time I've ever seen him back down a little bit from anyone. That speaks a lot about Mess. It says a lot about his char-acter and how much respect he had because Slats really admired him, the way he played with heart and desire."

The Oilers reflected Messier's heart and desire. They wanted to win in a hurry. They had so much to learn in so little time.

■ ■ ■

In 1979-80, the first season in the NHL for Messier and Gretzky, all of the attention was on Gretzky, who shared the league scoring title with Marcel Dionne of the Los Angeles Kings. The Oilers went 28-39-13, reached the playoffs, and were swept by the Philadelphia Flyers in the first round.

For his part, Messier, in his first NHL season, scored 33 points in 75 games. He was only 18 years old when he played his first NHL game on October 10, 1979, against the Chicago Blackhawks at Chicago Stadium, which would be the scene of his greatest game years later. Three days later in Edmonton, Messier scored his first NHL goal against the Detroit Red Wings. But the season would have its downside for

14

Messier, too: He was sent to Houston of the Central Hockey League for four games, the only four games he would ever play in the minor leagues.

The next season, the Oilers took a baby step. They swept the Montreal Canadiens, who were just two years removed from their own four-year dynasty, for the first NHL playoff series win in team history. Then the Oilers ran into the Islanders' dynasty. Edmonton had plenty of skill, but hadn't yet developed the defensive responsibility to beat a team like the Islanders.

During that series, some of the Islanders' veteran players were stunned to hear Messier and some of the baby Oilers on the bench singing "Here we go Oilers, here we go!" Despite his youth, Messier's had become the lead voice of the Oilers. He had already become a respected member of the team. His production was increasing, too. Messier scored 63 points in 72 games, then seven more in nine play-off games. He also scored his first NHL hat trick, on March 16, 1981, against the Penguins.

Then the Oilers made their move to the big-time. Gretzky began shattering important records in 1981-82, including 92 goals and 212 points. Messier also took a major step statistically. After scoring 23 goals in 1980-81, he scored 50 in 1981-82, the only 50-goal season of his career. Messier was more than a very good player. There were, and had been, players with more skill. There were, and had been, players who were tougher. There have been better skaters, but there may not have ever been a player that tough with so much skill and speed. There have been other power forwards, but not many with as much finesse. There have been players who could do things with the puck that Messier could not do, but none of them were 6'1" and a chiseled 205 pounds, huge by early 1980s standards. And not many players, of any size or skill level, had Messier's meanness, his menacing glare, his iron will, his chin of rock, and his leadership abilities.

The Oilers went 48-17-15 in 1981-82 for the second best record in the NHL behind the Islanders, but they had another lesson to learn about humility. They lost a best-of-five games first-round series to Los Angeles in which they allowed 23 goals in the three losses, including a 10-8 defeat in Game One.

Another piece of the puzzle joined the Oilers in 1982-83: John Muckler, whose coaching resume dated back to 1959-60 with the New York Rovers of the Eastern League, joined Sather as an assistant coach.

Sather, the master motivator, wonderful bench coach, and brilliant collector of talent, needed an Xs and Os guy, so he brought in Muckler.

The Oilers went 47-21-12, tied Philadelphia for the second most points in the regular season, and rolled through the first three rounds of the playoffs. They met the three-time defending Stanley Cup champion Islanders in the finals. And they were obliterated, four games to none. Gretzky didn't score a goal in the series. Messier scored one.

The final series was not without its humorous moments for the overwhelmed Oilers. Down 3-0 to the Islanders after the first period of Game Four, Messier walked into the locker room and delivered a semi-inspirational speech.

"All right," Messier said, "we got 'em right where we want 'em."

"Obviously, we were in a desperate situation and there was no reason to do anything but laugh about it and go out and play some hockey," goaltender Andy Moog recalled. "I remember that being one of Mark's favorite sayings, in a gravelly, salty old hockey voice, 'Let's play hockey!' I don't know where he first heard that or picked it up: 'Let's play hockey!'"

After the Islanders completed the sweep, the Oilers were criticized for having too much firepower and not enough defense. The experts questioned whether Gretzky and Messier, who excelled in the run-and-gun west, could handle the two-way, grind-it-out game played by the teams in the east.

"One thing about Mark and I, we never ran from the heat or the blame," Gretzky said. "We would always stand up, front and center. If we lost, we would never say, 'Well …' The unfortunate thing about the year we lost to the Islanders, first of all, was they were a great team, maybe one of the best teams in hockey history in depth, and they'd won four in a row. But remember, we were 22-year-old kids. We were babies. You look at 22-year-old kids now and you say, 'Well, can you play in the league?' And we were expected to carry a team to a championship, which was fine.

"The ironic thing about that year was, up until Game One of the finals, we'd played as good hockey as we'd ever played in our careers, as a team, as lines, as individuals. We dominated the first three series, romped to the finals, and we were sitting at home playing Game One against the Islanders, ready to go. The ironic thing was we maybe played one of our best games in the whole playoff. We lost 2-0 with an empty-net goal. [Goalie] Billy Smith was absolutely flawless, in the series and that game. We were a young team and we didn't know how to handle it. There was a lot of media pressure in Edmonton, and we weren't old enough and hadn't enough experience to understand where to go from there. But when you're the center of attention, you're going to take the heat, and we understood that. That didn't bother either Mark or I. It was a tough loss because we'd lost to a great team. But, again, we were babies."

The Oilers began preparing for 1983-84 the night they were eliminated. They watched the Islanders celebrate what would be the final Stanley Cup of their dynasty. That night, Gretzky told Paul Coffey that until you win a championship, you can never be considered a truly great player. Something else happened the following year that would have a profound effect on Messier's career and on the Oilers.

"We just had a good summer," Gretzky said. "Before we left for the couple of months, we were like, 'OK, let's be ready.' And we came back the next year and the thing that probably more than anything helped us win the Cup was that was the year I hurt my shoulder. I had a 51-game-point streak, and I played through a bunch of games I shouldn't have played because of the streak. Finally, I couldn't play anymore. We went on a five-game road trip and lost every game. We came back and I started skating with the team again, and that was the day Glen moved Mark to center. Up until that time, he was always a left winger. That turned around our team because that's when it became evident we had a one-two punch that other teams didn't have. We had two guys who could score; we had one guy who could score a lot and one guy who could play really physical and score. It worked out well because neither of us had any selfishness toward the other. He would come off, and he would push for me to go, and when I would come off, I would push for him to go. It was one of those unique situations not a lot of teams, maybe ever, were fortunate enough to have. I think that was the big turning point as far as winning the Stanley Cup goes."

Although Gretzky was the captain of the Oilers, Messier and Lowe could just as easily have worn the "C." All three players spoke from the heart, played hard every shift of every game, and weren't afraid to show their emotions. They were tougher than most people realized and able to play through severe pain. But mostly, they knew how to lead, how to say the right things when they needed to be said, and how to get the job done. Messier certainly didn't need a letter on his chest to be a leader. Indeed, already the Oilers were becoming Messier's team and many of the Edmonton players were saying that while Gretzky deserved to be captain, Messier was the team leader.

"I was quite content," said Messier. "I never thought twice about it. And to this day people couldn't believe that we could have that many quality players on one team and have absolutely no animosity towards each other. I firmly believe that animosity starts with character flaws. We had great character people on that team, and the great character people were the stars on our team, so all the role players naturally just filled in with the attitude that the team was first and everything else was second.

"But people were always trying to drive wedges into our team and concoct stories. We used to read the headlines in the tabloids and literally laugh to each other because never before have there been so many great players on one team that didn't have ulterior motives and weren't selfish."

The Oilers steamrolled to the 1984 finals, where they once again faced the Islanders. This time, they were ready.

"In '82-'83, when we lost to the Islanders four straight, we were a bunch of talented people looking for direction," said Muckler. "We could win a lot of games in the early days because we had the most talent. But when you get into the Stanley Cup finals, or even the semifinals, you're going to go against a team that's pretty well equal to what you are. The Islanders had an abundance of experience that year, and they beat us on experience, no question. We walked in there with a lot of swagger and thought we were a pretty good hockey club, and the Islanders, through the good coaching of Al Arbour and the experience of a lot of their players, kept control and beat us four straight. That was a great lesson for our hockey club.

"In '83-'84, we were focused, and we went back with a gameplan, and we all knew what we had to do. And we went there to win. The first time, I shouldn't say we didn't go to win, but I think we were happy being there. This was totally different. The first game of that series was one of the best games I've ever seen, the 1-0 game. Billy Smith was phenomenal and Grant Fuhr was better. Kevin McClelland scored the winning goal, on a rotation from the right side in the Islander end, and the puck went between the post and Billy Smith's foot."

The Oilers had learned that, despite their high-powered offense, they could only win with defense. But after winning Game One, 1-0, they lost Game Two, 6-1.

There was reason for the Oilers to be concerned. The Islanders had proven, in winning nineteen consecutive playoff series, that they were capable of bouncing back from a loss. The Oilers had to prove they could do the same thing. After Game Two, Lowe stood up in the locker room and spoke loudly and for a long time about commitment and about respecting the opponent. The veterans reminded the younger players to fear their opponent, and about the lessons they had learned the year before. The entire team was silent on the long flight from Long Island to Edmonton. There was fear in the Oilers' eyes. The next day, at practice, Lowe ripped into a few of the Oilers who he felt weren't pushing themselves hard enough.

Messier wasn't one of those people, but the time had come for one of his greatest moments. A trademark moment.

The Islanders were leading, 2-1, and were controlling Gretzky when, midway through the second period, Fogolin broke up a Brent Sutter rush. Messier skated to the Oilers blue line and yelled, "Give it to me!" Fogolin saw the fire in Messier's eyes, the look that said, "I'm going to do something." He would never forget that look. After taking the pass from Fogolin, Messier cut to the middle of the ice, as he approached the Islanders' blue line. With a burst of velocity, he split between defensemen Gord Dineen and future Hall of Famer Denis Potvin, putting an outside-in move on the rookie Dineen as he went by. Messier whipped a shot that flew past goalie Billy Smith on the short side. The shot rang off the post on its way into the net.

The game had turned. The Oilers went on to win, 7-2. They had turned the series in their favor.

"Messier just became a dominant player," Potvin said. "He took over the series. It was the turning point in the series, and a turning point in their franchise. And in ours. That was the emergence and arrival of an extremely talented player and exceptional leader. That was a defining moment in the way he was viewed by us and by the hockey world. It was a moment that impacted his career in terms of billing this leader as one of the greatest."

It was ironic that on the play that turned the Islanders' dynasty into the Oilers' dynasty, the play that defined Messier and so many great players in that series, Messier had taken the pass from Fogolin, the guy who had led the Oilers when they were in their infancy. Fogolin hadn't merely passed the puck. He had passed him the torch of leadership.

Messier played a dominant, physical, mean series. He cold-cocked Islanders defenseman Tomas Jonsson with a vicious open-ice elbow. He was a thunderous force.

"I was drafted by the Oilers in '83," said Beukeboom, "And I was fortunate enough to watch every Stanley Cup playoff game they played. The difference between the year before, when they got swept by the Islanders, was Mark. He dominated, and ever since then he's always been known as a force in the playoffs, maybe second to none."

Recalled Andy Moog: "Mark just decided against the Islanders that he was just going to play as hard physically as he'd played in any series or any game to that point. It started to show up, maybe not so much in Game One or Game Two, but it started to show up in Game Three. He was punishing people, and he was starting to find these new reserves of energy. In Game Three, he really took over that series. We were a great group of followers. If somebody did it, everybody else did it with him. We went along with him. Everyone else was right on top of their game as well."

Messier scored another goal in the third period of Game Three. In Game Four, he broke open a close game with another remarkable goal. Goalie Grant Fuhr whipped the puck out of the Edmonton zone and Messier skated after it in pursuit. He beat Potvin, Bryan Trottier, and Jonsson to the puck. Then he corralled the puck on his stick and put a shot past Smith. The Oilers were on their way to a 7-2 victory. In Game 5, Gretzky scored two goals and an assist in a 5-2 Oilers win that clinched the series. The Oilers, Messier, and Gretzky, had their first Stanley Cup.

Messier was voted the winner of the Conn Smythe Trophy as the most valuable player of the playoffs. He cried when he received the award. Afterward, in a TV interview, he spoke about his mom, and how "she felt it in her bones" that the Oilers would win this championship. He said that he and the Oilers had been inspired by a speech made by Gretzky, in which Gretzky said he'd trade all his trophies and records for the Stanley Cup. In his autobiography, Gretzky would say that he was happier about Messier winning the MVP than he was about any of the trophies he had won.

Gretzky was handed the Cup by league president John Ziegler, then he passed the Cup to every teammate to lift. Messier took his turn, and skated to the glass. He lifted the Cup in the direction of his family members so they could share the excitement. That would become his tradition. As Messier and Gretzky skated around the ice together, they couldn't stop screaming and laughing.

It wouldn't be the last time.

■ ■ ■

The Oilers repeated as champions in 1985. They went 15-3 in eighteen playoff games, including a four games to one victory over Philadelphia in the finals. Gretzky won his first playoff MVP with a mind-numbing 47 points in eighteen games. They clinched their second straight Cup with an 8-3 win over the Flyers.

The Oilers should have won three in a row, because in 1985-86, they were still the best team on the planet. But they ran into a fierce, hated, blood-rival, the Calgary Flames, in the second round. The incident for which the 1986 playoffs are remembered is an incident that, perhaps as much as the Oilers' victories, showed what kind of character the Oilers possessed.

In Game Seven, Edmonton defenseman Steve Smith accidentally banked the puck off goalie Grant Fuhr into his own net. The Oilers lost the game, 3-2, and the series, four games to three. Calgary went to the Stanley Cup finals and lost to Montreal. Yet, the Oilers never blamed Smith for the loss. Everybody shouldered the blame.

The Oilers shook off their 1986 disappointment and won again in 1987. They got through the first three rounds of the playoffs with twelve wins and two losses, then ran into a game Philadelphia Flyers team in the finals. Flyers goalie Ron Hextall won the Conn Smythe Trophy, but it didn't matter how well he played, because the Oilers were at the top of their game. Gretzky and Messier were only 26 and entering their prime years.

Prior to the final game, Gretzky had spoken with Messier and Lowe about who would be the first person to get the Cup after Gretzky. When the Oilers won, Gretzky handed the Cup to Steve Smith, the goat of the previous season. On the Oilers, all was easily forgiven.

■ ■ ■

The dismantling of the Oilers began in November of the 1987-88 season when Coffey, a future Hall of Famer, was traded to the Pittsburgh Penguins. That spring, the Oilers won their fourth Cup in five years. It was Gretzky's last.

The sports world was rocked on August 9, 1988. The news flashed from the farthest reaches of Canada to every part of America. Indeed, it received far more attention in the United States than any Stanley Cup victory had ever received, and it sent shock waves through a heart-broken Canada: The Oilers had traded Gretzky to the Los Angeles Kings. Sold him, really, although the official transaction read: Gretzky, Marty McSorley, and Mike Krushelnyski to the Kings for Jimmy Carson, Martin Gelinas, first-round draft picks in 1989, 1991, and 1993, and report-edly $15 million.

Gretzky had been advised about the deal in advance, and had some say about the inclusion of McSorley and Krushelnyski. He had been speaking to Pocklington and to Kings owner Bruce McNall in the days leading to the announcement, but kept it a secret. When Messier heard the rumor, he began calling Gretzky's home. He left several messages, but Gretzky didn't return the calls. He was worried that Messier would try to convince Pocklington to kill the deal. Gretzky knew Messier was powerful enough to nix the trade, and he didn't want that to happen.

Messier was playing golf at Edmonton Country Club on August 9, 1988, when he was informed about the trade. He spoke to Gretzky prior to Gretzky's press conference in Edmonton. At the press con-ference, Gretzky broke down and cried.

"I promised Mess I wouldn't do this," Gretzky said.

The *Edmonton Sun* captured Gretzky's emotions in a front-page pho-tograph that was accompanied by the headline: "99 TEARS!" That was followed by the teaser to the other stories about the trade: "Pages 2, 3, 4, 5, 6, 10, 11, 18, 19, 23, 30, 36, 37, 38, 39, 40, 41, 42, 43, 46 and 47." The only news that day was about Gretzky.

"It was really disappointing," Gretzky said years later. "It was dis-heartening because we had a legitimate shot to win four or five more championships, five or six more championships, who knows? It was disappointing for everyone. But who would have ever known that the team was broken up over money matters, basically, and not really through hockey decisions, but through business decisions.

"And the team being broken up did nothing but escalate salaries to a different level. In a lot of ways, there was a hard salary cap because of the contract I was under, and the contract Mark was under, and what Coffey was under. The league really had a salary cap. And when I was traded, basically that removed the salary cap. The ironic thing about it is the reason salaries are the way they are today, I believe, is because of the breakup of that team."

For Gretzky, the most difficult part about being traded was leaving behind Messier. Numbers 99 and 11 were no longer a duo.

"Probably one of the worst things of my career," Gretzky said. "Many days, as much as I enjoyed L.A. the first two or three years, I remember thinking, 'I wonder what's going on in Edmonton.'"

That summer, Gretzky had married actress Janet Jones in what would be known as Canada's Royal Wedding. Messier was part of the wedding party and would later be the godfather for Wayne and Janet's first child, Paulina. Messier and Gretzky were tight, and Messier was devastated by the trade. Over the next eight seasons, Gretzky and Messier would run up huge phone bills calling each other.

Gretzky needed some time to get over the trade. He was worried about being a $15 million bust, but he had another outstanding season with 54 goals, 114 assists, and a ninth Hart Trophy as the league's MVP.

The Oilers needed a full year to get over the loss of Gretzky. Indeed, as fate would have it, a little less than a year after the trade of the century, Gretzky's Los Angeles Kings faced Messier's Edmonton Oilers in the first round of the playoffs. Gretzky and the Kings rallied from a three games to one deficit to win the series in seven emotional games.

When Gretzky left for Los Angeles in 1988, the captainship of the Oilers had naturally gone to Messier, who by that time was considered one of the greatest leaders in sports. Finally, he was the official leader of his team.

Messier slumped to 94 points that season, but in 1989-90, he won his first Hart Trophy as the NHL's Most Valuable Player and carried the Oilers to their fifth Stanley Cup. When he received the Hart Trophy, he thanked his family and started crying. In the audience that night, seated with Messier, were Wayne and Janet Jones Gretzky. As Messier made his acceptance speech, the Gretzkys cried, too.

"He plays with his heart and speaks with his heart," Kevin Lowe said of Messier. "That's what makes him as great as he is."

Even then, two years after the breakup, Canada was still crying bittersweet tears over the breakup of one of the greatest combinations in hockey history: Gretz and Mess.

3

Born to Lead

Messier was a leader from the day he arrived in Edmonton. His hair was long. He pulled up to the rink on a motorcycle. He was a wild kid: big, strong, fast, and mean. Just like his father.

Doug Messier is the father of an extremely close family. He resembles former Major League Baseball manager Sparky Anderson with his white hair, tanned face, and eagle eyes. Be assured, though, that he's much tougher than Anderson. His sons, Mark and Paul, don't call him Dad. They call him Doug. He is a friend to his sons as much as he is a father, a buddy with whom the boys play a highly competitive game of golf. Doug is a lot like Mark in that he is tough on the outside but soft and kind on the inside.

The Messiers are a hockey family: Doug the father, Mary-Jean the mother, the two boys, Mark and Paul, and the two girls, Jenny and Mary-Kay. One distant relative, an uncle, was Murray Murdoch, who played for the New York Rangers' Stanley Cup championship teams in 1928 and 1933. A closer relative was Billy Dea, a former NHL player and Mary-Jean's cousin.

Mark, the third of Doug and Mary-Jean's children, was born on January 18, 1961, in Edmonton, three years after Paul, one year after Jennifer. While Mark was growing up, his father played for various minor-pro teams, including the Portland Buckaroos in the Western Hockey League and the Nottingham Panthers in England. While with Portland, Doug's strength earned him the nickname Magilla Gorilla. He was also active in the formation of the players' union.

Because Doug's career had him moving around so much, the family spent virtually all of its time together. They had few close friends, which solidified the family's bond. They depended upon each other. Whenever possible, Doug drove Paul to his junior hockey games. Mary-Jean drove Mark to his games. Because of this, Mark grew close to his mother.

In the summer, after hockey season and school, the whole family would pile into the station wagon and drive to California or Mount Hood, Oregon, where the Messiers had a cabin. During the season, the family lived on a five-acre farm in Beaverton, Oregon, outside of Portland. Young Mark would do farm chores, cleaning the horses' stalls, picking berries, and riding a Shetland pony named Billy. Mark would make his great-grandmother laugh by impersonating a monkey. He also imitated Miss Piggy and comedian Tim Conway.

On the ice, Doug was one of the most feared players in the WHL, a league leader in major penalties. Mark was eight when his father moved back to Edmonton to play for the Monarchs of the senior league. In one game, Mark and Paul watched as their father, the player-coach of the Monarchs, knocked out four opponents. Doug simply told his boys he was doing what was best for the team.

When Doug's playing career ended, the Messiers moved back to Edmonton. By then, Mark and Paul knew they wanted to be professional hockey players.

"I always remember the sound of the crowd," Mark said. "It did something for me. That feeling never left me. I remember being six years old and thinking, 'I'm going to be a hockey player and that's all there is to it.'"

From the time he was six, Mark rehearsed what he would do the first time he lifted the Stanley Cup over his head. He dreamt about skating around the ice with the Cup raised above him.

At first, however, Paul was the hockey star of the family, and Doug was his coach. Mark was merely the stickboy for the Spruce Grove, Alberta, Mets, but that gave him the chance to be in the locker room and listen to every speech between periods and before games, and to every bit of strategy. He was interested in what was being said and why. Doug was Mark's coach when he started playing junior hockey at age sixteen for the St. Albert Saints. Mark got seven dollars for a win, four dollars for a tie, and two dollars for a loss. More important than money, his listening had paid off.

"I'd go into the dressing room to give one of my talks, and it basically already had been done by Mark," Doug recalled.

"Mark had everything," Paul said. "He was big, strong, and very, very tough. Actually, he was a little bit mean. Not toward his family, but he could get mad when he was a kid. He always played with older kids, and he'd lose his temper. When he was seventeen, he already was 190 pounds. He was dominating the league, beating up everybody in Tier II."

He wasn't just mean, though. In the late 1970s, 6'1", 190 pounds was big, even by NHL standards. Mark already had a remarkably powerful skating stride, in which he held his back straight and swayed his arms from side-to-side, and held his stick with one hand as his legs pushed away. His acceleration from a standing stop was breathtaking. Mark also had the skills of a smaller man, good hands, and a wicked backhand shot from close range. He had the mental makeup to be a star, too. That came from his family.

"They're so close, and I think that's where he gets a lot of his inner strength, from the family," said Adam Graves, who joined the Oilers in 1989. "If there was ever anyone who's questioned the importance of family, they should spend a day with the Messiers. I remember back in Edmonton, when I first got there, how great he was. I remember Mark meeting us at the hotel, picking us up, and taking us to practice. During the day, if you were single, he'd tell you to come to his house for a pre-game meal. He'd have a pre-game meal for eight guys."

Doug's competitiveness rubbed off on the boys. Kevin Lowe once said: "Mark's father and his brother can't play a game of gin without standing up and getting ready to take each other's heads off."

They still go at it, tooth and nail, on the golf course or at anything they do.

"They're as tight-knit a family as I've ever seen," said defenseman Ken Daneyko, a close friend of the family who inherited the Magilla Gorilla nickname from Doug Messier. "When they go out, it's all for one. That's from his father. He started some good vibes. And his mother was very influential. They're all tight, and it's all family. They all stick together as a team. That helped along the way toward all he accomplished."

"The family has been my support system throughout my whole career," Messier told *Newsday*. "Because of it your self-esteem becomes greater, as does your confidence as a person. I don't think it's everything, but it gives you something to latch onto—your morals, your values, being compassionate toward other people."

Daneyko grew up with the Messier boys in Edmonton and dated Mary-Kay Messier. He went to Mark's hockey school and traveled with the Messiers to Greece and Hawaii.

"Even when he was twenty-three, he had the utmost respect," Daneyko said of Mark. "Even before he was a superstar, you could see the leadership, that pull, and the way people reacted. I remember going into restaurants and bars. People would crowd around him. That presence was always there. It spoke for itself on the ice, but you could see it away from the rink as well. He was very quiet or even shy. It was me and his other buddies who were rambunctious. We were more like bodyguards.

"He used to say to me when I was younger, 'I'll try to get you in Edmonton.' I used to go to Germany and train with Paul when he played there. You'd go over there to get a head start, and Mark would come over and practice. He was always helpful as far as keeping me positive. I'd get real down when I was in the minors and his father and Paul and Mark would help me keep my head up."

Paul made it to the NHL for a brief stint with the Colorado Rockies during the 1978-79 season, but played in only nine games and never scored a point. He finished his career by playing for seven seasons in West Germany. Mark wasn't a sure thing to make it in the NHL, either, until he actually arrived in the league. Hockey people knew he'd be tough, but some thought he might just be another tough guy.

"I remember his first fight," said Colin Campbell, an original Oiler. "He fought Al MacAdam. Al MacAdam was a tough fighter, a veteran, and a good puncher. Mark just hung in there with him. He wasn't a great fighter, Mark, he was just such a big, strong moose that he wouldn't get beat up in a fight. I remember the first time we tangled in the corner in training camp. He hit me and I elbowed him back and he pushed me. You can feel when a player's strong, and he was strong. For a kid of eighteen, he had tremendous strength on his skates."

During his brief stint with Cincinnati, Messier got Sather's attention when he beat up one of the Oilers, Dennis Sobchuk. "Even as a seventeen-year-old, there was no mistaking it," Sather said. "They talk about Maurice Richard. Well, Mark has the same look."

The look: His jaw juts to a lantern chin. The muscles and veins in his temples flex. His darting dark eyes are set deep beneath a dark, granite brow. His ears are pinned back alongside his head, and from the front can appear almost pointed at the top. His hair was long as a youngster, and began to get shorter later in his career. As it receded, Messier ultimately shaved himself bald. The look is topped off with a frightening, intimidating stare.

Yet Messier is known as a generous man who loves keeping his teammates happy. He is downright kind and gentle at times, often outwardly emotional, and his laugh can make a whole room laugh with him. His friends say he has the "big Joker's smile," referring to the character in *Batman*. He is loud and always makes his presence known. Messier can be vulgar when among men, but a refined gentleman when around women or children.

"When you look at Mark, can you imagine anyone, the older players, calling a player at 18 or 19 years old 'Moose?'" asked Lee Fogolin. "That's what we called him. Moose. Just the physique, the raw-boned physique. Everybody talks about Gordie Howe's physique, but Mark ... You looked at him, and you knew he was an athlete. You'd say, 'What does this guy do? Is he a baseball player, a football player, a hockey player?' His physique and strength would tell you that.

"At 18 or 19, he had the competitive attitude, and the character. You could see when he first came to camp that year that it was just a matter of time before he matured into one of the best who ever played. On the ice, he was as mean and tough as anybody I've ever seen, anybody I'd ever played with or against. Off the ice he was a gentleman, a great guy, that's for sure. But if somebody did something, boy, that toughness ... he was as mean as you'd ever see. But off the ice, his gentleness and caring, it was like a lot of athletes, you can't believe it's the same person."

Messier's mean streak earned him a lot of room, and his ferocity made him as much a force on the ice as did any of his other skills.

"He was feared," said Craig MacTavish, "not so much for what he could do with his gloves off, but for what he could do with them on, in terms of high sticking guys or elbows. He'd just take care of business, and every once in a while he'd make a statement that nobody was going to take liberties with him."

While with the Oilers, Messier was suspended three times. There could have been dozens more suspensions. In 1983-84, he received a six-game suspension for whacking Vancouver's Tomas Gradin over the head with his stick. In 1984-85, he broke the jaw of Calgary's Jamie

Macoun with a punch and was suspended for ten games. In 1988-89, he was suspended for six games for knocking out some of Rich Sutter's teeth with his stick.

"Messier is to hockey what Jim Brown once was to pro football," said the late Bob Johnson, the former Calgary and Pittsburgh coach. "He's a bull with finesse. He's a mean hombre."

Legend has it that one time, Kent Nilsson, the Oilers's skilled winger, had broken from the team concept and was playing too selfishly. Messier grabbed him by the throat and shook him.

"He just looks at you," Nilsson later said. "One of those looks and you know you better get going."

Nilsson did get going. He became an integral part of the 1987 team, which John Muckler called the best of Edmonton's five Cup teams.

Don Cherry, the former Boston coach who now is a legendary TV personality in Canada, compared Messier to Charles Manson.

"You look at his eyes, you think there's a screw loose," Cherry said. "I say that affectionately."

"The biggest compliment you can give a player now is that he has the Messier look," said Terry Crisp, who coached Calgary during the 1980s when the Flames had a heated rivalry with the Oilers. "If a player had the Messier look, watch out. Not many had it.

Recalled former Vancouver coach Harry Neale: "I remember Tomas Gradin, who was a very good little center for us in Vancouver. He won a draw cleanly from Messier, back to our guy, who scored. Messier just chopped him over the fuckin' wrist. Gradin came to the bench saying, 'Jesus Christ, all I did was win the draw.' I heard one of our guys on the bench say, 'Hey, usually he breaks your fuckin' wrist when you win a draw from him.'"

Although he was mean on the ice, Messier was a gentle bear off the ice. He is a fun-loving, emotional man who enjoys life. Lowe once called Messier wild.

"We had some great times, to say the least," Lowe wrote in a story he authored for The Hockey News in 1990. "Mark loves to have a good time. He and I probably went out on the town a little more than Wayne. Wayne did his share of it, but right from Day 1 he had a great sense of responsibility. But Mark and I were out more often because we weren't Wayne Gretzky."

Throughout his career, Messier has remained quiet about his private life. "There has to be a little bit of a line drawn there," he said.

He had a son, Lyon, who was born in 1988 to Lesley Young, a former model. Messier had met Young on one of the Oilers' road trips to New York. When Lyon was born, Young served Messier with a paternity suit. Although the parents would have another court fight ten years later over an increase in child support, Messier treated his son ... well, like a son. Lyon came to the games whenever his father was in Landover, Maryland, to play the Capitals. Often, he hung out in the locker room while his father talked to reporters after games. He regularly visited Messier's house in Hilton Head, South Carolina, and shared short vacations with his father.

Messier downplays the stories about his and his teammates' youthful indiscretions. But the young Oilers did some serious partying. Once, when asked about his social life, Messier said, "I didn't exactly go home after every game and bake cookies."

"Name me one kid who's eighteen and gets a fistful of money, a new car, new clothes and tell me he doesn't get into a little trouble," Sather once said.

"He was a free spirit," Campbell recalled. "He was honest and fun-loving. I remember one time we went on a road trip and he missed the plane. They sent him right to Houston, our farm team that year. I think he enjoyed it more than going on the road trip because it was warmer down there. He just loved life. You could see Sather took to him right away, just loved the kid. He loved to play."

Years later, when he started making a lot of money, Messier bought Gretzky's classic black Bentley. Then he bought a place in Hilton Head, South Carolina, where his family had a second home. It became their permanent base and a place where Messier could have his big toys: a championship golf course on a tiny island and a deep-sea fishing boat.

"Mess and Gretz were always best of buddies, but they were polar opposites in many ways," MacTavish said. "I remember one day, Gretz had this brand new, big Mercedes. Kevin Lowe, myself, Mark, and I think Glenn Anderson were there. We borrowed Gretz's car and we were going hunting. Gretz's car was always immaculately clean, and it still smelled brand new, and Mess was driving. We were just piling down the cornstalks in Gretz's brand new Mercedes. We were just laughing and Mark had a big mouthful of spit, and we were all kind of soiling Gretz's big limo Mercedes. We all went out hunting, and nobody got killed, which was an accomplishment."

It was a time for fun and games for the young Oilers superstars.

"You know what it was?" Gretzky said. "We were so young, I don't believe we realized the pressure we were under. There's no question that was a big factor in the whole situation. We'd all been faced with pressure in our lives, and grown up being the best player on our teams, and people expecting us to excel in junior hockey and so on. But I think when we got into pro hockey, we were so young, we just wanted to play hard. We practiced hard, we enjoyed each other's company. I don't believe we really understood or realized what the pressure was. And again, part of that was the coaching staff and management had taken that pressure away from us and let the older guys handle the pressure more than the younger guys.

"Yet they didn't completely shelter us from it, but they guarded us from it. If the team was playing poorly or we weren't winning the first couple of years, or the year L.A. beat us in the playoffs, people wanted to break up the Oilers: 'That team can't win; they're too offensive minded.' I remember that summer, Glen had to go a long way in protecting and guarding against breaking up that whole team, and protecting the players, and that's what he did. He always did that, and I don't think we realized it then when we were playing, but obviously he was a little wiser than we were."

Few could match Messier's infectious intensity. Paul Messier said that in the Messier house, you don't need a calendar to know it's playoff time.

"Maybe he's a little nervous, a bundle of nervous energy," Paul said. "It's not fun to hang around him. He channel surfs pretty good, you know? He can't seem to keep his attention on anything. I wouldn't say he's cranky or anything, but I don't think he even realizes what he's saying to you sometimes, or what you're saying to him. He's sort of there, but not there. My father was like that as a player, too. He used to lose his hair at playoff time."

By the mid-1980s, Messier's personality had melded with his on-ice persona. He wore an old, rounded WinnWell helmet that looked like a construction worker's hard hat. Very few players in the league wore that hat, but two who did idolized Messier: Daneyko and young Oilers forward Kelly Buchberger, who would become the team's captain a few seasons after the legends departed.

Messier, a left-handed shooter, developed a snap shot off the wrong foot, the back foot, a dangerous shot he'd often fire while skating down the right wing. Goalies, who are used to players shooting off the front foot, were fooled even when they knew it was coming. Messier learned the shot by watching the old Soviet hockey teams. His right leg would kick straight out toward the right-wing boards as he unleashed the shot, which often sliced. Often, the shot wasn't terribly hard, but it was always difficult to handle. Because Messier lifted his leg, goalies could not detect the moment of release by watching his skates.

Messier had other traits, like taking one hand off his stick as he accelerated while carrying the puck up ice, and his constant on-ice spitting. And he adopted some sayings. One was, "There's winning, and misery." Another was, "Winning isn't all flowers and fun and games. Winning sometimes is sheer hell."

"What was unique about our team was we grew up together, so nobody was scared of anybody," Gretzky said. "We became like a family. So if Mess was having a tough night, Kevin could say, 'Mess, we need you to get going.' If I was having an off night, Mess could stand in the locker room in front of everybody and say, 'Hey, Gretz, we need you. You've got to get going.' And nobody took that as an insult. Nobody took it as, 'Wow, you can't say that to him.' And everybody kind of had that for each other."

A big part of that group gathered every few years for Team Canada's training camp in preparation for what used to be known as the Canada Cup. It was a world-class, Olympic-style tournament involving the best hockey nations in the world. Canada won the gold in four of the five Canada Cup events, and finished second once.

In two of those years, 1987 and 1991, the coach of the victorious Canadian team was Mike Keenan. In 1987, Keenan was the coach of the Philadelphia Flyers, who lost to the Oilers in the finals. In 1990, he was the coach of the Blackhawks, who had lost to the Oilers in the conference final.

"In 1987, we had just played them in the final, through seven games in May," Keenan said. "A short time thereafter, early August or late July, we assembled for Team Canada '87. That was my first introduction to Mark from a coaching perspective. Quite frankly, my first reaction with seeing all those Oilers on the ice—Wayne Gretzky, Mark, Paul Coffey, Glenn Anderson—was, 'How the hell did we ever go seven games with these guys?'

"I was very impressed with the talent level. The thing that was most striking with Mark was his ability to mix with the group without taking away from anybody. And his relationship with Wayne. The chemistry they had as a group was one that was very respectful. You could also see the genuine like for each other at the same time. They had a lot of fun together.

"Mark was very instrumental in bringing that group together. And certainly, based on their talent and their success, they had a great deal of confidence. They had a good mix. They had enough respect for each other and each other's ability. They won a lot and they won often. And it's a lot easier on all of us in this business when you win."

The Canada Cup was a showcase for the best of the best, and nothing was better than in 1987, when Gretzky set up Mario Lemieux for the Canada Cup-winning goal against the Soviet Union. All three of the games in the best-of-three final series were decided by 6-5 scores.

"In both Canada Cups, Mark and Wayne were very instrumental," Keenan said. "In '87, Mario also played a huge role. There were so many great players, like Raymond Bourque, all these guys in their prime. And we also played a fabulous, fabulous team in the Red Army. It was communism vs. capitalism, and their players were in their prime, too, players like Slava Fetisov and Igor Larionov. It was some of the best hockey ever.

"Mark was very much an emotional leader. Wayne was an artist and an exceptional player. Mark was the passionate leader. The mix was fantastic. In '91, Wayne was hurt when Gary Suter hit him, and two guys stepped up. One was Mark, one was Paul Coffey, and they made a huge difference.

"Mark always had that connection with his teammates. There's no other player who had the same type of impact. I had some great players, great leaders—Mark Howe, Rick Tocchet, Chris Chelios, Steve Larmer, Michel Goulet, Dirk Graham, Jeremy Roenick, the Vezina Trophy goalies. Every great team has to have people who are very influential within the group. How Mark impacted his team was incredible. In Game Two in 1987, we were tied after regulation. He came in and just jacked the room right up. It was really an incredible experience. And the team stayed jacked up, even more so for Game Three. Honest to God, you could feel the energy in the room, like I've never experienced in any situation before or after. The energy was so high, it was like they were walking on air after he spoke."

The often-confrontational Keenan had his first face-to-face confrontation with Messier on that Canada Cup team.

"In '87, I was being very challenging with the group," Keenan recalled. "We were in Montreal, and they felt I was being a little bit demanding with them as a team. So Mark and Wayne and Raymond Bourque came up to see me in my hotel room. They said, 'This is our summer. You're working us awfully hard.' I said, 'I am? The tournament begins in two weeks, doesn't it?' They said, 'Yes.' I said, 'We're expected to win, aren't we?' They said, 'Yes.' I said, 'Do you expect to win?' They said, 'Yes.' Then they said, 'We're sorry we're here,' and they left. It just points out what good people they are. Mark said, 'It won't happen again. Forget we had this meeting.'"

In the 1984 Canada Cup, Messier infuriated the Russians when he elbowed Vladimir Kovin and opened a 26-stitch cut on Kovin's face.

"The Canadians play like Indians looking for scalps," said furious coach Viktor Tikhonov.

Another best vs. best tournament was Rendez-Vous 87 in Quebec City, when the NHL All-Stars played the Soviets.

"Mark took over the dressing room," recalled Dave Poulin, who played for the NHL. "I don't think there was any question about that. Of course, Gretzky's presence is always a factor, but Messier just stood up and took it over. He said, 'This is the way we're going to do this and this is how we'll warm up.' And then he said, 'OK?' He scared the hell out of me. You played your best because you were afraid of answering to Mark."

■ ■ ■

So much of Messier rubbed off on the Oilers, and vice versa. They won one last Stanley Cup, without Gretzky and Coffey, in 1990. In 1991, the Oilers lost to the Minnesota North Stars in the conference finals. Messier knew when he walked off the ice after the series clincher that he had played his final game as a member of the Oilers.

"We would have won seven or eight or more," said Muckler. "There's no doubt in my mind. Now they're all pieces of other organizations' Stanley Cup winners. If they all stayed in Edmonton, we'd still be winning there. But could you imagine the payroll? There was no way, economically. It just couldn't happen. That was the main reason I left. I knew that was coming. Mess left the same year I left. I went to Buffalo after we lost to Minnesota in the final four. Our team was all beat up, Mess was hurt, MacTavish was hurt that year, too. I knew it was going to break up."

Sather knew, too.

"Here was arguably the best team that had ever been put together in the world and it had an opportunity to do something for another five or six years, and it was dismantled," Sather said years later in a story in the Toronto *Globe and Mail*. "If we were in New York or Los Angeles or Toronto or Montreal, that team would never have been dismantled, believe me. The market wasn't big enough to handle it under the situation we were in. I knew the reality of all those decisions that had to be made. I didn't like it, but I understood it."

Gretzky and Messier were part of a special team. "The days when you go to work and come home and think about things, the things you think about are the guys you played with. Not the winning," Fogolin said. "The people you played with. And it's like the sun comes out whenever you see them or think about them."

4

The Big Deal

The young general manager had been nicknamed "No Deal Neil" when the Rangers floundered early in his first season. Neil Smith had been the third choice to become the Rangers' general manager during the chaotic summer of 1989, in what had become a 49-year-old Stanley Cup drought.

Phil Esposito, the Rangers' general manager the previous season, had fired coach Michel Bergeron for insubordination with two games remaining in the regular season, and the Rangers having lost seven of their past ten games. The firing came on April Fool's Day, and many people thought it was a joke. The joke was on the Rangers. Esposito named himself coach, and the Rangers lost the last two games of the regular season.

Their situation worsened in the playoffs. With the Rangers trailing, three games to none, in the best-of-seven first round series, Esposito summoned goalie prospect Mike Richter from the minors. Richter, who had never before played in an NHL game, made his debut in Game Four. The Pittsburgh Penguins won to complete the sweep.

Esposito's three-year run as general manager had been chaotic. He made forty-three trades, some of them absolute disasters. After receiving a vote of confidence from team vice president Jack Diller, Esposito was fired on May 24, 1989. Thus, the Rangers' merry-go-round of general managers and coaches continued, as did their dismal history of failure.

The summer-long search for a replacement was almost as comical as Esposito's April Fool's joke. Joe Bucchino, a former Rangers stickboy, headed the Rangers' table at the NHL Entry Draft. Diller wanted Scotty Bowman, the fabled former Montreal and Buffalo coach, to run the Rangers, but he turned down the job. The Rangers then offered the job to Herb Brooks, who had coached the United States Olympic team to the Miracle On Ice gold medal in the 1980 games at Lake Placid. Brooks turned down the job, too. So the Rangers and Diller were in a pickle. The search had become a subject of ridicule. One of the New York tabloids ran a photo of Jack Diller next to a photo of Phyllis Diller.

Finally, on July 17, Diller introduced the Rangers' new general manager: Neil Smith, a 35-year-old known best as a talent scout for the Islanders and the Detroit Red Wings. Smith was hardly a novice, but he was hardly Bowman, Brooks, or the high-profile type the Rangers almost always sought. Smith won the job by showing Diller a well-mapped plan for success and by promising to build a strong organization. He swore franchise stability would finally find a home at Madison Square Garden. Smith began his tenure by making some difficult decisions and by displaying toughness his soft-spoken nature might have led one to believe he did not have. Smith fired Bucchino, then hired an assistant, Larry Pleau, and a coach, veteran Roger Neilson.

Neilson is odd in some ways, yet he is a genuinely nice, likable, and knowledgeable man. Colin Campbell, who would come to New York as an assistant coach in 1990-91, often compared Neilson to a grandfatherly figure, or a friendly, kindly uncle. He was 55 when the Rangers hired him, and had been a head coach for four other NHL teams: the Toronto Maple Leafs, Buffalo Sabres, Vancouver Canucks, and Los Angeles Kings.

He is funny, loyal, and quirky. He could charm you with a story for any occasion. And he knows his hockey.

Neilson's style is simple: Defense first. He likes to trap opponents at center ice, a style which wasn't known as the neutral-zone trap until years later. He uses four lines. His checkers play as much as his stars. Neilson, as is often said, would rather lose 2-1 than win 5-4.

Neilson once crossed paths with Messier and the Edmonton Oilers. He had been fired by the Kings and the Oilers hired him to handle their video systems. Most of the Oilers liked Neilson. Some didn't.

"Roger, they hired Roger, yeah," said one of the former Oilers.

"We used to throw his fuckin' shit in the garbage. We just felt like we worked all year long, and this guy's coming in for the playoffs? Fuck him. He's not going to get to first base here."

In 1989-90, his first season with the Rangers, Neilson guided a team lacking stars and experience to a division title, the first championship of any kind for the Rangers since they won the regular-season league title in 1942. Playing without the burden of expectations, the young Rangers jumped out to an 8-1-3 start, and were sailing along until hitting an 0-8-2 freefall in December. That's when the "No Deal Neil" moniker was born.

Newspapers and fans urged Smith to trade for the center and offensive force the Rangers needed: A big-name, marquee player. He balked. Finally, Smith stole the show at the 1990 All-Star weekend in Pittsburgh. He traded youngsters Tomas Sandstrom and Tony Granato to Los Angeles for Bernie Nicholls, who had scored 70 goals and 150 points in 1988-89. Big as that deal was, it would seem insignificant compared to the Real Deal that would follow a year and a half later.

■ ■ ■

Neil Smith has a closet in his office.

"That's where we keep the ghosts," he said. "That's where the skeletons have lived for the last fifty years."

When Smith made his promises to Diller, he also had to promise to win a Stanley Cup. The Rangers hadn't won the Cup since 1940, a half century made more torturous for their fans by the success of the New York Islanders, who, playing less than forty-five minutes from Madison Square Garden, had won four consecutive Cups in the early 1980s. The Islanders' fans' chants of "1940!" taunted the Rangers and their fans. In the 1980s, the New Jersey Devils made it a three-way Metropolitan area rivalry, and their fans picked up the "1940" chant, too.

The curse, however, was older than the Islanders and the Devils. A famous black and white photo shows six tuxedoed men standing around the Stanley Cup in 1941, the year after the Rangers had won it all. The photo shows Col. John Reed Kilpatrick, the owner of the Rangers, burning the mortgage of the old Madison Square Garden in the Cup. Many say this act of hockey blasphemy was the start of the Rangers' long drought.

Then there's the story of Red Dutton, who ran the New York Americans in the late 1930s and early '40s. The Americans preceded the Rangers into the NHL and played at the old Garden. But when the Garden's owners decided to build their own team, the Rangers, and when the Rangers ran the Americans out of business, Dutton declared:

"The Rangers will never win the Cup again in my lifetime." Dutton was right: He died in 1987.

The Rangers had their chances. In 1950, they took the Detroit Red Wings to two overtimes in the decisive Game Seven before Pete Babando won it for the Wings. The Rangers didn't win another playoff series until 1971. In 1969-70, they were one of the league's top teams until future Hall of Fame defenseman Brad Park got his skate caught in a rut at the Garden and tore up his knee. In 1972, the Rangers were leading the league until March 12, when leading scorer Jean Ratelle broke his ankle. The Rangers lost in the Stanley Cup finals to the Boston Bruins. In 1979, they shocked the Islanders in the semifinals, then had a one game to none lead over the Canadiens in the finals, but didn't win another game.

At first, the fortunes for the Neilson-Smith regime didn't look any better. In 1990, the Rangers lost to the Washington Capitals in the division finals.

The wheels for the biggest trade in Rangers history were set in motion atop an old, wooden folding table outside the visitors' locker room at the Capital Center in Landover, Maryland. The entire history of the Rangers was about to be rewritten.

In April 1991, the Rangers had just bombed out of the playoffs for the second year in a row. They had been eliminated by the Washington Capitals in what was referred to as the Rangers' Wizard of Oz series: They showed no heart, no brains, and no courage. Before the third period of the final game, Smith stormed out of a men's room in the press lounge, angry and agitated.

"It's like I built a car to win the Indy 500 and somebody went and crashed it in the first turn," Smith said.

When Smith jogged down the Capital Center's long cement staircase after the game, he promised himself that he wasn't going to make any comments about what he had watched. But he couldn't help himself. The players had had their say. Now Smith would have his. As he sat on the folding table, the veins bulged in his forehead and neck.

"If I was still scouting for Detroit, I'd know which side had the talent," Smith said. "But I'd also know which side had the heart. It just wasn't there. This is totally unacceptable. I'm not saying there will be major shakeups because that would be a panic move. The fact is in the NHL the pressure is on in the playoffs. That's the climax of the season. We play six months to eliminate five teams. This is what separates the men from the boys. Well, you saw a lot of boys tonight."

When Smith referred to the Rangers as "high-profile, high-paid players," he clearly was talking about his veteran stars: Bernie Nicholls, Mike Gartner, and John Ogrodnick. The team also had a leadership problem. Captain Kelly Kisio was a terrific team player, but he hardly had a dynamic personality. When he got hurt, the captaincy went to James Patrick, a smart player, but no leader. When Patrick got hurt, the Rangers overlooked the other alternate captain, David Shaw, and gave the "C" to Gartner.

Smith reacted. In one of his first moves during the offseason, he left Kisio unprotected for the expansion draft. Kisio ended up with the expansion San Jose Sharks, leaving the Rangers without a captain. Soon, a rumor circulated that the Rangers were interested in obtaining Mark Messier from Edmonton. The rumor was too unbelievable to be true.

At age thirty, Messier was considered to be on the downside of his career. He had played twelve long seasons with long playoff runs, including six to the Stanley Cup finals. He had won two Canada Cup championships. He had logged plenty of ice time. His thirty years were more like thirty-five or forty to most hockey players. He had missed several weeks of the 1990-91 season with a troublesome knee. Gambling on Messier seemed like too big a risk for the Rangers. Besides, the Rangers would have to give up too much of their future to make the deal worthwhile for Edmonton.

On September 3, 1991, Smith made a move that didn't attract much attention. He signed 23-year-old Adam Graves, a free agent from Edmonton. Graves, a center/winger, had scored seven goals and 18 assists in 1990-91, and helped Edmonton win the Stanley Cup in 1990. Only Smith, who had drafted Graves for Detroit, and those who had played with Graves or seen him regularly, knew that his value to a team would not be measured in statistics. There are only a handful of such players, whose goals and assists don't come close to telling the whole story. A few of the Rangers players were going through unofficial pre-camp practices at the Rangers' practice facility in Rye, New York, when a reporter walked in with the news of the Graves signing. Two of the players, Joey Kocur and Kris King, had played with Graves in the Detroit organization.

"Gravy!" King and Kocur screamed at one another as they high-fived. "We got Gravy!"

James Patrick called Ron Low, the Edmonton assistant coach, who told him that Graves was not only a great player, but a great fighter.

Low told Patrick that Graves' most notable bouts came against the much bigger Joel Otto of Calgary, who regularly harassed, whacked, and hacked Messier in the legendary Edmonton-Calgary wars. Graves would then beat the daylights out of Otto.

So here was Smith, still a young man in a business dominated by older men, knocking heads with Edmonton's veteran boss, Glen Sather. Smith knew that Type One free agents came with a catch. An independent arbitrator would decide upon the Oilers' compensation for the loss. Team A, the signing team, would submit its offer. Team B, the team losing the player, would submit its demand. The arbitrator would take one or the other. Smith figured that Sather would go after his young players. Smith also knew that Graves' statistics could sway the arbitrator to take his low-ball offer. Smith figured that Sather wouldn't try for Tony Amonte or Doug Weight, two of the Rangers' organizational diamonds; going after too much could force Judge Edward Houston of Toronto to side with the Rangers' offer. Sather wanted to work out a trade and agree on compensation before going to arbitration. He offered to take second-tier prospects Louie DeBrusk and Steven Rice. Smith declined.

The signing showed Smith had some guts. Challenging Sather at arbitration showed even more courage.

Sather wasn't happy. He pointed out that Graves was the heir to Messier as captain of the Oilers. The Detroit Red Wings, Los Angeles Kings, and Philadelphia Flyers had been interested in Graves, but Smith and the big-money Rangers had come along and signed him.

Sather's immediate reaction sounded a siren.

"Tell Neil," Sather said, "that he just cost himself a chance to get Mark Messier."

Mark Messier?

At the time, this much was known: Messier wanted a new contract and wasn't going to get big money from the Oilers, who had been dumping payroll. Until Sather's remark, nobody believed Messier could be coming to New York. Later, Graves admitted he chose the Rangers over the other three teams because he knew Messier was coming right behind him. But at the time, when Smith was asked if the Graves deal had taken him out of the Messier ballgame, he responded: "I never said I was in that ballgame."

In the compensation case, the Rangers offered Edmonton Troy Mallette, 21, who was young, enthusiastic, and whose statistics were similar to Graves'. Edmonton wanted Rice, 20, and DeBrusk, 20, a monstrous fighter. Smith considered Sather's proposal ridiculous. The arbitrator obviously agreed. The Oilers were awarded Mallette. Smith had beaten Sather.

For his part, Smith didn't believe for a minute that he had cost himself a chance to get Messier. He was convinced Edmonton couldn't keep Messier and that Messier was ready to leave. Smith kept moving forward. He obtained big Tim Kerr, an injury prone mountain of a man who regularly scored fifty goals for Philadelphia. The best, however, was yet to come.

■ ■ ■

When Smith finally admitted to talking to Sather about Messier, he said he wasn't optimistic about getting the deal done.

"If you feel you can help the organization and the team with a player, you've got to go out and get him," he said. "But, the premier players in this league, there's a big price you pay for them. I can't sit here and say, 'I don't want Mark Messier, we're not interested.' You can draft for a hundred years and not get a Mark Messier. But how much of your nose do you cut off?"

Sather wanted three of the Rangers' young players in return for Messier: Some combination of Rice, Tony Amonte, Doug Weight, Louie DeBrusk, and Alexei Kovalev. Smith was willing to part with Nicholls and no more than two of the young players. Nobody thought that would be enough to sway Sather, and the Rangers would also have to send a pile of money to the financially strapped Oilers.

Messier spent the later part of his summer playing for Team Canada, alongside Gretzky, in the Canada Cup. When the Canada Cup ended with another championship for Canada, Messier went home to Hilton Head, South Carolina, rather than to Oilers training camp. The trade watch was on. At the very least, Messier's days in Edmonton were over.

■ ■ ■

The sun glimmered off the Long Island Sound and through the big window of Neil Smith's office at the Rangers' practice rink in Rye. One September day in 1991, Smith gazed out the window and pondered a magnificent opportunity.

Smith had several hockey preview magazines spread out on a coffee table in the middle of the room. As he picked up each magazine, he couldn't help but notice that each one prominently featured color photos of Messier, Gretzky, and Mario Lemieux. These three players, Smith realized, were the giants of the game. And one of them was available.

But Smith wasn't completely comfortable with the idea of getting a 30-year-old whose body had endured so much wear and tear. Concerned about Messier's knee, Smith talked to other general managers, coaches, scouts, players, television analysts, and writers. He talked to doctors, too.

Messier had played in only fifty-three games the previous season, and in many of those he was in less than one hundred percent physical condition. Were injuries and age the reason the Oilers had made him available? Or was this really a chance to get a five-time champ, the ultimate leader in his sport, the man who had won the MVP just sixteen months earlier?

Despite the "No Deal Neil" moniker, Smith is relentless. If he thinks an available player can help his team win the Stanley Cup, he will get that player. Sometimes he might spend too much. Sometimes he might put the present ahead of the future. Sometimes he might overestimate what the player will actually deliver. But he will get the player.

As for Sather, rival general managers had learned to check their wallets after talking trade with him, even over the telephone. Sather is cagey, pushy, stubborn, and street-smart. He will get something for nothing, or more than he should get for something. He has never let his team die, even though he has been forced by circumstances, finances, and a cash-poor owner to trade Gretzky, Paul Coffey, Jari Kurri, Glenn Anderson, and Grant Fuhr. Sather wasn't going to give up Messier for nothing.

Messier wanted to play in New York. He knew the Oilers' future was nothing like its glorious past. His salary would be a burden to the franchise. Gretzky was gone. He wanted to play where he'd get $2 million a year plus endorsements, somewhere far away from Edmonton. By saying he'd never again play for the Oilers, and by hinting to friends he wanted to come to New York, Messier had played right into Sather's hands. And because the Rangers had what Sather wanted—the money to pay Messier, the money to mail to Edmonton, and young prospects—a Rangers-Oilers trade made sense.

Sather, a former Ranger, placed the pressure squarely on Smith's shoulders by publicly negotiating the trade. Sather got Rangers fans all worked up. WFAN radio in New York tracked down Sather during the summer and arranged for an interview on short notice. Questions about the trade were answered somewhat honestly and vaguely. Later, it was learned that Sather had handed off the phone to Oilers radio voice Rod Phillips, who handled the entire interview.

The pressure on Smith was building. Then Messier said he wanted to help the Rangers win the Cup, and that he wanted to play ten more years, bum knee and all. Smith seemed to be in an almost-no-win predicament. If he got Messier and Messier's knee didn't hold up, he would be the loser. If he gave up the team's future for Messier and the Rangers didn't win the Cup, he would lose. If he didn't get Messier and Messier had another MVP season somewhere else, he would lose. The only way Smith could win was if the Rangers won the Cup, with or without Messier. And they probably weren't going to win it without him.

■ ■ ■

Neilson still had not named a captain on the eve of the 1991-92 season. When asked about it, he twitched and nervously looked away. He knew what the questioner was getting at. Neilson, who has always been bad when it came to fibbing, said two of his top candidates for captain were Brian Leetch and Mike Gartner, and they had both missed most of training camp. But it had become obvious that the captain-to-be wasn't yet a Ranger.

Boston Garden was still almost empty hours before the opener. Smith sat in the yellow, wooden arena seats and answered reporters' questions. He said he had spoken to Sather once, for about ten minutes, that day. He added with a look of disgust that the chances of getting Messier were fifty-fifty. He didn't want to tip his hand.

Throughout the Rangers' 5-3 loss to the Bruins, Smith was on the phone in the creaky press box. The person on the other end of the line was Dr. Bart Nisonson.

Smith had phoned Messier while Mark was playing golf with his father and brother in Hilton Head, South Carolina. By the time their game had reached the fifteenth tee, Messier was told he was about to become a Ranger. Messier quickly flew out of town and snuck into New York for a physical on his left knee, which had twice been severely sprained the previous season. The trade between the Rangers and Oilers was nearly complete. The only missing ingredient was for Messier to pass his physical.

Smith phoned Dr. Nisonson over and over. Finally, he got through. "How's he doing?" Smith asked.

"You have quite a specimen here," Dr. Nisonson said. "A specimen." That's all Smith needed to hear. His next phone call was to Sather. "Let's do it," he said.

5

The Captain

Early the next morning, October 4, 1991, the Rangers called an impromptu press conference in the lobby of the Boston Long Wharf Marriott. A few yards from the front desk, with hotel patrons curiously looking over their shoulders, Neil Smith announced he had acquired Mark Messier.

The Rangers traded Bernie Nicholls, Louie DeBrusk, Steven Rice, and millions of dollars to Edmonton for Messier and future considerations. The future considerations would be a later trade that sent David Shaw to the Oilers for enormous defenseman Jeff Beukeboom.

The history of the Rangers was about to change. They would never be the same again.

Messier joined the team in Montreal. He was introduced at a press conference in an old oak-walled lounge at the fabled Montreal Forum. Smith couldn't have been prouder to introduce Messier and have him pull on the Rangers jersey. Messier slipped into a blue Rangers jersey with No. 11 on the back and sleeves. Cameras flashed away and Messier flashed a smile, but mostly he stared straight ahead. His thinning hair stood up on his head. He stuck out his chin. His posture defined confidence.

"The thing you get Mark Messier for is not to score 50 goals or 120 points," Smith said. "You get him because he lifts the rest of your players to another level. He's going to have an impact on a Brian Leetch and a James Patrick, and he's going to have an impact on a Doug Weight and a Tony Amonte. He's going to make them believe in themselves.

"Another exciting thing is whenever he leaves here, if it's seven months or seven years from now, he'll leave us with something we didn't have before he arrived. We'll be a better organization for having had him. He will put something into the Rangers logo that you won't be able to see. He will make the Rangers believe they can win, and I'm not sure anybody has ever made the Rangers believe they can win. You will sit there and say there is something dramatically different about this team.

"At training camp, in the opening speech, I said to everyone, not just the veterans, 'Prove to us you will do anything to win, and you'll be on the hockey club. Because I'll tell you, we will do anything to win. And that means trade you, cut you, send you down. We'll do anything to win.' And I think this again reinforces that message."

Trading for Messier was a fantasy when Smith first discussed it in July. Actually, getting Messier felt like a fantasy to Smith.

Messier had wanted $2 million a year from Edmonton, an amount the Oilers couldn't possibly come up with. But it was more than money that Messier wanted. He wanted a change of scenery.

"It was time," he said. "It was just time. In the end, the Oilers offered a pretty substantial contract. But I've been playing in Edmonton for twelve years and it was going to be sooner or later. Both the Oilers and myself recognized that fact and we were able to get things done."

Said Sather: "It's sad for me to trade Mark Messier, but it becomes more complex than that. We've traded a lot of players, but we acquired a lot of young players in return. If you don't trade players when they still have some value you can never recover."

Loyalty can be fatal in team sports, but the Oilers' decisions had more to do with fiscal responsibility than with player evaluation. Messier had seen Gretzky, Paul Coffey, Marty McSorley, and Mike Krushelnyski depart earlier. That summer, the team was further gutted with the departures of Grant Fuhr, Glenn Anderson, Steve Smith, Charlie Huddy, and Ken Linseman. Then they lost Graves to the Rangers. Messier, playing hurt when he played at all, had meager totals of 12 goals and 64 points.

"He's a great competitor," said John Muckler. "He was the leader of the pack the year I coached. They got the best person available to captain and be a leader of their team. He's played on five Cup winners and, with Wayne, was a leader on all of them."

Joel Otto, the big, mean checking center for the Calgary Flames, said: "I'm glad he's gone. Hey, he's an unbelievable player. Any time you can get him out of the division it's a benefit for us."

Said former Rangers captain Andy Bathgate, long retired: "If you can get an impact player, you can only wait so long. Messier has that look in his eye that tells you he's there to play."

Said Rangers Hall of Famer Rod Gilbert: "How can you pass on a person who on all of his five fingers has a Stanley Cup ring?"

Smith couldn't pass on Messier. He knew that Messier was more than an MVP-type player.

"Even after we made the trade, Slats told me, 'He will solve every problem you have, every time something comes up,' meaning in the locker room," Smith said. "That's what everybody says: 'Messier will always find a way to lead the team.' It sounds almost too good to be true or ridiculous to listen to people talk about a player like that, but every hockey person you talk to agrees.

"I spoke to Wayne Gretzky and Marty McSorley and they swear by Messier. You talk to Mike Keenan, Pat Burns, or Cliff Fletcher, who don't have a stake in this thing, and they all have seen his leadership work. It's amazing. I can't wait to see how it works for us."

Smith wouldn't have to wait long. Messier said all the right things right from the start.

"I accept the challenge and everything that goes with New York," he said. "I'm looking forward to it. I say, 'Let's go, then, and do what we have to do to make it work.' Everybody seems to want to tip-toe around the issue, that the Rangers haven't won a Stanley Cup in fifty-one years or whatever it is. Well, in Edmonton I always felt pressure was good for us. I've met every challenge I've ever faced head-on. I never want to duck any issue or challenge that comes my way. I welcome this one.

"I lived in Edmonton for thirty years and this was one of the biggest decisions of my life. This is a big move for me. It was a fantastic twelve years, but I'm looking more than forward to the new challenge in front of me. I'm starting a so-called second career. And I'm every bit as confident my second career will be as good as my first."

His first career had been remarkable and included five Stanley Cups, 392 goals, 1,034 points, and another 80 goals and 215 points in 166 play-off games. He had played in nine all-star games and won three Canada Cup championships. But this was New York. Wouldn't this be different?

"New York is the media mecca of sports," Messier said. "They want to win, but I don't worry about pressure. Edmonton has only 500,000 or 600,000 people, but they expected a lot, too, coming into the league with Wayne Gretzky. But a team isn't built in a day. You don't become a team in one day. They've made a lot of changes here and we'll need some time, a month or so, to settle in and start becoming the best team we can be. The key word is team. It's not the best players that win, it's the best team that wins. It is important to keep team in capital letters. It takes a while to become a team. We've got six months to do that now."

The process began immediately. Messier suited up for his first practice at the Montreal Forum shortly after the press conference. He shook a few hands, introduced himself to his new teammates, and skated onto the ice. Every players' attention immediately shifted. Messier skated with his powerful stride, slowly at first with both arms swaying his stick. His eyes stared straight ahead. He circled the ice over and over again, and a few teammates sidled up to him for a few words. The rest just watched from a distance as they circled the rink. They looked like sheep in a lion's cage.

There was uncertainty, yet a very positive feeling, to the drills. Messier's presence dominated the session. Veterans such as John Ogrodnick, Tim Kerr, and Mike Gartner—all former 50-goal scorers—appeared to be in awe of their new teammate. Younger players watched in wide-eyed fascination. Leetch skated up to his buddy, James Patrick, and said, "Do you believe Mark Messier is on our team? Can you believe it?" Then Leetch went to rookie Tony Amonte and told him, "Tony, you're going to be his winger." Amonte nervously stammered in reply, "I don't know. I don't think I'm going to be able to do it."

Messier's every move was recorded and remembered by the dozens of reporters from New York, Montreal, and various parts of Canada, and by the players who didn't want to miss a thing on this memorable day. The Rangers were certainly different. They looked like a team that believed it could now win.

"What he has," Gartner said, "what he was born with and has developed, is leadership qualities. And when you put those qualities together with five Stanley Cups and three Canada Cups, it puts an aura around those qualities. It just adds to the mystery, the mystique. I don't think it's anything magic. He's just a good leader, a quality person who has been part of winners his whole career. When he stands up and says something in the room, guys tend to listen."

Suddenly, Leetch looked like a better player. So did Gartner and the other players. Graves beamed. He had played with Messier in Edmonton, but that didn't mean he was any less awe-struck. He was just too happy to show it. Said Neilson: "I know Adam Graves hasn't stopped grinning since the trade was announced because he knows the impact Mark will have on the team."

Graves repeated one line over and over: "Aside from my father, there is nobody I respect more than Mark Messier, and I've only known him a few years. I'd tell you some negative things about him, but I don't know any."

The following night, in front of a *Hockey Night in Canada* television audience, a curious audience watching on TV in New York, and a soldout Montreal Forum, Messier made his debut against the Canadiens. The Rangers hadn't won at the Forum in their last twelve trips. It was something Messier would have to get used to quickly: things the Rangers hadn't done in a long time.

Messier pulled on his sweater with No. 11 on the back. Graves, who had kept No. 11 warm the night before in Boston, switched to Bernie Nicholls' now-available No. 9, and the Rangers went to work. Ogrodnick rammed one of the Canadiens into the corner boards. The hit was so atypical of Ogrodnick, it could only have been attributed to Messier's presence. Late in the third period, Messier stepped out of the penalty box and assisted on Doug Weight's tying goal. Then Sergei Nemchinov, in his second NHL game, won it in overtime with his first NHL goal.

One little dragon was dead. Messier had slayed the first one he had faced.

■ ■ ■

The whirlwind weekend wound up on Monday at Madison Square Garden. This was the official opener of the remodeled Garden, but it was also an opener of another kind: of the Messier era. Several former Rangers captains were invited. Among those in attendance were Barry Beck (Rangers captain from 1981-86), Ron Greschner (1986-87), and Dave Maloney (1978-80), along with Gilbert and Murray Murdoch, a distant relative of Messier's. All of the honorees wore jerseys with a C sewn onto the upper left side of the chest.

The moment that defined the night came after the players were introduced. Nobody was surprised, but the scene was still climactic, when master of ceremonies John Davidson announced, "Your new captain, five-time Stanley Cup champion, Mark Messier!"

Messier skated across the ice with his arms raised. The crowd roared. He shook hands with the other Rangers greats. Suddenly, the Garden was his.

"It was one of the greatest nights of my life," said Mary-Jean Messier, Mark's mother.

So, with the C firmly sewn onto Messier's new shirt, the new era in the new Garden began. Leetch made a rink-long rush for the Rangers' first goal by John Ogrodnick, and Messier assisted on both goals in a 2-1 overtime win over Boston. Messier stole a pass along the boards and fed Mike Gartner for Gartner's 499th career goal and the win in overtime.

Two games with Messier, two overtime victories for the Rangers.

"If we play eighty games like this," Messier said, running a hand over his nearly-bald head, "I might lose a lot more hair."

The Rangers felt good. They felt something magical.

"I wish anybody could work magic like that," Gartner said. "But truthfully, you need some breaks and we've gotten some. There might be a different feeling now, that we can win in overtime. The best thing about it is I think we can play a lot better than this. When the team chemistry comes, I think we'll be much better than we are now."

Now the lessons would begin. How To Win, 101. Professor Messier.

■ ■ ■

When Messier walked into the Rangers' locker room at Madison Square Garden, he noticed a huge table in the middle of the room. The table had been there for as long as anybody could remember. The trouble was, when Messier sat in his stall, he couldn't see the Rangers defensemen. So Messier moved the coolers and most of the equipment from the table. By the next game, the entire table was gone. Messier wanted to be able to address the team before games, during intermissions, and after games. And when he did, Messier told the equipment staff, "I want to be able to make eye contact with all my teammates."

Messier freely talked about the Rangers' tradition. Nobody had ever talked about the tradition of the Rangers because it was a tradition often mocked for failure. But Messier talked about the pride of this Original Six franchise, of the team that battled for years with only Montreal, Toronto, Detroit, Chicago, and Boston until the league expanded in 1967. He talked about the great players who had passed through Madison Square Garden, and the team's rich history, despite the Cup drought. In a matter of days, old pictures and plaques, commemorating the Rangers' history, were framed and hanging in the hallways outside the Rangers locker room and inside the room.

Messier, a Ranger for about a week, had turned the shame of the past fifty-one years into something the Rangers could be proud of. He had changed the images of past players from fallen losers into heroes and Hall of Famers. They hadn't won the big prize, but Messier wanted the Rangers organization to be proud, not embarrassed, of its history.

Messier had left most of his trophies, awards, and Stanley Cup rings behind when he moved from Edmonton to New York. His sister offered to ship his awards to New York, but Messier didn't want them. He wanted to make a clean break. Only later, when his house in Edmonton was sold, did Messier have his memorabilia sent to Hilton Head.

One day during practice, the players formed a semicircle around Neilson. Messier noticed something, reached with his stick to the chalkboard, and made a point of his own. Neilson watched intently. The other players, who had been shuffling about or bending for a breather, suddenly stopped shuffling and listened. Messier talked, they listened.

Not only fear of Messier's wrath made the players listen. They also deeply respected him for having won five Stanley Cups.

"It's like some guy talking about a diet," Gartner said. "If he stands up and he's overweight, you dismiss what he says. But if he stands up and looks like Arnold Schwarzenegger, you pay attention."

Messier commuted back and forth from his new Manhattan home to the Rangers' practice facility in Rye with Leetch, who he roomed with on the road. Messier latched onto Leetch, and Leetch didn't seem the least bit star struck. They talked about everything, including hockey, and quickly became friends. Much of their drive time was spent with Messier telling the young defenseman what it takes to achieve greatness. Messier told Leetch not to be afraid of making mistakes, to take chances. Messier convinced Leetch that great players sometimes make great mistakes trying to make great plays. With Messier's encouragement, Leetch suddenly became a force on the ice, joining the play in the offensive zone, and being the trailer on a play usually created by Messier's speed.

Unlike many of his teammates, Leetch wasn't in awe of Messier. If Messier had said, "Drop and give me fifty," more than a few Rangers would have been doing pushups. After the Rangers failed to score an even-strength goal in two games, Messier said, "We have to find a way to score, even if that means we have to put the puck between our teeth and carry it into the net." Everybody was sure that if that's what it took, that's what he'd do.

In his first eleven games, Messier not only had an 11-game point streak, but he was cut in three different places on his face. The players couldn't help but stare as Messier continued his bullish play with blood dripping from his face and onto the front of his uniform.

"The support he has is, like, if he said, 'There's a burning building, let's go in and see if there's anybody we can pull out,' they'd all go, 'Yeah!'" said assistant coach Colin Campbell. "Or he'd say, 'There are sharks in that water; let's go swimming,' and everybody would go, 'Yeah, all right!' It's an all-for-one, one-for-all thing. It's like we might really go swimming with the sharks and survive. It's a feeling that everything is possible if we do it together."

The fourth game of the season was another nail-biter. Messier's first sermon came after the first period, and every word of it was positive and corny. "We're outplaying them," Messier told the Rangers, who were trailing the arch-rival Islanders 2-1 before a disgruntled crowd at the Garden.

"The guys were a little down," said Kris King. "He just put it straight. He said that we certainly outplayed them. And that we had to work hard. And then he comes out and scores the big goal. You can talk a lot and say some things. But you've got to go out on the ice and do it."

Messier did it. He scored his first goal as a Ranger in the second period, and his second goal in the third. King got the winner with fifteen seconds left and Patrick added an empty-netter five seconds later to complete a 5-3 victory.

"The feeling is we can win every game, no matter what the circumstances," Messier said. "We got behind the other night in Montreal and we got behind tonight. We know we can't win eighty games, but that's the attitude we want to take, that we can. Winning is an attitude. You've got to believe in yourself."

Neilson appreciated Messier's presence and power in the locker room. Having Messier was like having a coach in the locker room.

"He's just gone into the dressing room and said, 'Hey, we've got to turn it around this period,'" Neilson said. "That's really important to a coaching staff. The players hear our voices enough. When a player of his stature stands up, players listen. Not all captains can do that."

The Rangers didn't need a long time to see another side of Messier. In a 5-3 loss to Washington, Joey Kocur received three minor penalties. Kocur was one of the most feared fighters in league history. His right fist was a jackhammer that not only won him a lot of fights, but sometimes left opponents severely injured. In the Washington game, Kocur received a charging penalty for a sequence in which he not only ran over one of the Capitals players, but also got a piece of teammate Doug Weight, sending him out of action with an elbow injury. Kocur was also called for roughing and for tripping on a play so far away from the puck that almost nobody saw it, except referee Terry Gregson.

On the resulting power play, Washington's Kevin Hatcher scored the winning goal.

Messier skated up to Gregson after the goal and showered him with obscenities. Gregson awarded Messier a misconduct penalty.

"I was just disappointed with the calls on Joey," Messier said. "He played a good, hard game. His reputation preceded him. He got us off to a good start his first shift, then after that . . . it's frustrating to see Joey play as hard as he did . . . we need that kind of effort."

Winning is everything to Messier.

"And I don't think you should settle for anything less," Messier barked. "Anything less is unacceptable. I think you've got to learn. Winning isn't something that happens by accident. It's a well thought-out plan and it starts in camp, and everything you do all year is to get as best prepared for the playoffs as you can. That's something we had to learn in Edmonton. We went through a lot of learning processes because we never had anybody who went through it. You come to camp with one goal—to win the Cup—and everything you do from that point is toward that purpose. Every practice. Every game."

Messier loved talking about the Stanley Cup. He relished the prospect of ending the Rangers' drought. Their failure had become his challenge.

"When you talk about it, think about it, what it would be like to have a parade down Fifth Avenue, that would be great," he said. "You have to think about winning. You think it, you talk it, you eat it, you breathe it, and it becomes consuming. You can't be coming to the rink for three hours for practice, or for three hours for a game. It's more than that, and sometimes it's hard on people around you and families, but that's the way it has to be done."

■ ■ ■

Messier's closed-door, players-only, peel-the-paint-off-the-walls, single-voice meetings were few and far between early in the 1991-92 season, but he held one during a game against Minnesota. The Rangers trailed, 2-1, after the second period, when Messier ripped into his teammates. They'd go on to win, 3-2.

"Let's put it this way," Mike Richter said of the meeting. "We listened. And we went out in the right frame of mind for the third period."

Following a 6-1 loss in Los Angeles, Messier spoke to his teammates about commitment and what it took to be champions.

"I will not take losing as a habit," Messier said. "I won't stand for it." Messier said that every player should look no further than himself after a loss. He broke into tears, and virtually every Ranger in the room cried. Two nights later, Richter shut out the Blues in St. Louis. On the way back to the hotel, Messier ordered the team bus driver to pull over at a tavern. The captain then took the entire team inside for a celebration. After Messier's speech in Los Angeles, the Rangers played twenty-one games over .500 the rest of the season.

Yet, all was not well. Neilson used a form of the neutral-zone trap long before it became the curse of the 1990s, when lousy teams employed the boring style to shut down teams that had more talent. In the trap, instead of forechecking and attacking, the defending team backs off and lets the other team come at them. Then it tries to trap the puck-carrier in the neutral zone and cause a turnover.

Edmonton never used anything resembling the trap in its glory years. With all their speed and skill, the Oilers never backed off. They went full steam ahead, chased the puck in all areas of the rink, and forced teams to back off from them.

The first signs of Messier's unhappiness with Neilson's passive system appeared in November. For the fourth time, the Rangers played poorly in the third period and blew a lead.

"The wheels came completely off the bus," Messier said. "We stopped skating and when you stop skating in this league, it's like playing football and kicking from your own end zone all the time. Sooner or later, they're going to put it in your end zone. I'm not trying to be negative, but you can't play hockey without skating. You can't keep just defending. We had zero forechecking, and they kept coming at us. We left John Vanbiesbrouck to the wolves."

■ ■ ■

The NHL Players Association salary survey became public as the Rangers and Messier discussed his new contract. The survey would have an enormous effect on salaries in hockey because, for the first time, everybody knew what everybody else was making. Suddenly, there was a means for comparison and setting market values.

Messier's contract with the Oilers had him scheduled to earn $1.084 million in 1991-92, making him one of only sixteen millionaires in the NHL. Yet, Messier was far down on this list of the NHL's richest players. Gretzky made $3 million, Lemieux made $2.38 million, and Buffalo's Pat LaFontaine made $1.6 million. Messier was fourteenth on the list, behind Luc Robitaille at $1.1 million, even though he was far superior to many of the players making more money.

The Rangers fixed that situation. Messier's new deal included a $1 million signing bonus and annual salaries of $1.75 million in 1991-92, $2.35 million in 1992-93; $2.5 million in 1993-94; $2.65 million in 1994-95; and $2.75 million in 1995-96. It offered a $60,000 bonus for winning the first round of the playoffs, $60,000 for winning the second round, $100,000 for getting to the Stanley Cup finals, and another $100,000 for winning the Cup. The most significant clause allowed Messier to ask to renegotiate his contract if the Rangers won the Stanley Cup. This was a vital clause, but the Rangers could not envision any amount too great for winning the Cup.

Smith didn't have a problem with the contract, which was negotiated by Doug Messier. When he traded for Messier, Smith had promised to rip up the old contract.

"This is a player that, in my mind, is every bit as good and probably a lot better than I thought he was," Smith said. "He certainly has lived up to his billing, and probably surpassed it in my mind. He has played with injuries, he has gone out and single-handedly beat a team on at least one occasion. I put him on a level with the elite."

Messier had a sore wrist that wasn't getting better. He played in St. Louis, and planned to skip a game in Winnipeg, which would have given him six days off in a row. Besides, he had personal business to attend to in Edmonton.

Instead, he went to Edmonton, took care of business, then played in Winnipeg. This was typical Messier. He would not sit down unless he could not stand up.

He was also becoming a New York celebrity. When Messier and Leetch appeared on David Letterman's show, Letterman had the two players shoot pucks at a camera mounted inside a net at Madison Square Garden. Letterman mocked Messier and Leetch as they repeatedly failed to wreck the camera.

That was the first real national TV attention for Messier, Leetch, and these Rangers. Messier would become a frequent guest on Letterman's show.

Messier kept making impressions off the ice. He hosted a team Christmas party, and arranged for the players to chip in and buy luggage for all of the coaches. He organized a midnight team champagne toast on New Year's Eve, and a team trip to Paramount studios in Los Angeles.

Good things were happening for the Rangers as the season hit its mid-point. A new era had arrived. Negative streaks were ending. The Rangers reached the all-star break with a win over Calgary that improved their record to 30-17-1 and put them a point behind the Canadiens for the best record in the NHL. When the final game before the break ended, Messier closed the locker room door and addressed his teammates.

"Just stay focused and get your rest," he said. "The season hasn't started yet. We've played well, but the real fun stuff starts when we get back."

But a dark cloud was looming over the Rangers and the entire league. The players' union and the league's owners, who were trying to work out a new collective bargaining agreement, had pointed to the all-star break as their key negotiating period. The negotiations never happened. Suddenly, a strike was possible.

■ ■ ■

When the season resumed after the break, the Rangers kept piling up improbable victories. On February 17, Messier shot the puck into a scramble of bodies and Darren Turcotte scored with half a second left to earn a 3-3 tie with Vancouver. In a 5-4 win over Minnesota, Messier scored twice in the final six minutes to rally the Rangers from a 4-1 deficit. Two days later, the Rangers were tied 1-1 with Philadelphia when Messier put on a show.

The play began when Graves, who was becoming Robin to Messier's Batman, belted Philadelphia's Terry Carkner and caused a turnover.

Messier, who had been hounded and annoyed all night by the Flyers' checkers, found himself free and sped up the right wing boards. As Messier approached the net with the puck on his backhand, he made a move as if he was going to skate around the back of the net. Flyers goalie Dominic Roussel and defenseman Steve Duchesne slid across the front of the net to cut off a wraparound. But Messier flipped the puck backward, over the base of the goal net, and onto Amonte's stick. Amonte knocked the puck into the vacated side of the net for the game-winner.

"That was a fabulous pass," said Amonte, who had escaped from several of his teammates so he could get to Messier in the post-goal celebration. "Mess has said that I should just lay low, play cool, lay silent out there so no one will notice you. He likes to pass over the back of the net like that, and he attracts so much attention it leaves people open. It is a little Magic Johnson, but he's a fabulous player and he's got the moves, and he knows what to do at all times."

The move was nothing new to Messier. He and Glenn Anderson had used it several times in Edmonton. Now Messier and Amonte were clicking.

Two nights after the victory over Philadelphia, the Rangers beat Chicago, 4-1, for their fortieth win of the season and improved their record to twenty games over .500 for the first time since 1972-73. Just as importantly, Messier's preachings were taking root. Messier's teammates were starting to sound like Messier.

"As soon as you start reveling in what you do, it starts to come apart for you," Vanbiesbrouck said. "Paper-checking isn't going to do you any good. We have to focus on what we have to do. Numbers are numbers, but we haven't totally accomplished anything yet."

Yet, history had turned the Rangers fans into a pessimistic lot, and as March arrived, the fans feared the worst. The Rangers' chances to end their curse were starting to look too good. A players strike was inching closer to reality. To Rangers fans, the looming strike was just another form of the jinx. And Messier was unwaveringly behind the union.

"I think at this point in time we have to make a stand," Messier said. "I don't think they're going to give us anything without taking us seriously. It seems it has to come down to the last minute to make them feel we're serious."

The fatalistic fans might have thought the cave-in was coming when the Rangers lost three in a row. A loss at home to Washington conjured up memories of a late-season eight-game losing streak in 1990-91. The losses, along with the strike talk, inspired panic in New York.

The Rangers rebounded with an impressive 7-1 win over Chicago at the Garden in which Messier had three assists. With the win, the Rangers had ninety points for the first time since 1983-84.

Messier had become the heavy favorite for the Hart Trophy as league MVP. Thanks in part to Messier, Leetch was a favorite for the Norris Trophy as the league's best defenseman. Neilson was among the favorites for the Adams Trophy as coach of the year. Amonte, Messier's right winger, was a candidate for rookie of the year.

As if to cement his credentials, Messier scored four goals on March 22 in a 6-3 win over the Devils. The four goals made Messier the fourth player in team history to top a hundred points in one season.

"I'd say he just gift-wrapped the Hart Trophy with a big bow on it," Graves said. "Actually I am a little surprised. Having me on his wing and getting 100 points . . . he's better than we thought he was."

The Rangers clinched the Patrick Division title on March 24 with a 4-3 win in Philadelphia. When Vancouver lost to Pittsburgh on March 26, the Rangers clinched the Presidents' Trophy for having the best record in the regular season. They hadn't done that since 1941-42, when the NHL had only seven teams.

Two nights later, the Rangers lost a meaningless game to the Islanders, 4-1 at Nassau Coliseum. More meaningful was the strike deadline, which was only two days away. With his head bowed, Messier spoke to reporters about the looming deadline. His teammates, too, were aware of the bleak reality of the situation.

"You can't think that this is it, because you'll just depress yourself," Kris King said.

By a vote of 560-4, the NHL Players Association struck down the owners' last proposal and went on strike on April Fools Day. The Rangers took a few days off, then most of the players began working out in Rye. For two days, most of them skated and had fun. But, as the players wrapped up their workout on Day Two, a long, black limousine pulled up to the arena. Messier, who hadn't been skating with the team, emerged from the limo. He wasn't happy.

When Messier walked to the bench, the players came over to see their captain and find out what he had to say. Messier told them that by working out and remaining prepared for the season, the players were sending a bad message to the owners. Messier, a pro-union man like his father, said the union didn't want the owners to think that the players could be ready to play at a moment's notice. The Rangers stopped skating. Within days, thanks to Messier, every other team had stopped skating, too.

Messier had spent two days in Hilton Head, where he, Graves, Weight, and Richter played golf on challenging courses. Messier is a pretty good golfer, but Richter, Graves, and Weight are not. They claimed to have lost forty-two goals balls in two days.

"Not that the shots were that bad," Graves said, "but there were signs, 'Alligator area, beware!' and we didn't bother looking for too many balls."

Instead, they put on roller skates and skated around the island.

■ ■ ■

The strike continued. Gretzky and Lowe joined Messier in New York. Messier, Gretzky, and Lowe would walk down the streets of New York, three abreast, chased by photographers and TV cameras. Messier talked about forming a rebel league. The owners and the players union made ultimatums and final offers. A deadline was set. The owners threatened to cancel the playoffs. When the deadline passed on April 7, NHL president John Zielger declared that the playoffs would be canceled.

A day later, Ziegler received permission from the owners to renew negotiations with NHLPA President Bob Goodenow, who had returned to his office in Toronto. Goodenow boarded another plane and returned to New York. Ziegler and Goodenow met for fifteen hours, until past midnight on April 10. Finally, they hammered out an agreement. This round of negotiations was believed to have been pushed by a small faction of players. The key players were Gretzky, Lowe, and Messier. The season had been saved.

Eighteen days after they had last played, the Rangers resumed their season in Toronto with a predictably rusty 4-2 loss to the Maple Leafs. The Rangers returned to the Garden for the final game of the regular season, received the Presidents' Trophy, and trounced Pittsburgh, 7-1, for their fiftieth win. The Garden crowd got a big kick out of Messier accepting the Presidents' Trophy. They had visions of Messier holding a bigger, better trophy in two months.

Messier was not impressed. He thanked Ziegler and barely lifted the trophy. Later, he placed it in a remote corner of the locker room. The message was clear: the Presidents' Trophy was not the prize the Rangers wanted.

Messier finished his first season in New York with 107 points, two short of the Jean Ratelle's team record. Leetch scored a career-high 102 points and joined Bobby Orr, Denis Potvin, Paul Coffey, and Al MacInnis as the only defensemen to have scored 100 points. The Rangers had 105 points, their best season since 1971-72.

But, as Messier had pointed out, these were not the prizes they most desired.

■ ■ ■

The Rangers opened the playoffs with a 2-1 victory over the Devils, who had finished eighteen points behind them during the regular season. Messier looked mean right from the start. He glared at Claude Lemieux on the first shift, beginning what would be a classic battle between two of the league's greatest playoff performers.

The war escalated in Game Two. Messier scored two shorthanded goals, extending his Stanley Cup record to thirteen shorthanded goals, and an assist. But he was on the ice for all three Devils goals in the second period of a 7-3 win for New Jersey. Messier and Lemieux, the Devils' most potent scorer as well as their most effective checker, exchanged more than goals. They exchanged nasty slashes, spears, and crosschecks. Lemieux, who loves to talk trash, insulted and aggravated Messier, who seemed frustrated. Messier's frustration grew when the Rangers lost Game Three in New Jersey.

"When you're favored, this is not the way it's supposed to be," Messier said. "We're not supposed to be trailing. We were supposed to win our first two games at home and win one in New Jersey. We finished with 105 points, and they had 87. This is not the way the script was written, so there are a lot of alarms going off. There is nothing harder than playing a team that wants to be a dragon slayer. They have no pressure and nothing to lose."

Richter swung the series back to the Rangers' side with a 3-0 shutout at the Meadowlands in Game Four, tying the series at two games each. Messier got away from Lemieux a few times, and also set up checking winger Jan Erixon for the goal that broke a scoreless tie in the third period.

After the game, Lemieux was livid as he relived the Messier spear in Game Two, and recalled an incident in Game Four. Lemieux had lined up Messier for a blind-side hit, but Messier saw him out of the corner of his eye. At the last moment, Messier jumped and nearly took off Lemieux's head with his stick and elbow.

"I guess it was just another one of those invisible things," Lemieux said, referring to Messier's reputation for getting away with fouls.

The Rangers won Game Five, 8-5, and returned to New Jersey with a chance to end the series. Neilson said the Rangers wanted to win Game Six "for one main reason: So we don't have to hear how long it's been, if ever, since the Rangers won a seventh game."

The Rangers had never won a Game Seven, but that's what they faced after the Devils beat them, 5-3, in Game Six. The Rangers, who had been carried by Messier all season, needed him to pull up his game. He had been shut down by Lemieux for much of the series and was ordinary in Game Six.

"I feel that it's a big game for myself and I'm certainly looking to have a big game, just as I am going into every game," Messier said, downplaying his role.

Messier had his big game. He scored twice in an 8-4 win that clinched the series. Next up was the Pittsburgh Penguins, who had another star named Lemieux: Mario.

In a game that featured virtually no emotion or passion, the Penguins skated into the Garden and won Game One, 4-2. The Rangers didn't check and refused to dump the puck into the Penguins' zone, angering Neilson. But that wasn't Messier's style. He wanted to rush the puck, make drop passes, hit the late man, and work give-and-gos. He wanted to forecheck and pursue the puck. Neilson wanted to play dump-and-trap against the powerful Penguins, whose offense was the best in the NHL.

Messier, however, couldn't play anything in Game Two. He had hurt his back during a run-in with Claude Lemieux, and would miss a play-off game for only the second time in his career.

But by the time the game ended, Messier's back was a secondary story. Five minutes into the first period, Graves had slashed Mario Lemieux's left hand, sending Lemieux crumpling to the ice. The Rangers went on to win, 4-2, but the slash on Lemieux was the big story. Graves proclaimed his innocence and said he wasn't trying to hurt Lemieux. When the next day the Penguins revealed that Lemieux had a broken hand, Neilson was painted as a contract killer who had sent out his goon to get rid of the best player on the Penguins. Graves was painted as the hitman who had carried out the order.

For the following forty-eight hours, all of the talk was about Lemieux and Graves. Lost in the shuffle was this note: Messier had a torn back muscle.

With Messier and Lemieux on the sidelines nursing injuries, the Rangers won Game Three in overtime, 6-5. The following day, the NHL suspended Graves for four games.

Losing Graves was a crushing blow for the Rangers. Neilson held a team meeting to discuss how they would make up for his loss. As Neilson spoke, Messier looked down at the floor and shook his head.

Oh, boy, we're in trouble, Colin Campbell thought. He knew if Messier wasn't buying into Neilson's plan, then nobody was.

■ ■ ■

Messier returned for Game Four, but the Rangers blew a 4-2 lead in the third period and lost in overtime, 5-4. Messier coughed up the puck in his own end and Ron Francis, who earlier had scored on Mike Richter from seventy feet out, scored the winner for the Penguins. The Rangers were in trouble. In Game Five at the Garden, Jaromir Jagr beat Vanbiesbrouck on a penalty shot and the Penguins won, 3-2, to take a three games to two lead in the series.

Messier was silently angry. He didn't like the way the Rangers were playing. They were backing off and playing Neilson's passive trap. The trap went against his instincts to play a high-risk, high-reward, pressure-in-all-zones style.

What bothered Messier even more was that Neilson was trying to win a battle of matching lines with Penguins coach Scotty Bowman, an expert at matching lines. By insisting that his checking line of Turcotte, King, and Paul Broten played against Francis and Jagr as often as possible, Neilson had reduced his best players' ice time. Including Messier's.

Messier thought Neilson was being stubborn. The coach had players jumping on and off the bench every time Jagr stepped on or off the ice. This led to chaos and enabled Bowman to keep Messier on the bench by playing Jagr. Messier's ego would never accept less playing time. He could never accept that he was incapable of playing against anybody.

In a way, Messier knew the Rangers couldn't beat the Penguins, and his fears were realized when the Rangers ended their season with a 5-1 loss to Pittsburgh in Game Six. The Penguins, who almost always attacked, would not lose another game en route to their second consecutive Stanley Cup. The Rangers, who had played so conservatively, were left thinking about 1940. Again.

"When you play the champs, you can't just beat them, you have to knock them out," Messier said. "We were up 4-2 with ten minutes left in Game Four and let them off the ropes. I've tasted the bitterness of defeat before and bounced back. I certainly count on bouncing back from this bit of bitterness. Sometimes, in the end, to taste the sweetness of winning you have to taste some of the bitterness of defeat first."

That had happened in Edmonton, when the Oilers lost to the Islanders in the 1983 finals, then came back in 1984 to win the Cup. Maybe, Messier thought, this was the lesson year. Sure, there were legitimate excuses: the strike, the slash on Lemieux, and Messier's back. But, said Messier, "when you lose, there are a million and one reasons."

Although he didn't say so, one reason stood out in Messier's mind: the coach.

6

Roger, Over and Out

"**W**ait till next year—Part 52" was the headline a couple of days after the Rangers skated off the ice in Pittsburgh to the Penguins' fans' taunting and waving of yellow and black signs that read "1940." It was breakup day and the Rangers were clearing out their lockers, undergoing physicals, and meeting with coaches and trainers before going home. Neil Smith gave Roger Neilson a vote of confidence and Messier tried to put a positive spin on the past season.

"This is a team whose nucleus is going to be around for ten years," Messier said. "That alone is encouraging, when you know there doesn't have to be a lot of changes. I don't like speaking about the past, but I know the lessons we learned are all going to come into play. I still think this is a team that is going to win a Stanley Cup, no question about that. But it's going to be a long, hard fight to get back to this point. With the talent and desire here, I think there is no question we're going to win a Stanley Cup.

"I look back at how we started back in October, to the team we had at the end of the year, and there's no comparison. I think the way the whole team dedicated themselves and made a commitment, you can't replace that. You don't get that often. Guys like Randy Gilhen, Kris King, and Paul Broten played their hearts out this year. That's what you need."

Messier sounded good, but he also sounded as if he was saying the team was good enough to win, but didn't. He sounded like he was trying to place the blame elsewhere.

The night before, Messier had sat courtside at Madison Square Garden as the New York Knicks beat the Chicago Bulls to force a seventh game

64

in their NBA Eastern semifinal playoff series. Messier had admired the way Knicks coach Pat Riley handled the game. Perhaps he simply admired Riley, who is more Messier's type of coach than Neilson. Riley is a dapper, high profile, it's-all-about-winning coach who has a strong personality to go along with his championship rings.

"Obviously, he has proven he's an incredible coach at this time of year," Messier said of Riley. "On top of that, he's got the commitment of the players."

Messier never talked about Neilson, even when pressed on the subject. He was given five or six opportunities to say one decent thing about Neilson, and never did, almost steadfastly refusing to do so.

Smith and Neilson both addressed the players at the team's breakup dinner. Messier was asked to speak, but refused. He was angry, as were most of the players.

"This isn't right," Messier grumbled. "We're celebrating losing." Thirty minutes later, he grabbed Adam Graves, Brian Leetch, and Tie Domi and left. They got into Messier's limo and went out for a few beers.

A month later, most of the key Rangers attended the NHL's awards night in Toronto. Messier won the Hart Trophy as the league's most valuable player. Leetch collected his first Norris Trophy as the league's best defenseman. Tony Amonte, a finalist for the Calder Trophy as rookie of the year, was there. So was Neilson, a finalist for coach of the year. And Neil Smith was there because this was a big night for the Rangers.

Messier grinned widely when he was called up to receive his award. He politely congratulated Mario Lemieux and the Penguins on their second straight Cup. He congratulated MVP finalists Brett Hull of St. Louis and Patrick Roy of Montreal. He cracked a joke.

"I keep telling the fans in New York to be patient, we're going to win the Stanley Cup," Messier said as a smile crept across his face. "But I don't think they like the patient part too much."

Messier thanked his teammates, Smith, the fans of New York, and the hockey writers who voted for him. As in 1990, he got choked up when he thanked his family. He thanked everybody except Neilson, who was in the audience.

Messier didn't think he had anything to thank Neilson for.

Smith spoke to Neilson and Messier during the summer and both insisted there was no problem between them. Knowing this, Smith couldn't try to patch up a relationship that neither person would admit needed patching.

With nothing to do on the Neilson-Messier front, Smith had a busy, unproductive, and frustrating summer. His attempt to trade for Eric Lindros, the highly regarded 19-year-old center who had sat out the 1991-92 season after getting drafted by Quebec, was controversial. The Rangers thought they had traded for Lindros. The Flyers claimed they had already traded for him. The case went to arbitration, where the Flyers won.

The night before training camp opened for the 1992-93 season, Neilson and Messier had a private meeting. They talked about differences in philosophy and Messier publicly proclaimed that there wasn't a problem.

"If I can help in certain areas and we can blend some ideas, it will be best for the team," Messier said. "Ultimately, he's the one who makes the decisions. He's the one who sets the tone for the team and the style of play and the personality of the team. That's how it should be. I respect my coach, as I've been taught my whole career, and I told Roger, 'I'm here to work my butt off, as I did last year.' More important, he's the coach of the team and I'm a player, and I don't think that has been or ever was in doubt."

The Rangers had a gifted team, which enabled them to defy Neilson's attempts at putting in a conservative system. Although they got off to a good start in October, they rarely won prettily or easily. They held their own in the standings, but their play indicated something was wrong. Messier was scoring goals and piling up assists, but, more than ever, he was playing on the perimeter. The team seemed caught between Neilson's trap and the puck-pursuit style preferred by Messier.

The situation came to a head on November 9, when the Rangers lost, 5-1, at home to the first-year Tampa Bay Lightning. Earlier in the day, the Rangers had announced that Neilson had signed a three-year contract extension. After the humiliated Rangers skated off the ice, Messier decided it was time to get some things off his chest. According to Messier, the constant shuffling, mostly of the fourth line, was a distraction.

"I don't think it's anyone's fault," Messier said. "It's something that's been coming for a long time. We have three or four guys out of the lineup. Last year we had pretty much the same lineup game in and game out and everyone knew his role and did it. Instead of having four players unhappy, we have twenty-four players unhappy, and it's been a problem for a long time now and it's starting to catch up to us. We have guys in and out of the lineup for no unforeseen reason, and it's unsettling. Talent is only going to take you so far if you don't have good feelings in the dressing room, coming from everyone. To tell you the truth, we're a long way from that right now. I certainly don't blame any of the players at all. If they didn't want to play, there'd be something wrong.

"We're a quarter of the way through the season, and I don't see us improving. Twenty-four guys for depth is fine, but that's what a farm team is for. On paper, it might seem to be an ideal situation. In my estimation, it's going to get worse. That's just the way I see it. I'm in the dressing room and I have my finger on the pulse of the team. I don't think it's Roger's fault, or Neil's fault, or the players' fault. Don't get me wrong. I'm not blaming the coaching staff or Roger or anybody. I just think realistically it's not going to work this way."

Smith was exploring the possibilities of a multi-player trade without using all of his depth on the wrong trade. Neilson had said all along that having extra players was a problem. He knew he was on the hotseat. Regarding his new contract, Neilson said: "I'm glad I signed it before the game."

Both Neilson and Smith tried to act as if there was no controversy. Messier insisted he had an obligation to stick up for his teammates. The next day, Neilson put the team through a rigorous hour and a half practice during which he hammered home the need for the team to play a dump-and-chase style. The repetitive dump-in drills were obviously aimed at Messier. After the team wore itself out by throwing the puck into the corner and chasing it, Neilson had the players do exhausting sprints. Some of the players fell to their knees. Then Neilson left the ice and Messier took his teammates to a corner of the rink for a lengthy discussion. He was the only one who talked.

Neilson dryly summed up the controversy. "I can't believe a loss to Tampa Bay could cause such a furor," he said. "Geez, you'd think we'd lost the Stanley Cup."

Two nights after the Tampa Bay loss, the Rangers blew a 4-2 lead and lost to Washington, 7-4, at the Garden. Afterward, one couldn't tell whether Messier was trying to end the controversy or start a new one.

"It took a month and a half to get to this point, so it's not going to rectify itself overnight," Messier said.

Messier sounded off again later in the week. He insisted that he had to stand up and say something.

"Perhaps that's why this team's never won, because they never addressed a problem, because they masked their problems instead of having somebody stand up and speak out," he said. "I'm the guy

everybody's counting on to bring that successful feeling and the togeth-
erness, and to bring a championship. If there's a problem with that,
then maybe they brought the wrong guy in. These are things I've always
done, and I feel I'm the guy to do that here. The relationship between
management and team is important, and the captain and the alternate
captains are important to bring that relationship.

"You look straight down the barrel and face it, deal with it, fix it, and
move on. When the next problem comes up, you face it and deal with
it and move on. There are always going to be problems. I've faced them
for fifteen years. There are even problems with championship teams.
It's human nature."

Unsure of how to handle the problem, Smith flew to Toronto for
the general managers' meetings. The players insisted that Messier was-
n't lying down in an attempt to get Neilson fired, but they also said the
rift was too obvious to ignore and beyond repair. After one practice,
Neilson and Messier had a closed-door meeting that lasted an hour. Smith
tried to arbitrate the matter and get player and coach to make up.

Smith found himself involved in the controversy, too. He was in
Philadelphia for the Rangers' game against the Flyers on November
19, accompanied by Madison Garden president Bob Gutkowski. Smith
downplayed the significance of Gutkowski making the trip and tried
to downplay the Neilson-Messier rift.

"I've always been monitoring it, only because I talk to Roger all the
time, a couple times a day," Smith said. "I believe now the same as
what I believed in the summer. If we hadn't lost a few games in a
row, like we have, there wouldn't be any supposed situation. But we've
lost a few games, so there are all these pimples popping out."

The Rangers' complexion got worse. Messier broke out of a prolonged
slump with two goals, but the Rangers were clobbered 7-3, extending
their winless streak to five games. Two days later in Winnipeg, Neilson
called in most of his players for one-on-one meetings. He asked them
what they thought was wrong with the team. Only a few indicated that
Messier was the problem, or that the relationship between the coach
and the captain was creating turmoil. Neilson knew otherwise.

One of those not invited in for a meeting was Mike Richter, who
earlier in the season had an argument with Neilson when he decided
to move into New York City. Neilson thought Richter should stay in
the suburbs. Richter found out about the meetings and was angered
by his exclusion. His season had become as nightmarish as the team's.

Neilson was enraged by the Rangers' 4-2 loss to Minnesota on November 30 at the Garden. The defensive mishaps bothered him greatly. Two weeks later, the Rangers acquired Kevin Lowe from the Oilers in a deal that figured to improve their defense. Columnists in Canada suggested that Lowe had been brought in to serve as a buffer between Neilson and Messier, a suggestion Lowe angrily denied. Messier welcomed the arrival of his friend and former teammate.

On December 17, the Rangers lost their best defenseman when Leetch went head-first into the boards at St. Louis Arena. The Rangers feared Leetch had suffered a career-ending injury; the injury turned out to be irritation and compression of a nerve in his neck and shoulder. Leetch had trouble lifting his arm and nobody knew how long he'd be out of action. There was little question, however, that the Rangers would go nowhere without him. And Messier was playing, but not practicing, because of an injured ribcage. The Rangers kept struggling.

Neilson, who rarely raises his voice, was as angry as he had been all season after the Rangers watched the Devils bounce back for a 5-4 overtime victory at the Garden two days before Christmas.

"I don't think there was a turning point," Neilson said. "We were outplayed all three periods. If there was ever a game we didn't deserve to win, this was it. We went back to our river game, and we didn't deserve to win by any stretch of the imagination."

The river game, as Neilson put it, was his way of saying the Rangers had played pitiful defense. At the same time, Neilson sounded as if he was defining Messier's preferred style. Neilson, who had bent far from his defensive nature as the Rangers became more talented over the past two years, had seen enough.

"Our team, far too often, takes the offensive option every time," he said. "Eventually that has to catch up to you in this league. At the end of last year, if there was one thing we wanted to do, it was to be better defensively. So far this year, it hasn't happened."

Neilson took a direct verbal shot at Messier, who cheated to the offensive side more than any other Ranger. A pass had hit Messier in the skates as he looked for a breakaway. The Devils' Stephane Richer picked up the loose puck and scored. Said Neilson: "We're just leaving the defensive zone too early. That's something we've tried to remedy. We've got a lot of forwards who aren't doing the job defensively. That's the problem. They're not doing it."

The Rangers kept losing, to the Islanders, Washington, and then 11-6 to Buffalo on New Year's Eve. The season was falling apart. Prior to a 5-2 loss in Pittsburgh on January 2, Neilson made a bold move: He called in Graves, Lowe, and Gartner for a private meeting. "We need you guys to lead us, because Mess isn't leading us," Neilson told them. News of the meeting got right back to Messier. He wasn't happy.

"I room with Kevin Lowe, so of course I knew about it," Messier said. "It was obviously one of the problems I had with Roger. Our relationship obviously deteriorated, and having a meeting like that behind my back certainly proved that. I'm the captain of this team, and until somebody takes that away from me, that's not the way to do it."

The best team in hockey the previous season was merely two games over .500. Smith was on a plane, heading home from the World Junior Championships in Sweden. The Neilson Watch had begun.

Smith hated the situation. He wanted to run a stable organization, not like the franchise he had inherited three and a half years earlier. He did not want to fire Neilson, a friend who had been a loyal and hard-working employee, and whose only crime was that he had worn out his effectiveness. But he couldn't deny this fact: Neilson's days were numbered.

On January 4, 1993, Neilson was fired and replaced by Ron Smith, his former assistant coach. Afterward, Neilson and Messier finally aired their differences. The former coach knew exactly where to place the blame for his dismissal, and he didn't pull any punches.

"Last year Mark came in and gave us all hope for a Stanley Cup, and he was really as good a leader as you could ever get," Neilson said. "This year he didn't lead us. I think there was a difference as far as his contributions. Last year he was right on top of all the little things, talking to the guys at the right moments, being up on everything that was happening, and noting everything. This year those things didn't seem to be getting done."

Messier, speaking defensively, hated being accused of quitting on Neilson.

"I challenge anybody to say it to my face, that we laid down for Roger," he said. "I certainly don't want to coach this team. I never wanted to when Roger was here. I think there are things we could have done differently over the course of a season. When you play teams in your division seven times, you become familiar, and they start taking things away. You have to change and counterattack. We were being predictable, and our record in the division indicates that. We can't be so bullheaded to think you can keep running through a wall. You've got to learn and adjust and go on."

The Rangers had no choice but to go on. Neilson was gone. Messier was still a Ranger. Colin Campbell summed up the scenario in two words: "Mess won."

■ ■ ■

Messier was happy with his first game under Ron Smith, a 3-3 tie with the Devils on the night of Neilson's firing. He got the ice time he desired. The Rangers played an up-tempo style that seemed to invigorate him. Messier had an extra spring in his stride. He played a hard, alert game.

"He got me involved," Messier said of his new coach. "I knew I was more involved than I've been in a month and a half, and it felt great. You can say all you want, make all the speeches you want, but if you've got to be put into situation where you can get the opportunity to lead by example. Tonight I felt I was."

The main topic of the night, of course, was the firing, and Messier again answered all of the questions about Neilson. He never wavered from his position. Then, when all of the reporters were gone, he slumped in a chair in the back of the players' lounge and exhaled deeply. His eyes were aimed at the floor.

"I don't feel so good right now," he allowed.

"What the fuck was I supposed to do?" he said.

Messier cursed and mumbled in a verbal stream of consciousness, allowing what he was really feeling to surface: The Rangers had brought him to New York and told him to win a Stanley Cup. Messier truly believed that would never happen playing Neilson's passive style. Messier pointed out that Neilson had never won anything. He wasn't trying to insult the ex-coach, but rather trying to emphasize that Neilson's system couldn't win, and that his own puck-pursuit, high-stakes style had won many times. And that Messier, like all superstars, needed to play a lot in all situations.

These points were difficult to argue. Messier didn't get Neilson fired because he didn't like him. Messier got Neilson fired because he thought it was necessary.

"Should I have just shut up and finished out my career?" Messier asked. "Should I have said, 'Nice try, Mark?' It was my obligation to stand up and act."

71

Said Paul Messier: "Do you sit there and collect money, or do you make it right?"

Messier didn't like being blamed for Neilson's firing. He told some of his teammates that he would never again put himself in this position.

"What hurt him most was that they brought Mark in for a reason, and the team was making some improvements and he was giving his opinion like he had before," Leetch said. "Roger had different opinions. When it all started to become public, and Roger had those meetings behind his back, Mark bit his tongue. It wasn't until things started to come out the opposite way that he started to clam up and not give an opinion either way. He wouldn't give a negative, but he started to not say anything positive, either. It hurt because they trusted him when he came here, and to not use his opinion, or not go about things the same way as when he first got there, they hurt him. He felt that trust was a little bit betrayed. He said, 'I'll never let that happen again. I won't put myself in that position and get so involved, where all of a sudden things can turn on me like they did.'

"It didn't affect him, though. There's nothing Mark can't handle. There are disappointments he faces and things he deals with, but I think Mark sees a certain number of years in his career and he wants every year to be successful. He felt he was losing a year because he was almost being betrayed by those who listened to him when he first came in."

With Neilson gone and Ron Smith in charge, Messier returned to his old self. He brought to practice a framed plaque of a seven-paragraph essay entitled "What It Takes To Be No. 1" by Vince Lombardi. The plaque, which was hung in the Rangers' dressing room at Madison Square Garden, reads:

> *Winning is not a sometime thing; it's an all the time thing.*
>
> *You don't win once in a while; you don't do things right once in a while; you do them right all the time. Winning is a habit.*
>
> *Unfortunately, so is losing.*
>
> *There is no room for second place. There is only one place in my game, and that's first place. I have finished second twice in my time at Green Bay, and I don't ever want to finish second again. There is a second place bowl game, but it is a game for losers played by losers. It is and always has been an American zeal to be first*

in anything we do, and to win, and to win, and to win.

*Every time a football player goes to ply his trade he's
got to play from the ground up—from the soles of his
feet right up to his head. Every inch of him has to play.
Some guys play with their heads. That's OK. You've got
to be smart to be number one in any business. But more
importantly, you've got to play with your heart, with
every fiber of your body. If you're lucky enough to find
a guy with a lot of head and a lot of heart, he's never
going to come off the field second.*

*Running a football team is no different than run-
ning any other kind of organization—any army, a
political party or a business. The principles are the same.
The object is to win—to beat the other guy. Maybe that
sounds hard or cruel. I don't think it is.*

*It is a reality of life that men are competitive and the
most competitive games draw the most competitive men.
That's why they are there—to compete. To know the rules
and objectives when they get in the game. The object is
to win fairly, squarely, by the rules—but to win.*

*And in truth, I've never known a man worth his salt
who in the long run, deep down in his heart, didn't
appreciate the grind, the discipline. There is something
in good men that really yearns for discipline and the
harsh reality of head to head combat.*

*I don't say these things because I believe in the "brute"
nature of man or that men must be brutalized to be com-
bative. I believe in God, and I believe in human decency.
But I firmly believe that any man's finest hour—his
greatest fulfillment to all he holds dear—is that moment
when he has to work his heart out in a good cause and
he's exhausted on the field of battle—victorious.*

—*Vincent Lombardi*

■ ■ ■

Since arriving in New York fifteen months earlier, Messier had wanted
the green light to play his style. Now he had it, and he started to play
like a bullish power forward again. He had a goal and three assists,
and ten shots in a 5-4 win over Washington on January 13.

73

The game was Messier's most physical game as a Ranger. Todd Krygier nailed him from behind with a shoulder, sending him hard into the corner boards. Krygier, who was not known for such tactics, skated away from James Patrick's challenge, but didn't see Messier coming at him as he headed to the bench. With referee Dan Marouelli looking the other way, Messier skated over and squashed Krygier.

But just as Ron Smith was settling in and Leetch was getting closer to returning—just when Messier was starting to relish his new freedom on the ice—Messier suffered strained ligaments in his right wrist. He was tripped by Detroit's Yves Racine during a game in Detroit on January 19, one day after his thirty-second birthday.

Messier missed six games before returning on February 8. A few days later, he, Graves, and Amonte sat in a video room at the Rangers' practice rink and went over tapes of how they used to play together. After watching the tapes, they went out and combined for three goals and four assists in a slump-snapping 4-3 victory over the Islanders.

Despite wearing a protective soft cast on his wrist, Messier scored two goals and 13 assists in ten games. In the final game of that stretch on February 27 in Edmonton, he was checked hard by defenseman Igor Kravchuk and dislocated a rib. Although the injury was first diagnosed as a strained ribcage muscle, it would become a chronic problem.

The Rangers pushed their luck the next week by allowing him to play in a 3-1 win over Pittsburgh. Although he scored a goal, he appeared to be in great pain. When Ulf Samuelsson of the Penguins, who was known as the nastiest player in the league, hit Messier in the ribcage, Messier responded by raking the butt-end of his stick across Samuelsson's face. The fracas cost Samuelsson some blood and three teeth, and cost Messier a game misconduct.

A week later, Messier and Samuelsson were each suspended for three non-game days. Messier would lose more than $25,000 in pay. Samuelsson lost less than $9,000. Messier wasn't mad at the decision, but he was mad at Samuelsson.

"I've said all along that we should play without referees and let the players settle all those scores themselves, and you'd probably see a lot less violence if they looked after themselves," Messier said. "I've always felt that way, and I still do."

He also said that if he had known he would get suspended, he would have gotten more for his money.

On an off-day between games, Messier had his ribs treated by doctors, then strolled into the locker room. He was dressed casually in clothes that appeared to be beat up and old, but were actually quite pricey. He wore an expensive hat that a rap star might have worn. It was floppy with a brim all the way around. The brim was bent upwards. The top was black leather, as was part of the brim. The rest of the hat consisted of patches of corduroy prints: purple with green, green with gold, and gold with orange. Hats like that aren't often seen in the NHL. When Messier was asked if he'd play in the next game, against Los Angeles, he said: "Absolutely, unless I get hit by a car on my way home today."

This seemed like a natural response coming from Messier, who didn't seem to know the meaning of precaution or of taking an extra day to heal.

"I don't even know how to think along those lines," he said. "I'm a hockey player. I'm a Ranger. And if I can play, I'm playing."

Playing in pain was one of Messier's greatest faults. He never allowed his body to heal. If he could play, he played.

For the first time since becoming head coach, Ron Smith had both Messier and Leetch in the lineup for a 4-3 victory over the Kings on March 9. Two nights later, the Rangers won their second straight by beating Chicago. Then the Rangers' budding optimism was buried under a blanket of snow.

A huge snowstorm in the northeast forced the cancellation of the Rangers' next game in Washington. A seven-hour train ride back to New York didn't help Messier's ribcage. He missed the next night's game, a 3-1 loss to the Bruins. Before long, Messier needed anti-inflammatory drugs and painkillers in order to play. The medication made him light-headed, dizzy, and nauseous. Messier was in a Catch-22: On one hand, he couldn't take the drugs all the time. On the other hand, he couldn't play without them.

Making matters worse, he twice had to confront tough guy Dave Manson, who roughed up Amonte during a game against Edmonton on March 17. Messier found the strength to get revenge against Kravchuk, who had initially caused his rib injury, but he hardly enjoyed the act.

"I really wanted to give him a good one," Messier said, "but I couldn't. Payback will have to wait until next year."

■ ■ ■

The Rangers acquired forward Esa Tikkanen from the Oilers on March 17, giving their locker room even more of an Edmonton East look. Neil Smith bristled when it was suggested that he was just buying all of the old Edmonton players.

"Who the fuck am I supposed to get, ex-San Jose Sharks?" he asked.

At practice that day, Mark Hardy of the Rangers taped over all the nameplates above the locker stalls and wrote in "Fogolin," "Semenko," "Lumley," and "Moog"—players from the Oilers of the early 1980s.

Two nights later, the Rangers salvaged one win out of a three-game homestand by beating San Jose, 8-1, at the Garden. The city streets were still covered in snow and ice from the great storm. For all intents and purposes, it was the Rangers' final night of the season.

7

Black Ice

Messier wanted nothing more than to fix the Rangers' season. He wanted to make amends for all that had transpired between himself and Neilson. The only way to do that was by rebounding from the Rangers' horrible first half and making the playoffs. Until the wee hours of March 20, there was reason to believe that might happen.

Messier often said he didn't believe in curses, jinxes, and ghosts, although he occasionally referred to such things as "the dragons" that hovered over the Rangers. But if there ever was any truth to the idea that a curse hung over the Rangers, it showed itself on Saturday, March 20.

The snowstorm six days earlier had left ice all over New York City. In the early hours of that Saturday morning, only a few hours after the Rangers' win over San Jose the night before, Leetch got out of a taxi in front of his Manhattan apartment. He stepped over a pile of snow, planted his right foot onto a patch of black ice, slipped, and twisted his right ankle.

Leetch was helped to his apartment and went to practice the next morning with what he thought was a bad sprain. He underwent treatment on the injured ankle, then went for X-rays, where doctors discovered he had a broken right fibula. He would be out for eight weeks. Only four weeks remained in the regular season. For the Rangers, all hope of salvaging their season was gone.

As bad as the season had been, the Rangers believed they still had a prayer. After missing thirty-four games, Leetch had returned five games earlier from his neck and shoulder nerve injury. Messier seemed happy.

anen and Lowe were fitting in. Leetch's injury was the latest set-back in a disastrous season.

Most of the Rangers didn't know of the severity of Leetch's injury until that night, when they attended the Rangers' Fan Club dinner at a Westchester hotel.

"It's absolutely . . . I mean . . . what do you say?" stumbled Messier. He gulped and tried to paint a positive picture of the situation, but his facial expression belied his words. He knew the Rangers couldn't win without Leetch. "It goes without saying what he means to our team," he added. "It's incredible, just incredible. This is just going to be one of those years that's going to test our perseverance to the bitter end."

The bitter end for Leetch was a familiar reminder of other bitter ends for good Rangers teams of the past: Jean Ratelle's broken ankle, Brad Park's knee, Ulf Nilsson's knee, Leetch's broken left ankle three seasons earlier, and the 1992 players strike.

"I keep hearing those things," Ron Smith said. "You wonder about it sometimes. I might believe in extra terrestrial life, but I don't know if I believe in jinxes. We felt we were ready to make our move. Now it's a tougher task, but I'm not going to say it's impossible."

Messier was one of the few Rangers who knew about the injury prior to the fan club dinner. He had spoken to Leetch who, he reported, was devastated. But Messier refused to buy into the jinx talk.

"Nope, not one bit," he said. "If you're surrounded by enough talent, and the people are all pulling on the same rope, you're going to be the master of your own destiny. This organization has been thinking along those lines since I've been here. Jinx is just another excuse for whatever, a lack of motivation or talent. If you push yourself, you put an end to all those jinxes."

Over the next twenty-four hours, several people called radio station WFAN in New York and claimed to have seen Leetch and Messier in a Manhattan bar late that night. The callers said the two most important Rangers had been horsing around and roughhousing. Some said Leetch got hurt when Messier picked him up and dropped him. One said Leetch fell down a flight of steps. There were whispers from unnamed bartenders and patrons about Leetch jumping off the bar. The rumors were angrily and steadfastly denied by Leetch, who admitted he had a few beers at two bars in New York after the game, but maintained that the injury occurred when he slipped on a patch of ice.

"There's absolutely no way anybody can say I hurt myself in the bar," Leetch insisted. "I don't know how people can say that unless they saw you do it. I went out with Mess and Tony Amonte and a couple of friends of Tony's. I had a couple of beers. That was it. A couple at dinner downtown, and a couple at a place uptown. We all left. Tony gave Mess a ride home, and I took a cab crosstown."

In any event, the Rangers were in trouble. They won their next game in Ottawa, but lost at home to Philadelphia. Ron Smith left Messier on the bench during a four-on-four, a situation in which Messier usually excelled.

"I'm not going to get into that," Messier said. "That's a coaching decision."

As April rolled around, the losses mounted and rumors surfaced.

A published report said that Neil Smith had called unemployed coach Mike Keenan "a dictator." Smith explained that he had been questioned about the type of coach the Rangers needed and whether the Rangers needed a disciplinarian. According to Smith, he replied: "No, I don't think we need a dictator."

Keenan reacted angrily and called Smith disrespectful. The story spread across Canada in newspapers and on television. Smith called Keenan to clear up the misunderstanding. Keenan and Neilson, a close friend, attended that night's game between the Rangers and Islanders.

It wouldn't be the last time that Keenan's name surfaced in relation to the Rangers.

■ ■ ■

Messier wore only a towel and skates as he went through his daily locker room routine. No piece of equipment meant as much to Messier as his skates, and he spent a great deal of time and energy making sure they were in perfect condition. He worked with the team's equipment managers and with skate salesmen. Every millimeter of his skates had to feel just right. He could feel a nick in the blade or the tiniest bit of dullness. He never wasted time getting the problem rectified.

One day, Messier stood in front of his locker wearing only his skates and a towel. Then he put on a pair of baggy white boxer shorts covered with big red lips. Next, he put on a pair of dark, thin, wraparound sunglasses, and a soft leather jacket. Wearing nothing else, Messier motioned to the reporters.

"We put ourselves in this position," Messier said before a question could be posed. "We shouldn't be here. No words left. Nothing left to say. All the clichés are used up."

Messier, along with his four former Oilers teammates, had never missed the playoffs. When asked if he feared not making the playoffs, Messier said: "No. I fear not attaining our goal."

Messier's 1,000th career NHL game was a 5-2 loss to the Devils on April 7. It was not a memorable night.

"You keep getting kicked in the teeth," he said, "and it's tough."

The situation was tough for all of the Rangers. Graves had gone several nights without sleeping more than an hour and a half. He looked awful as he walked sadly past the big fountain in front of the practice rink. His hair was uncombed. A baseball hat was pulled down near his eyes.

Graves insisted people were crazy to think about trading Messier, an idea that had been raised by the media. Messier would finish the season with 91 points, despite missing nine games and playing many others while on painkillers and anti-inflammatory medication. He had a bump under his ribcage that was about the size of a tennis ball. His back ached so much, he often sat during interviews.

But he had angered some people earlier in the season with his stubborn approach to the team's style and his part in the Neilson firing. Both Neil Smith and Ron Smith suggested that Messier often forced awful passes on the power play. They blamed Messier for the team's follow-the-leader mentality, in which the Rangers always looked for breakaways and made dangerous passes, regardless of the situation and the possible consequences.

The Rangers wanted to have a ceremony to commemorate Messier's 1,000th game, but he declined. He didn't think it was much of an accomplishment. And he knew what kind of reception he'd get from the Rangers fans who, only a year ago, had cheered him loudly and lustily.

On April 9 at the Garden, the fans gave a standing ovation to Mario Lemieux, who scored five goals in a 10-4 win by the Penguins. They chanted, "Let's Go Penguins!" and sang "Hey, hey good-bye" to the Rangers. They chanted, "1940!" They booed Messier.

A 1-0 loss in Philadelphia three days later mathematically eliminated the Rangers from the playoffs and assured that they would go from first to last in the Patrick Division. Neil Smith was in the pressbox at the end of the game when a drunken Flyers fan ran past yelling, "1940!" When the fan spotted Smith, he picked up the volume a few notches.

"Fuck you!" Smith hollered at the fan. The veins in his forehead and neck bulged.

"This is as low as it gets," Messier said later. "I played my whole career feeling responsible for the way things are, or the outcome of whatever happens. I just take it very personally. It's hard right now. It's a tough pill to swallow. I just couldn't get anything done, and to me that was more frustrating than anything."

Messier had taken the fall for Neilson's firing, and he was certain to take a great deal of the blame for Ron Smith's inevitable dismissal. Neil Smith and his bosses knew they had to hire a coach who could handle Messier, rather than a coach who would get handled by Messier. A coach such as Mike Keenan, Scotty Bowman, or John Muckler could tell Messier: "I'm the coach, and this is how it is." But that coach would also have to understand and respect Messier, and realize that Messier had to have input into the team's style of play, lineup decisions, and virtually everything that happened in the locker room.

■ ■ ■

Messier probably shouldn't have tried to play through his injuries. The drugs he took made him vomit and lightheaded. He tried to play without them, but he'd get involved in a collision on the ice and have no choice but to resume taking painkillers.

"I don't want to make it sound like I was rolling over nails to get in the lineup," he said. "But it has been pretty tough."

Ron Smith should have told him to sit out a few games. After all, even if Messier got the Rangers into the post-season, he'd have nothing left for the playoffs. It was a no-win situation. Messier was going to sit out several more games going into a game against the Bruins, but the team was on a losing streak. Messier felt he had to play.

"I had no strength," he said. "I couldn't knock anybody off the puck, and that's the way I have to be able to play to be effective."

During the final home game, a 2-0 loss to Washington, Messier was booed mercilessly.

"A lot of people probably think it doesn't affect him, that he doesn't care," Richter said. "It was killing him. It was really hurting him deeply that we weren't doing better all season. The fans didn't understand that."

Messier laughed when asked how he felt. He felt lousy. He had been criticized by the fans, the newspapers, and on radio and TV. Messier always read the papers and watched the TV news. He listened to sports radio. He had heard the fans booing him. How could he not feel lousy?

But Leetch and Graves, two of Messier's most influential teammates, were on his side. Both said the Rangers would be crazy to trade their captain.

"It's one of those things, I guess," Graves said. "Everybody looks to him to do everything. When the team doesn't do well, everyone blames it on Mess. That's not fair. You depend on everyone on a team, and I know Mess plays as hard as he can every night. You don't realize it, but he was really badly hurt. He couldn't even breathe before some games because his ribs hurt so much. It's tough for me to see everything come down on him.

"I've said this before, but the last seven years, nobody has helped me more than Mark Messier. And when he's healthy, which he wasn't very much, he's still an awesome player."

Leetch didn't buy into the popular theory that Messier alone had been the cause of Neilson's firing.

"Mark made it clear, when asked his opinion about the coaching style, that he disagreed with a lot of what Roger did," Leetch said. "Neil Smith talked to Mark and Neil believed that Roger was the right guy, and stuck with him. But I don't think Mark said anything until he was asked, and then he said, 'This isn't the system I would play.' But he certainly played hard for Roger, and he played hurt for Roger. Mark never went to anybody and said, 'Something's got to be done with the coaching.' When the question came up to him, he gave the answers he thought were right."

■ ■ ■

Keenan and Neilson were at The Spectrum when the Rangers lost to the Flyers on April 12 in Philadelphia. Keenan was reportedly close to signing a deal to return to the Flyers as coach, but other rumors had him going to Detroit, which was about to have a coaching vacancy.

The rumors were wrong. Keenan, who left the game with Neil Smith and Neilson, was talking to the Rangers about becoming their next coach. Just four days later, prior to the Rangers' final game of the season in Washington, the Rangers signed Keenan, 43, a three-time Stanley Cup finalist.

Messier, who had played for Keenan in the Canada Cup, respected him, even though a lot of hockey people considered him an out-of-control dictator who had to have his way. Then again, maybe that's exactly what the Rangers needed. Messier would say that when Keenan arrived, he felt he "could be the captain again, the top guy."

"All the experience I've had with him was the two Canada Cups, where he had a pretty good set of circumstances," Messier said. "It's altogether different to have your own team. But I think any time you're able to win, and you share a winning experience with someone, there's a certain bond created. Mike stepped into the Canada Cup, and that's not an easy situation by any means, but he made it enjoyable for everybody and, at the same time, we were well prepared to play."

Like Neilson, Ron Smith didn't go quietly. He sent a parting shot to his former players.

"We were talking about training camp the other day, and I said it would be a good idea to go to West Point and let the guys see people who go around and follow orders," Smith said.

The Rangers were about to find out what that was like.

8

Iron Mike

To play for Mike Keenan, you have to "embrace change." You have to possess "intrinsic values." You have to "adapt to the core group." Those are some of Keenan's clichés. To play for Keenan, you need vast aerobic capacity and recovery ability. You can't even think about being a smoker or of being out of shape. You need to be tough on and off the ice. Keenan seemingly prefers that his players are either single or don't let their families get in the way of their goals.

There is no perfect Keenan player . . . except Mark Messier.

Otherwise, anybody can be a Keenan player, and anybody can certainly not be a Keenan player. To play for Keenan is to constantly be confronted and challenged. To play for Keenan is to be pushed beyond the point you might think necessary. When he asks a question, he demands an answer. When he makes a demand, he expects it to be fulfilled. To Keenan, belittlement is a form of motivation and a way of finding out what a player is strong enough to endure.

Sometimes his style works. Often it doesn't. Some players improve because of Keenan, while others can't deal with him. Life around Iron Mike is a lot of things, but it is never gentle, and it is rarely pleasant. It is never boring. Yet, he wins, almost all of the time. At least for a while . . . until the newness of his style wears off.

When Keenan arrived, he assured the Rangers that 1993-94 would not be the same as 1992-93. He was going to make absolutely certain that the players would not relax as they had at times the previous season. He would set goals. Anything short of those goals was unacceptable.

This was music to Messier's ears, as was the reunion with Keenan. Keenan loved Messier's type of player and leader. Partly because of that, Messier had the utmost respect for Keenan.

Keenan would be gentle, or as gentle as he could be, with Messier. He rarely challenged or disagreed with him. Keenan gave Messier and Kevin Lowe enormous input into decisions. He played Messier like a violin, and thus got the best music from his star, who had been embarrassed by the events of the previous season.

Although Keenan had never won the Cup, he had plenty of success. In eight NHL seasons, he had a .590 winning percentage, fifth among all coaches in league history. He was the first coach to win more than forty-five games in each of his first three seasons. He had been to the finals three times, with the Flyers in 1985 and 1987, and with Chicago in 1992. He had won five division titles, and twice had the best record in the league. As a rookie coach in 1985, he won the Jack Adams Award as coach of the year. He also won two Canada Cups, a Canadian collegiate championship with the University of Toronto, and the American League championship in 1983.

So, on the day after the Rangers' 1992-93 season ended in shame, Iron Mike Keenan was introduced at Madison Square Garden as the Rangers' new coach. He wore a black leather Rangers' bikers' jacket. He claimed to be more mature and to have toned-down his personality, and tried hard to argue that his reputation as a hated whip-cracker was undeserved.

"I think that abrasive stuff is overstated," Keenan said. "From time to time, I will openly admit, I went close to or over the line too often. But I've grown and matured as a coach, and I think you'll be surprised to see that development as far as my ability to relate to players."

Keenan got to work right away. He had always liked having a clear-cut No. 1 goalie who played at least seventy-five percent of the games. Because two new teams were entering the league, one of the Rangers' goalies, Mike Richter or John Vanbiesbrouck, would have to be left unprotected in the expansion draft. Keenan and Neil Smith decided to trade Vanbiesbrouck, who was later selected by the Florida Panthers. Richter was the Rangers' No. 1 goalie.

The Rangers opened their pre-season in London, England, where they played in a two-game exhibition tournament against the Toronto Maple Leafs. Keenan was warm, positive, and upbeat to his players. He encouraged and taught. He wore a microphone behind the bench for the MSG Network's telecasts and was heard encouraging his players: "That's it, boys!" "Do this, boys!"

The Rangers, starving for a positive experience after the previous season, bonded instantly. They won both games in London and a trophy. The Rangers laughed at their championship and its seeming insignificance, but winning made the Rangers feel good. The two games in London got the Keenan era off to a positive start. Messier called it a great experience.

Part of Keenan's plan was to set high goals for the Rangers. He sounded a little like Messier when Messier joined the Rangers. First, he went to Joe Whelan, a producer for the MSG Network, and asked him to handle a project. Keenan wanted a video of past ticker-tape parades in downtown New York City's Canyon of Heroes.

"I want the players to be able to visualize it," Keenan told Whelan. "If you can't see it, you'll never achieve it."

Whelan edited a video of the championship parades for the 1969 Mets, the 1978 Yankees, the 1986 Mets, astronauts, and war heroes, and put it to music. Keenan gathered the Rangers into a room and showed them what he hoped would be their crowning moment, nine months before the fact.

Keenan then took the team to Glens Falls, New York, for a week of training camp. During the first four years that the Rangers had made the trek to upstate New York, Neilson had divided the roster into four teams for a tournament. Neilson not only had the teams play every day, but he also had them compete in flag football, softball, and volleyball. The winning teams won gift certificates and electronic equipment.

Camp Keenan had no tournament, no other organized sports, and no prizes. He divided the team into three groups, each of which played four games in three days. There were no prizes. Nothing was at stake, Keenan pointed out, "except pride. And jobs."

One day, Messier bummed a ride back to the team hotel with a reporter.

"I really like this team," Messier said convincingly. "I really like the feeling on this team."

Messier looked different. He had shaved his head and was completely bald. He looked even more menacing than before.

As he spoke during the short ride back to the hotel, Messier said the Rangers needed to add some size and muscle, along with some checking and overall depth. But his optimism was obvious. He sounded like a captain who was truly excited about his upcoming season of redemption. And he wasn't being interviewed. He was speaking from the heart. He truly felt that something big was about to happen.

Not that there weren't some bumps in the road. After a preseason game against the Islanders, Keenan challenged Smith to make the Rangers tougher. This was the first of several times during the season that Keenan, in his role as coach, would try to play general manager.

While Keenan tried to influence Smith, the Rangers tried to figure out what their coach was all about. Keenan benched Tony Amonte and Darren Turcotte for stretches in the Rangers' season opener, a 4-3 loss to Boston. Keenan blamed James Patrick for a loss in Pittsburgh, saying, "He let his teammates down." Patrick was scratched for the next game. The Rangers were an edgy team, but it seemed to be working to their advantage. Their play had improved from the year before.

A year earlier, Messier had said the Rangers were unhappy because of their lineup problems. Under Keenan, the Rangers viewed the competition for lineup spots as a positive.

"The situation can be healthy, and should be healthy," said Messier, who got off to a strong start playing Keenan's up-tempo, puck pursuit game. "I don't want to see anybody happy that they're not playing. It's important they see the situation and are supportive of the guys who are playing. Then it's a good competition, not a competition where guys are trying to out-do each other, but one where you push each other as far as you can."

Keenan didn't play favorites with his in-game benchings. He even benched Leetch for several shifts.

"Nothing's automatic with him," Leetch said of Keenan. "He doesn't want anybody to go onto the ice unless you're told to. It has you just paying a lot more attention on the bench."

The Rangers, however, weren't winning. Two days after an embarrassing 4-2 loss to the first-year Mighty Ducks of Anaheim, Keenan had his first tirade as Rangers coach. The Rangers had practiced for only fifteen minutes when Keenan decided he didn't like their effort. He slammed down his stick over the crossbar of one of the nets, breaking the stick into pieces. Then he threw the Rangers off the ice. When the team got back to the locker room, Keenan lectured them behind closed doors. Then he sent them back onto the ice for more abuse. When practice resumed, he repeatedly yelled at several players.

A few of the players believed that Keenan's rant was premeditated and for effect, and that he had sawed partly through his hockey stick before practice so that it would shatter.

The Rangers were uneasy. Nobody was willing to criticize the coach, at least publicly, but there was a lot of grumbling. Keenan had never worried about who liked him and who didn't like him. Yet, he had annoyed several players for his repeated benchings of Leetch, who was viewed by the others as a scapegoat. Keenan often screamed at Leetch: "You're no Chelios!" Defenseman Chris Chelios of the Blackhawks was one of Keenan's favorites.

Leetch shrugged off the criticism. He didn't care for Keenan's tactics. He didn't think he needed anyone to motivate him.

Keenan refused to buy into the theory that his constant benching and blaming had his team playing uptight hockey. The Rangers followed the Anaheim loss and the practice tirade with a humiliating 4-1 loss in Tampa Bay on October 22. Suddenly, the Rangers looked like a team that was playing scared because of the coach's tactics.

"It's better to find out who can handle those situations in October than in the springtime," Keenan insisted. "As I've said before, the people in New York expect you to win, and the upper management in New York expects us to win. If people prefer to not be in this type of program, it's better to find out now while there's time to address the overall makeup of the team. They had one of the nicest men in hockey coach them last year and you saw their response. Their response to me hasn't fundamentally changed that much. Ask the players why they didn't play for a coach who was a real gentleman in Roger Neilson, and I'm sure Ron Smith was as well."

One day after he was benched, Amonte was called into Keenan's office. Amonte would remember this as "the day he broke me." Keenan had listed all of the Rangers' forwards on a chalkboard. Amonte's name was second from the bottom.

"Who do you think you should play over?" Keenan challenged. "Who do you think you're better than? Go up to the chalkboard. Are you better than him? No, you're not better than him. You're not better than him. And you're not better than him."

Amonte, who was only 23, didn't know how to respond.

"My biggest difficulty with Mike Keenan was not standing up for myself," Amonte said. "He seems to respect guys who stand up for themselves and guys who don't back down from him. He told me I was a rich kid from Boston, and I didn't know how to work hard because I never had to, and that couldn't be further from the truth."

Amonte left the office in tears.

Nobody could have guessed that the loss to Tampa Bay was a turning point in the Rangers' season. Keenan gave Richter his third straight start and the Rangers beat Los Angeles, 3-2, at the Garden. The win started an 18-1-3 streak that carried the Rangers to the top of the NHL. They were on the verge of going from first-to-worst-to-first in three seasons. Somehow, Keenan's tactics were working.

The players weren't the only ones who feared Keenan. The Rangers had a buffet in a room across from their locker room at Madison Square Garden. Keenan liked a type of roll that was usually on the buffet. One night, there were no rolls.

"No rolls tonight?" Keenan asked calmly.

In a heartbeat, eight members of the public relations department, the training staff, and the security staff, got up and went scurrying around the Garden, trying to find rolls for the coach.

■ ■ ■

Messier didn't have many enemies in the Eastern Conference, but he started a new feud on October 28, 1993, when Montreal defenseman Kevin Haller was assigned to handle Messier during a dramatic, rugged 3-3 tie at the Garden.

Haller had taken some shots at Messier earlier in the game. With the scored tied, 1-1, late in the second period, Graves and Messier broke in two-on-one on a shorthanded rush. Haller, who couldn't catch them, raised his stick above his head and slashed Messier's hand. Messier reacted and Graves immediately challenged Haller, who dropped to his knees.

Messier returned to the locker room to have his left hand checked. Although he returned for the third period, his thumb had been hurt.

Haller had been illegally physical with Messier all game. One hit resulted in a delayed penalty against Haller, during which Messier scored. During a Montreal power play, Haller gave Messier a couple of extra shots after the whistle. Keenan looked down the bench to Joey Kocur, then nodded toward Haller. At first, Kocur didn't move. Then Keenan said, "Joey, get out there."

"But we're killing a pen . . ." Kocur started.

Barked Keenan: "Get the fuck out there."

Kocur jumped over the boards, skated up to Haller, threatened to kill him, then skated back to the bench. Kocur's actions were illegal. If Kocur had succeeded in goading Haller into a fight, both he and Keenan could have been given long suspensions. But there was no penalty called against Kocur, who returned to the bench to Keenan's approval.

■ ■ ■

The Rangers were in Halifax, Nova Scotia, for a neutral-site game against the Devils, so Messier decided to bring home two big boxes of lobsters. The lobsters were packaged live and placed in boxes designed to keep them cold.

After their victory over the Devils, the Rangers boarded their charter for what promised to be a frightening flight home. The weather forecast was so bad that the flight attendant on the small jet passed out air sickness pills and went around with a basket of fruit, warning the passengers that they had better eat before the plane was airborne.

The flight was long and bumpy. During some of the calmer moments, Messier sidled up next to Keenan at the front of the plane. Keenan was in a good mood after the win, and he and Messier had a pleasant conversation. This wasn't unusual. Messier frequently spoke with Keenan during road trips. The captain would size up the mood and needs of the team and make suggestions about, for example, whether it was necessary to practice the next day. They'd also talk about whether beer should be distributed on a flight.

While Keenan and Messier talked, two players broke into Messier's lobster boxes and removed the lobsters. The thieves stuffed the live lobsters into their own suitcases and filled the empty boxes with magazines.

Usually when the Rangers' charter flight landed in New York, the jet parked on the runway. The team bus would drive onto the tarmac, pick up the players, and take them back to the practice rink in Rye, where their cars were parked. The exceptions were Messier, Leetch, and Richter, all of whom lived in Manhattan and arranged for a limo.

On this rainy night, the limo had not yet arrived. As the Rye-bound players loaded onto the bus, they snickered and whispered to each other. The bus slowly drove away. The players' laughter got louder. Several players ran to the back of the bus and pressed their faces against the rear window. Messier and Co. were still waiting for the limo, and Messier had his two lobster boxes at his side.

"Bye Mess. See ya Mess," the players yelled. Messier, looking oblivious, waved good-bye. He smiled, but he didn't know why everybody was laughing. Messier had two boxes full of magazines. His teammates had tomorrow's supper.

"Enjoy the lobsters, Mess," a player yelled out the window. "See ya tomorrow!"

Keenan laughed loudly at the prank. But in order to avoid paying a dear price for the good laugh, the perpetrators prepared the lobsters and brought them to the practice rink the next day for an unplanned team lunch.

■ ■ ■

On November 2, two days after their adventure in Halifax, the Rangers completed a three-team, eight-player trade in which they unloaded Patrick and Turcotte, both of whom didn't fit into Keenan's plans. They acquired Steve Larmer and tough Nick Kypreos. On the same day, Smith laid the groundwork for finalizing a new contract for holdout defenseman Jeff Beukeboom, who had returned home after training camp.

With Larmer, Kypreos, and Beukeboom added to a team already on a winning streak, the Rangers felt good. They were playing well and having fun. Suddenly, they were bigger, tougher, and grittier. But Keenan still wasn't satisfied. Although he was getting the team he needed and wanted, every day he would say to his assistants, Colin Campbell and Dick Todd: "Do you think we can win the Stanley Cup with this team? What do we need to do to win the Stanley Cup?" He challenged them to come up with answers.

Neil Smith wasn't sure the Rangers had what they needed, either. "I don't think this team is a finished product," he said. "I know from experience that you always have to make improvements."

As usual, Smith and Keenan wouldn't sit tight.

9

Redemption

Everything was so bright and cheery between Keenan and Messier that Messier didn't mind when he was benched during a game in Miami. Keenan could get away with benching Messier on two conditions: That he did it rarely and that the Rangers were winning. This was the first time he had crossed Messier, and the Rangers were on a 9-0-2 streak when Keenan sat his captain.

Keenan took this extreme step after pulling Mike Richter, who had allowed one goal on eighteen shots. Messier sat for five minutes, waiting for Keenan to call his name. Those five minutes contained a brief power play, a brief penalty kill, and two short four-on-fours, all situations in which Messier normally played.

Nobody would have been surprised had Messier lashed back at Keenan. The coach of the opposing Panthers was Roger Neilson, and benching Messier in front of Neilson took guts by Keenan. But Messier giggled when asked about his benching. And Keenan claimed Messier wasn't being benched; he was being rested after logging about twenty-seven minutes in each of the last three games. Messier knew otherwise.

"I got a breather all right," Messier said. "I just think we were trying to shake things up. I think what it tells our team is, twenty games into a season, it doesn't matter how you get it done as long as you get it done. This was different, but there's more than one way to skin a cat and winning games is more important than whatever might be happening on the ice."

The Rangers responded and beat the Panthers. After the game, one Ranger after another filed past the Panthers' dressing room on their way to the team bus and stopped to shake hands with Neilson. All but Messier, who stared straight ahead as he briskly walked right past him.

The Rangers' unbeaten streak ended at 12-0-2 when they lost to the Islanders, 6-4. The worst player on the Rangers was either Messier or Leetch, and you would have had to fight one of them if you claimed it was the other. After the game, Leetch and Messier returned to Manhattan and settled into a Broadway restaurant for dinner, a few beers, and some self-analysis.

"We spent a couple of hours telling each other that we were the worst players on earth," Leetch said.

The one-downsmanship carried on for hours with each player claiming he was far more horrid than the other, and pointing to a particular boneheaded play he had made that afternoon.

In the next two games, Messier and Leetch took turns dominating in a pair of victories, 3-1 over the Capitals and 3-1 over the Devils.

There were many magic and unusual moments in what was quickly turning into a magical and unusual season. In Los Angeles on January 27, the Rangers were in overtime after blowing a 4-1 lead. Messier hadn't done much and was struggling emotionally, as was usual when he went head-to-head with Wayne Gretzky. With eleven seconds remaining in overtime, Amonte was stopped on a penalty shot by goaltender Kelly Hrudey. The game looked as if it would end in a tie until Messier lost a faceoff to Jari Kurri and headed to the net. The Rangers forced a turnover, Hrudey stopped Sergei Zubov's first shot, and Messier knocked in the rebound for a 5-4 victory with only 1.5 seconds remaining.

One night in Detroit, Keenan was concerned about the Rangers getting bullied out of Joe Louis Arena, where they had won only once in their last ten visits. Before the game, Keenan told Kocur that if Bob Probert, the NHL's heavyweight champion, acted up, Kocur was to fight back. The problem was, Kocur was being ordered to fight his friend. When the inevitable confrontation occurred, Kocur and Probert battled to a draw. But Kocur didn't like fighting Probert, and he liked it less when he saw Probert's mother, who had been like a mother to him, after the game.

That was life under Keenan. You did what you had to do to win.

A game in Dallas was a perfect example. Although the Stars had a big, mean team, Kocur was not in the lineup. Gord Donnelly, Shane Churla, and Jim McKenzie were roughing up the Rangers' stars. Leetch got run over a couple of times in the first period, infuriating Messier, who yelled at his teammates between periods.

"Don't let them do that," Messier told the Rangers. "Don't worry about their goons. Just go after their good guys. Just fuckin' go right after them."

Messier then went out and set an example. He caught Mike Modano, the speedy Dallas center, cutting across the middle of the ice. Messier hit Modano with a clean, hard shoulder check. Modano crashed faced-down to the ice.

"They were running Leetchie and trying to run us," recalled Adam Graves. "It was a battle-filled first two periods. Mess basically said, 'They're going after us. We've got to start hitting their guys.' First shift out, Modano came across the ice, and everyone was just like, 'Ooooh.' I never like to see anybody get hurt, but it scared me and I was on his team. He means business, and I'll never forget that. It calmed the whole game down. He had the ability to say something, and then go out, and I must emphasize, his meaning wasn't to hurt someone. But it was a perfectly clean hit, and you kind of just went, 'Wow!' It was scary.

"He's so strong," Graves continued. "He's like a bull. But he understood the game, all the facets of the game, probably better than anyone. His skill and his mindset gave him the ability to back it up and make the right play. But I think his knowledge and his experience gave him the ability to know what was needed at all times. That's something that can't be taught, when you need this or need that. Sure, there are going to be situations where, at key times, somebody's got to do something, Then it's fairly obvious. But he had that ability to always be there at the right time."

Added Colin Campbell: "Mess's sense of timing was uncanny. No one could say it and could go out and do it like him. Wayne Gretzky had God's gift of the touch. The assembly line stopped and the talent just poured into Wayne. Same with Mess for his uncanny sense of timing. He went right out the next period and he nailed Modano with a clean check and dropped him. The other guys just shut right down. It was fair, it was clean. He didn't spear the guy or punch him in the head. He hit him with a great shoulder and dropped him. Gone, right out on the stretcher. It was just a sense of timing. He said it and went out and did it. You couldn't challenge him, because he would back it up and do it."

Messier had a hand in creating an unusual relationship in the locker room. Eddie Olczyk became the leader of the Black Aces, a group of players who weren't playing much. Messier, Graves, and Lowe created an environment in which everybody felt like they were part of the team, even though Keenan used few players and liked to play his stars as much as possible. A year earlier, Messier had called for something to be done because, "instead of having four or five players unhappy, everybody's unhappy." Now everybody was happy, or at least understanding.

"It's amazing how positive they've all been," Keenan said. "All of them. We cannot win without that group. They bring everybody a step up. It's human nature: You see somebody there waiting to take your job, you stay ready. There's no animosity, no being negative; and that's a reflection of their integrity. They're all quality people."

Olcyzk had enough skill to be a regular for another team, but he accepted his limited role. In the locker room, he wasn't just the top man on the Black Aces, a group of players who rarely played, but one of the top guys on the team. He regularly sprung for a lunch buffet delivered to the practice rink. He retained a positive attitude. When the Rangers finished practicing, Olczyk led them in a group stretch at center ice. As they finished, Olcyzk would shout, "Heave, ho, heave, ho, heave ho!" as the players made rowing motions and joined in. They were like a group of rowers in a boat, pulling the oars together toward a goal.

Messier always smiled proudly whenever Olcyzk started the "Heave ho!" chant. He knew how valuable such a little thing could be to a team. He knew how important it was for the team to be so together, focused, and single-minded in its purpose.

■ ■ ■

By mid-December, the Rangers were on an 18-1-3 streak and Messier was piling up impressive numbers. He moved into eleventh place on the all-time NHL scoring list with 1,266 points, passing former Rangers center Jean Ratelle. But he was hurting. Although he admitted to having only a bruised foot after a game in Florida on December 22, he was also suffering from sprained wrist ligaments, probably caused by a series of confrontations with the Panthers' Brian Skrudland.

The Rangers had learned a lot of lessons the hard way over the past two years. One of those was the importance of Messier and Leetch being healthy. Messier had been hurt during the 1992 playoffs and the Rangers, the best team in the league that year, went down in the second round. Messier and Leetch were both hurt for virtually all of the

1992-93 season and the Rangers missed the playoffs. The Rangers knew they couldn't fool around with Messier when it came to injuries.

Messier couldn't sleep the night after the game in Florida. He wanted to play the next night in Washington and went out for warmups, but he couldn't hold his stick. Messier vowed to return to the lineup as soon as he could hold his stick, but the question was: Why would he want to rush back? And why wouldn't Keenan order Messier to take a brief vacation? This seemed like a risky attitude for a player and coach who both knew that winning in April, May, and June was far more important than winning in December.

Graves wore the "C" while Messier sat out five games. Prior to a 3-2 win over Florida on January 3, 1994, at the Garden, the Rangers presented Mike Gartner with a silver stick for scoring his 600th NHL goal. Then they surprised the injured Messier by commemorating his 800th NHL assist and 1,000th game. Messier, who had declined such a ceremony the previous season, was stunned by the honor. When his parents and grandmother unexpectedly appeared, Messier broke into tears.

After an emotional 5-1 victory over the Blackhawks on January 16, Messier made a face when asked about his ailing wrist. He indicated that the wrist was extremely bothersome, but that he wasn't terribly concerned about whether it would heal.

Two days later, a back page headline in the *New York Post* blared: "Wrist Shot? Achin' Messier Considers Surgery." The story said Messier was deciding whether to undergo surgery that could end, or hamper, his season. So, prior to the Rangers' final game before the all-star break, on his thirty-third birthday, Messier called a news conference to announce that, after consulting with doctors, he wasn't considering surgery.

"They don't think it's necessary now," Messier said. "They think the wrist will heal sufficiently. They think with rest and treatment, I can regain the full range of motion."

Messier said he planned on participating in the all-star festivities that weekend.

"I can handle the pain," he said.

He could take a joke, too. The Rangers were back in their locker room after the game, a 4-1 victory over the Blues, when Messier's eyes darted around the room. He knew something was happening, but he didn't know what. Then—WHAP!—Joey Kocur hit him from behind, square in the face, with a towel full of shaving cream. It was Kocur's way of saying, "Happy Birthday, Mess."

After wiping the cream off of his face, Messier said he planned on celebrating his birthday quietly. Then he winked and smiled, indicating that he planned to do just the opposite at a party in Manhattan.

"Well," he joked, "I'm just twenty-one for one night."

Messier's birthday celebration continued when Gretzky, Brett Hull, and some of his old Edmonton pals came to New York City for all-star weekend. Messier was terrific and had three points in the game at Madison Square Garden.

■ ■ ■

Messier joined the NHL's top ten all-time scorers in a 5-3 win over Pittsburgh on January 31, passing Alex Delvecchio. He tried to be humble.

"Oh, Alex Delvecchio only used to sharpen his skates twice a year," cracked Messier, who had a knack for NHL history.

Messier, who probably holds the NHL record for having his skates sharpened in a period, game, season, and career, was reminded that Delvecchio made only about $2,300 a year.

"That's why he only had his skates sharpened twice," Messier said. "I'm sure it will mean a lot more to me when I'm finished. I feel I've got a lot of hockey left. But if you think about it, a lot of guys have come through the National Hockey League, and to be in the top ten is a pretty nice feeling. Hockey has been my whole life, so obviously for me to be up there with those guys is pretty special."

The accomplishment was special for the Rangers, who needed Messier to have another MVP-type year and still be at the top of his game when the playoffs started. Despite his aching wrist, he scored six goals in four games after the break.

"Mess is flying," Gartner said. "He has been all year, but since the all-star break in particular, it's like he's shifted it into another gear. Hey, when your big guy's going like that, you just follow along."

He was a leader in other ways, too. Fighter Darren Langdon, a shy kid from Newfoundland, didn't have a major league wardrobe when the Rangers recalled him from the American League. His first game was in Montreal and his parents were going to be there, but Langdon didn't have a suit. So Messier went out and bought him two Hugo Boss suits. When Langdon arrived in the locker room at the Forum, the suits were hanging in his stall.

"They're from the guys," Messier told Langdon.

"It was his way of making Darren feel comfortable and not out of place, and part of our team," Richter said. "You know, Darren's a good guy and he got some laughs out of it, but he felt part of the team. It was always like that with Mark, trying to get more people involved. He made your family feel like part of the team, made your friends feel like part of the team. There was a real identity to the group and that's a great thing to have, because it certainly makes everybody more supportive.

"All of it goes toward being a better team and winning. Think about how important that is for a younger guy coming up. It's important for older guys. If a new guy comes to the team, he's the same way. Mark probably gets a lot of heat from some people for speaking his mind too much, but while he's playing he's always making sure he's making everybody—players, coaches, trainers—feel included."

Messier affected them all. Graves, whose previous career high was 36 goals, was on pace to break Vic Hadfield's Rangers record of 50 goals in a season. Playing on Messier's left wing, Graves had become a classic power forward.

Although Graves and Messier differed greatly in playing style, they were similar in other ways. Graves would have been the Rangers' captain if Messier wasn't there.

"He's probably a better goal scorer than I ever was," said Messier, who scored 50 goals once, when he was twenty-one. "But he's his own individual. That's what's great about Adam. You can't compare him to anybody because he does everything in his own style. I don't think anybody ever really has played like him before."

But for all the good that was happening, Keenan's antagonism was affecting the team. Keenan had a run-in with backup goalie Glenn Healy. His relationship with Neil Smith was worsening. As the trade deadline approached, the stress between Smith and Keenan heightened. Both men wanted the Stanley Cup, but they had different ideas of how to go about getting it.

Keenan didn't raise his voice or seem angry after the Rangers lost to Detroit, 6-3, on March 7, but his blood was racing. Again, he challenged Smith to fix the team.

"They are far bigger than we are, and far more physical than we are," Keenan said. "If you're asking me, I don't know that we can compete with them in a seven-game series."

When asked if something should be done to improve the team's size, Keenan alluded to Smith. "That's up to the general manager," he said. "I'm just coaching the hockey club and the players who are here."

Rangers fans surely were having nightmares about a first-place season coming down to the final games and Messier leaving the Garden on crutches. The nightmare nearly came true on March 16 in a game against Hartford, when Messier was hit hard and cleanly by Todd Harkins. Fortunately for the Rangers, Messier's charley horse wasn't the dream-wrecker it might have been.

"I think, if we got Mark Messier hurt, no matter who I traded for, we're going to be badly damaged," Smith said as the trading deadline neared. "I don't care who you acquire, your team's not going to be nearly as good. I won't be able to make up for a guy like that."

One player the Rangers were very interested in acquiring was Edmonton center Craig MacTavish, the only player in the NHL who didn't wear a helmet and a key member of the Edmonton dynasty.

The Rangers went into the deadline coming off of their worst loss of the season, 7-3 to Chicago on March 18 at the Garden. Graves was one goal short of Hadfield's record with twelve games remaining. Messier missed the Chicago game and would miss the first game of a five-game road trip, having not scored a goal in twenty-three games.

Messier's thumb, hip, wrist, and thigh had been hurting all season, but he had still managed to score 24 goals and 77 points. There was no explanation for his goal-scoring drought, other than that the Rangers had played seventeen games in twenty-nine days, an extremely busy stretch.

Nobody seemed concerned except for Keenan and Smith. And make no mistake about it: The Rangers' activities on deadline day, March 21, had Keenan's fingerprints all over them.

Despite being in first place, the Rangers made five trades on deadline day. While the Rangers didn't get the second-line center they had sought, or another defenseman, they did get bigger, grittier, and more experienced for the playoffs.

Were Smith's deadline moves a sign of idiocy, panic, or genius? Was it lunacy to tear up the best team in the NHL and bring in four new players while dealing three? What about the team's fragile chemistry? Was there enough time in the final twelve games for the new players to fit in? Or was this the move that would put the Rangers over the top, give Keenan the depth and size he needed, and give Messier the foot soldiers he required to end the Rangers' Cup drought?

Smith, the man behind the moves, wouldn't jinx himself by claiming he had acquired the final pieces of the Rangers' befuddling Stanley Cup puzzle.

"I said that once and I swore I won't ever say it again," Smith said. "I just think we're a better hockey club right now than when I woke up this morning. We've got more depth, we're grittier and nastier, and that's what it's going to take. You're not going to get through a twenty-six-game playoff run without good depth."

The Rangers sent Gartner, a sure-fire future Hall of Famer, to Toronto for winger Glenn Anderson and a fourth-round pick in the 1994 draft. They also sent Amonte to Chicago for winger Brian Noonan and left winger Stephane Matteau. Minutes before the three o'clock p.m. deadline, the Rangers succumbed to Edmonton's demand for United States Olympic Team center Todd Marchant and acquired MacTavish.

Keenan had classified Amonte and Gartner, two of the Rangers' speediest scoring wingers, as "soft." Smith, who had no interest in trading either player, agreed that the Rangers needed the size and rugged style provided by Noonan and Matteau, who had been two of Keenan's favorites in Chicago.

As for Gartner, Keenan had lost faith in the 611-goal scorer. He implored Smith to trade Gartner for anything, or for nothing. When Smith resisted, Keenan resorted to threats.

"If you don't trade him," Keenan said, "he'll just sit and sit and sit. I'm not going to play him."

Smith succumbed and got Anderson in return. Getting Messier's former Edmonton winger, along with the respected MacTavish, had the captain smiling, too. Messier saw Anderson as a big game player.

"He's always been that kind of player," said Messier, who for eight years was the center on a line with Anderson. "The kind of guy who always wants to make the last basket. You look at the Dallas Cowboys, and how everybody talks about how they have all these big-play players. Glenn's the same way."

The additions of MacTavish and Anderson gave the Rangers eight ex-Oilers, joining Messier, Graves, Beukeboom, Lowe, Esa Tikkanen, and Mike Hudson. The Rangers also had six ex-Chicago Blackhawks, in addition to Keenan: Larmer, Olczyk, Greg Gilbert, Hudson, Matteau, and Noonan.

Within minutes, people were calling the Rangers the OilHawks.

■ ■ ■

The post-trade period opened on a positive note. Matteau's goal with 13.9 seconds remaining in regulation earned the Rangers a 4-4 tie in

Calgary on March 22. Anderson scored twice and Keenan placed Larmer on a line with Kovalev and Matteau. The line would be wonderfully effective. When he returned, Messier would center Graves and Anderson. That would leave Tikkanen, MacTavish, Noonan, and Nemchinov to rotate and fill up the third and fourth lines. The trades would allow Messier, Leetch, and Graves to scale back their ice time down the stretch.

Messier, who had five days to rest his wrist and elbow, came back for the next game in Edmonton on March 23. He promised that among his first priorities was "to get Gravy his fiftieth goal." Sure enough, late in the first period, Messier broke in on a two-on-one and passed to Graves for No. 50, tying the team record. On the next shift, while being leveled by big defenseman Luke Richardson, Graves knocked in the rebound of a shot by Alexander Karpovtsev for No. 51 and the Rangers record for goals in a season.

Meanwhile, a bigger, more significant record was falling that same night in Los Angeles. The record meant just as much to Messier as Graves' record. Maybe more. Gretzky scored his 802nd career NHL goal, breaking Gordie Howe's NHL record.

"People say Lou Gehrig or Joe DiMaggio were the greatest athletes ever," said Messier. "But when you look at all Wayne has done, it has to be him. Look at the championships, look at the records, look at the statistical achievements. They're mind-boggling. Look at what he's done for a franchise. Look how he saved a league, a whole league. How he changed the game and its image."

Having shared four Stanley Cups with Gretzky, Messier felt something special from a distance. "I think the things we shared, those were enough," he said. "The championships. Growing up as kids and learning how to be champions together. All that is enough for me to know in some small way I was part of 801 and 802. But he's the one who deserves all the credit, and he's the one who probably will be spreading the accolades around.

"I've learned a lot from him. His will to win since he was eighteen, his will to prove everybody wrong. When you're so young and so small as he was, and everybody's saying, 'You can't, you can't, you can't,' he was saying, 'I'll show you, I'll show you, I'll show you.' And he has shown everybody for fifteen or sixteen years."

■ ■ ■

The Rangers went into Vancouver on March 25 for a game that meant virtually nothing at the time, but would have significance in June. The Rangers had a 5-2 lead when the Canucks went on a power play in the final minute of the game. Canucks coach Pat Quinn put all of his musclemen on the ice: Shawn Antoski, Gino Odjick, and Tim Hunter.

Sure enough, a near riot ensued, which spilled over to the bench. Keenan and Quinn screamed at one another. Messier repeatedly hollered at Quinn, "Why the fuck did you have those fuckin' guys on the power play?" Odjick swiped at him with his stick. The swipe breezed past Keenan's mustache. Keenan sent out his tough guys and more fights broke out. Kocur chased Sergio Momesso around the ice. Momesso, fearing for his life, took two baseball swings at Kocur's legs. Kocur, showing remarkable agility, leaped over each hatchet-swing.

The trip concluded with a 3-1 loss in Winnipeg and a 4-3 victory in Philadelphia. The win over the Flyers put the Rangers over one hundred points for the fifth time in team history and set a club record with twenty-three road victories. As the season wound down, and the Rangers played one meaningless game after another, only one goal remained: To finish first in the league.

The Rangers beat the Devils, 4-2, on April 2 to sweep the season series, 6-0, and just about wrap up first place in the league and home-ice advantage throughout the playoffs. They clinched the Presidents' Trophy with a 5-3 win over Toronto on April 8. The Rangers received the trophy prior to their next home game. Messier, again downplaying its significance, as he had two years earlier, placed the trophy in a corner of the locker room.

"This is not our main goal," Messier said. "But it's a step in that direction. I can't remember having a season as enjoyable as the one I've had this year. This team itself, the camaraderie, it's been a real treat to come to the rink every day."

Messier finally broke his scoring drought by scoring twice against the Islanders on April 10. The Rangers would face their cross-river rivals in the first round of the playoffs as they started on their long road to ending the 1940 jinx. They finished the season with 112 points, the best in team history.

The day before the regular season ended marked the anniversary of the Rangers' last Stanley Cup victory, when Bryan Hextall's overtime goal gave the Rangers the championship on April 13, 1940.

The curse was fifty-four years old.

Another attempt to slay the dragon was about to begin.

10

"We Will Win"

As April 17, 1994, and the start of the playoffs arrived, several dates were significant to the Rangers. The most obvious was April 13, 1940, when the Rangers had last won the Stanley Cup. Another was one year ago to the day, when Mike Keenan was hired to coach a team that had gone from first-to-worst in the Patrick Division. Like Messier, Keenan had set a goal, and this was the next step toward achieving that goal: The playoffs, which would produce the Stanley Cup champion.

"When I got here, nobody wanted to say we wanted to win the Cup," Messier said. "This year, we came to camp and that was our goal. We knew the expectations were going to be big, and the pressure was going to be big whether we admitted it or not. You might as well say, 'Yeah, we have pressure to win, so we're not satisfied to be in the final eight, or to win the next series.' You have your long-term goal, then you can set your short-term goal, which right now is the first period."

The Rangers needed little prodding. For many of them, including Messier, the previous season had been their first spring without a play-off. Messier and his teammates had been ready for a while. The Islanders were waiting.

The Rangers knew that if they dictated the tempo of the games and played their best, they should eliminate their arch-rivals, who had finished twenty-eight points behind them in the regular season. While Messier, Lowe, and MacTavish refused to allow the other Rangers to even think disrespectfully about the Islanders, they also knew not to change what they had been doing. The Rangers' ideal tempo was high speed, applying pressure in all three zones, working the forecheck along the boards, and winning battles in front of the nets.

"The emotion will only pick up the game we like to play," Messier said. "From experience, when we've played in emotional, intense games, we've played our best hockey."

Emotion is a guarantee for playoff games, which are twice as intense as regular season games. Said Keenan on the final day of the regular season: "Let the games begin."

■ ■ ■

Lowe drove to the first playoff game from Westchester with Jeff Beukeboom and MacTavish. Nobody said much. Lowe drove like a maniac. The other players were too scared to talk, but all three were thinking the same thing: It was nice to be back in the playoffs.

The Islanders, however, barely offered them a challenge. The Rangers dominated them in the first three games, winning the first two in back-to-back shutouts by Richter, and winning the three by a cumulative score of 17-1. They clinched the series with a 5-2 win at Nassau Coliseum in the only close game of the series. The Rangers trailed, 2-0, before Messier scored two of the Rangers' five consecutive goals. They were a quarter of the way to the Cup.

Meanwhile, the Washington Capitals were removing one of the Rangers' roadblocks to the Cup by upsetting the 1991 and 1992 champion Penguins. Washington would be the Rangers' next opponent. Also going down in the first round were the best team in the west, the Detroit Red Wings, and the defending Stanley Cup champion Montreal Canadiens. The cards were coming out right for the Rangers, but Messier wasn't fooled.

"It doesn't really matter if it's Detroit or the Red Army," he said. "You've got to respect the teams that are left."

The Rangers continued their roll by winning the first two games at home against the Capitals. Keenan made several adjustments in Game Two that turned the game in the Rangers' favor. He shuffled lines and shortened shifts to thirty-five seconds.

The Rangers were hot and so was Messier. Peter Bondra of the Capitals had called them old, but the Rangers didn't look old when they played. Messier scored his sixth goal of the playoffs and the Rangers won Game Three, 3-0, to extend their winning streak to seven games. Messier made a face when a reporter pointed out that the Rangers had benefited from a few breaks in the game.

"Yeah," he said in mock agreement. "The harder we work, the luckier we seem to get."

The Rangers lost Game Four in Washington, but came back to clinch the series with a 4-3 win at the Garden. Leetch was outstanding in the clincher. He assisted on the first three goals, then scored the goal that snapped a 3-3 tie with 3:28 remaining in the third period.

"That was one of the single best playoff performances I've seen since I've been around," said Messier, who had seen some great performances during his career. "He did it all. It was as incredible as anything I've ever seen."

The Rangers were halfway home.

"We took the next step on a long journey," Messier said. "It's a step this team hasn't taken in a long time."

In 1991-92, when the Rangers won the Presidents' Trophy and lost in the second round of the playoffs, they had plenty of representation at the NHL awards ceremony. Messier won the Hart Trophy, Leetch won the Norris, Tony Amonte was a finalist for rookie of the year, and Roger Neilson a finalist for coach of the year. But in 1993-94, not a single Ranger was among the finalists for any of the NHL's awards, which were announced during the Rangers-Caps series.

"That's OK," Messier said. "I think everyone on our team has earned the respect of each other. It was just such a year when everybody contributed so much. It wasn't one guy carrying the team the whole year. I mean, Mike Richter played unbelievable, but we really had a balanced attack all year. Maybe that's why, but at this point . . ."

At this point, who cares, a reporter pointed out.

"Exactly," Messier said.

■ ■ ■

The Rangers' opponent in the Eastern Conference finals was the New Jersey Devils, meaning the highest profile series of the playoffs would be played prior to the finals: The Rangers vs. their cross-river rivals.

At the Rangers' final pre-series practice, Keenan noticed an extra jump in the Rangers' step, and saw Messier call the players into a corner of the rink after practice for an animated talk. This was a special time of year to be a hockey player.

The Tunnel Series quickly became a war. Keenan was angry after Game One because the Rangers blew a lead in the third period for the first time all season. They allowed Claude Lemieux to score the tying goal with 42.7 seconds left in regulation, then Stephane Richer scored at 15:23 of the second overtime, giving the Devils a 4-3 victory.

With the Rangers in trouble, Messier set the tone for Game Two. In the opening 1:13 of the game, he delivered two crunching hits and scored a goal. On his first shift, he knocked Devils captain Scott Stevens to the seat of his pants behind the net. Then he hit his boyhood pal, Ken Daneyko. Then he stole the puck and stuffed it past goalie Martin Brodeur.

The body checks never stopped, and while the Rangers had some ugly moments, the bad moments were far outnumbered by the things they did right in a 4-0 shutout win by Richter that evened the series at one game apiece.

Messier stretched his playoff point streak to twelve games in Game Three, but Stephane Matteau was the hero. Matteau scored in the second overtime to give the Rangers a two-games-to-one lead in the series. So far, the series hadn't been easy for either team. Game Three was nastier than Game Two, which was nastier than Game One.

The Rangers were in a good position. This was no time to panic. Nonetheless, Keenan chose Game Four in New Jersey as the time to do some very strange things.

Keenan's actions in that game have never been completely explained or understood. Nobody ever figured out why he dismantled a lineup that had won ten out of twelve playoff games. Keenan benched Leetch, Graves, MacTavish, and Brian Noonan at various times. Then he benched Messier. Keenan also pulled Richter. Keenan refused to back off from his decisions, even when the Rangers were battling to tie the game late in the second period and in the third period.

Later, after a 3-1 victory by the Devils evened the series, Keenan said he was unhappy with Noonan and MacTavish, who didn't play after the first period. The coach would not be so specific about Leetch, which raised the possibility that the Rangers were hiding a serious injury. Leetch had been relegated to the second unit on both the power-play and the penalty kill and his ice time had been dramatically reduced. Between periods, veteran Jay Wells, who had never won a Stanley Cup, turned to Colin Campbell and said, "Bench me. Get Leetchie out there. I want to win. Tell Mike we want to win."

"It was very obvious we weren't getting a very good response to start the game," Keenan explained. "They came out with authority and took it to us right from the beginning of the first shift. Throughout the first period, they were by far the best team and that proved to be enough for them to win."

106

Leetch, who was playing with a sore shoulder, had been hit early in the game by Claude Lemieux. The Devils had begun to suspect that something was wrong with Messier, too. They thought he had an injured back, ribcage, or groin. They would have loved to have known exactly what the injury was, but they were sure it was something. At one point, Messier skated to the bench without being called off. He later claimed it was for a skate repair, but the Devils suspected he wasn't being forthright.

Keenan's shuffling continued in the second period. Leetch, Noonan, and MacTavish remained on the bench, although Leetch took a couple of shifts with the second power-play unit. One of two things became evident: Either Keenan was a raving maniac who would risk a chance to win the Stanley Cup in order to prove a petty point, or Leetch was hurting badly. Messier, too. Keenan had been called a raving maniac before, but there may have been nobody on earth with more of a thirst for the Stanley Cup.

The Rangers were apparently hiding injuries to their two best players. Keenan's playoff policy was not to disclose injuries unless a player missed a game. When Keenan was asked whether Leetch's benching was injury-related or based on performance, he simply said: "It's related to one or the other, but I'm not going to expound upon it."

He didn't have to. The visitors' locker room at Meadowlands Arena is divided into three sections. In the back is the shower/bathroom area. In the front are the two main rooms: one where the players get medical treatment and hang their streetclothes, and one where they change into their equipment. The room where they hang their clothes is closed to the media.

Leetch was in that room after Game Four. He lay face-down on his stomach while team doctors and trainers examined his left shoulder and gently bent his left arm. The doctors looked concerned as they asked him questions. Apparently, Keenan wasn't lying. Leetch was hurting, and hurting badly.

But what about Noonan, MacTavish, and Graves? Nobody knew for sure because nobody was talking. Maybe Keenan knew about the injuries, maybe he was making them up, maybe he was creating excuses, or maybe he was just panicking. A few Rangers had another question for Iron Mike: Why, down 3-1 in the final minute, didn't he pull goalie Glenn Healy for an extra skater? Had he committed the ultimate sin and given up?

When Leetch finally emerged from the trainer's room, he insisted his injury wouldn't affect his play. Then he explained his reduced ice time by saying, "I didn't play very well my first five or six shifts. It was Mike's reaction to my play."

If it was as simple as that, it was unconscionable that Leetch was not out with the first power play unit in the third period when the Rangers were desperately trying to tie the game. Keenan had apparently quit on the Rangers.

Keenan knew that a reporter had seen Leetch on the trainer's table and that there would be questions about the injuries. The next day at the Rangers' practice rink in Rye, New York, hundreds of media members wanted to know what was going on. Keenan disregarded the throng of reporters. He called the six regular beat reporters into his office and left the other reporters standing outside.

"Turn off the recorders. Put down the notebooks," Keenan demanded.

Keenan hadn't gone off the record in a group session with reporters all season. By demanding that the pens and recorders be put aside, he was asking the small group to go off the record with the most important story of the year.

"Brian Leetch's shoulder is totally fucked," Keenan revealed. "He's having it frozen before every game." Messier had an injured rib and hip, just as the Devils had suspected. Graves had a deep, serious cut on the back of his leg. He had also injured his back, which would eventually require surgery. Noonan had a bad knee. MacTavish had a bad shoulder.

As Keenan talked on and on, the reporters didn't know what to do. Did he think that by talking off the record he would prevent this news from being reported? Was he trying to cover up something else? Was he trying to create a smokescreen? Was he making excuses in case the Rangers lost the series? Or was he flipping out? Had he completely lost control of the team?

Another side of the story didn't come to light until later: Keenan's relationship with Neil Smith had fallen apart. Perhaps Keenan knew that either he or Smith would get fired, and it would surely be him if the Rangers lost in the third round after being the NHL's best team all year. Unless, of course, he had a solid reason for losing.

The Rangers beat reporters didn't know what to do with the story. Outside the office, watching practice and waiting for Keenan's press conference to begin, were a hundred other media members. They wanted to know what happened in the office, but none of the privileged reporters were going to spill a story this good, even if none of them knew how they would write it.

Shortly afterward, in his official, on-the-record press conference, Keenan said the Rangers had only minor injuries, except for the one to Leetch, which he wouldn't disclose. Messier said he wasn't hurt. Leetch said he wasn't hurting so badly that it would affect his play. Graves said he was hurting, but no more than most players at this stage of the playoffs. Noonan said he wasn't hurt at all. MacTavish said the same thing.

Most of the beat reporters who had been present at Keenan's off-the-record session reported the injuries as fact without revealing their source. But the Rangers had a bigger problem. They would go into their most important game of the year not knowing how much or how well Leetch would be able to play, if he played at all.

The next night, on the front page of the Rangers' media notes for Game Five, under the heading "Injuries," the following sentence was typed: "The Rangers have no injuries to report."

Which was true. They had injuries. Just none to report.

Leetch and Messier both played in Game Five, but the Rangers lost, 4-1. The Devils had a three games to two lead in the series heading back to the Meadowlands for Game Six. They were a strong, confident team with a solid, nearly impenetrable young goalie in Martin Brodeur. The Rangers were in trouble.

"We were in a good situation after the double-overtime win in Game Three," Leetch said. "They responded and won two in a row. That's what we have to do now. We don't deserve to be in the Stanley Cup final if we don't win."

It was as simple as that.

■ ■ ■

The day before Game Six, Messier stood in front of his locker at the Rangers' practice facility. He faced a huddle of reporters holding microphones, cameras, and notebooks. Messier had been brought to New York for dire situations such as these, and everybody wanted to know what he had to say.

"We're going to go in there and win Game Six," he declared unblinking into the glare. "We've responded all year. We've won games we've had to win. We know we're going in there to win Game Six and bringing it back for Game Seven. We feel we can win it, and we feel we are going to win it."

Messier didn't sound as convincing and confident as his words would appear in print. When he finished talking, several reporters asked each other, "Did he actually say that?" Several considered not even leading with Messier's declaration because he didn't sound convincing enough. Most of the TV newscasts that day didn't use the soundbite.

Later, Messier admitted that the Rangers' confidence was wavering for the first time all season, and he wanted to make a statement that would show his teammates he still felt supremely confident in them. So he said, "We're going to win." He certainly didn't say, as the *New York Post* declared on its back page, "WE'LL WIN TONIGHT." He couldn't have said that. The game wasn't played until the next day. There was no game that night. But he did say, "We're going to win."

On the surface, the Rangers appeared to be in an impossible situation. Without Leetch and Messier at full strength, they didn't stand much chance of beating the Devils on any given night, never mind twice in a row. And the Rangers could hardly hope to compete with the Devils, the NHL's best even-strength team, unless their special teams beat the Devils' special teams. Without Leetch and Messier at full strength, the special teams, as was made clear in Games Four and Five, were not so special.

"It's important that, as a team, we focus on the first period of the next game and not think about the 1940 thing or the great-year-going-sour thing, or about Game Seven, or about the last game," Lowe said. "We have to think only about eliminating our mistakes and playing the style that made us successful all year. Guys have asked me, 'Have you been through this?' Yes. 'Have you been successful?' Yes. 'Does that make it any easier?' No."

Messier woke up the next morning saw the newspaper headlines, and said to himself, "Oh no." Years later, he would say: "At the time, I was so focused on trying to find the way to get us jump-started again that I forgot that every New Yorker, plus every Devil, would be reading that story. But, you know, it doesn't ally matter at that point anyway. My point, ultimately, was to instill the confidence back in the team, so if it did that job I didn't care about the rest of the burden that might have followed."

The game started . . . and the weight of the burden increased. The Rangers, one loss away from their fifty-fourth and most painful year of failure, fell behind 2-0 in the first period. At that point, it wouldn't have been a stretch to have called Messier heroic. It would have been a lie. He was awful, as were his teammates. There was no reason to think anything would change. The Rangers had been limited to two goals in the previous two games, and, in each, had been checked into oblivion once the Devils grabbed the lead.

Richter was under siege from the opening faceoff. The Devils took eight of the first nine shots and Richter handled all of them until Scott Niedermayer scored with 8:03 gone to give the Devils a 1-0 lead. Then, during a delayed penalty, Claude Lemieux deflected a shot past Richter for a 2-0 lead. The Rangers were on the brink of another long summer.

Keenan seemed lost. He called timeout during the chaotic first thirty-seven minutes, but said nothing. Assistant coaches Campbell and Dick Todd both stared at Keenan, then looked away as he stared back at them. Several Rangers huddled around Messier, as if they were begging for his leadership.

The Rangers got worse after the timeout. Messier, frustrated, got tangled up with Bernie Nicholls behind the net, and had a glove-in-the-face confrontation with the gathering of Devils that quickly formed. One of those Devils was Ken Daneyko, who knew Messier as well as anybody.

"He thought it was over," Daneyko recalled. "You could see he was frustrated. I saw it in his face behind the net when he took that roughing penalty with Bernie. He thought it was over."

Then, as if somebody had turned the clock back to Edmonton 1990, and dipped the Rangers' injured players in Lourdes, as if the Messier of 1990 had switched uniforms with the beaten-up Messier of 1994, the Rangers rallied.

Messier and Richter—who could not afford to give up one more goal—pulled them from the grave, with a big helping hand from the one-armed Leetch, who recaptured his brilliance. Keenan replaced Glenn Anderson with Alexei Kovalev on Messier's right wing. Kovalev, who had been terrific against the Islanders and Capitals, had done nothing against the Devils. Then, just when it looked as if the Rangers would die a quiet death, smothered by the Devils' trap defense, they mounted an improbable rally.

With less than two minutes remaining in the second period, Messier stole the puck at center ice and carried it into the Devils' end. He made a drop pass to Kovalev, then drew two Devils to the net. Graves also went to the net, creating traffic in front of Brodeur. Kovalev blasted a shot inside the left post to make it 2-1.

Messier took over. In the third period, Leetch lugged the puck out of the Rangers zone and blew past forechecker Bobby Carpenter. Leetch gave the puck to Kovalev, who carried it over the blue line and found Messier speeding to the net. Messier shot a backhander that eluded Brodeur's left skate and snuck in with 2:48 gone.

The game was tied and the Devils needed to respond, but they couldn't stop Messier, who was exceeding even his own speed limit. His bursts had the Devils backing off and out of their trap.

During a four-on-four with 12:12 gone in the third, Leetch again sent Kovalev into the Devils' zone for a hard shot that hit Brodeur's arm. Messier blew in past Game Five hero Bernie Nicholls—the man for whom he had been traded—and batted the rebound past Brodeur, giving the Rangers their first lead. Late in the game, Anderson took a needless penalty to put the Devils on a power play. Coach Jacques Lemaire pulled Brodeur early to create a six-on-four advantage for the Devils, but Messier completed his hat trick with a 140-foot shot into the empty net.

Impossibly, unpredictably, the Rangers had evened the series. Messier had followed through on his "guarantee" with one of the greatest games of his career.

"When Mike threw Alex on our line, it really helped open things up," Messier said. "His goal was huge. Then we were one shot away going into the third period and we felt the game opened up and we were hitting our stride."

Said Leetch: "It was basically him and Mike Richter, because our season was over if we go down 3-0 there. Mark was going down the other end, setting up plays or putting the puck in the net himself. I didn't even think about what was in the papers, the 'We will win.' He was going to play that type of game regardless of anything going on around it, because we had to have it."

Keenan, who as the coach of the Blackhawks was the victim of Messier's signature game in 1990, said: "That has to be one of the most impressive performances by any hockey player in the history of this league. I knew that 1990 game was one of the greatest games I had seen to that date. People will be talking about Mark Messier for many years to come, the way they talk about Gordie Howe, Bobby Orr, Wayne Gretzky, and Mario Lemieux. Maybe even Mark more than Mario because of his tenure and his five Stanley Cups."

The rave reviews for Messier came pouring in, conjuring up memories of that game in 1990, when Messier had singlehandedly rescued the Oilers from the brink of elimination. Now he had done it again, but for the Rangers against the Devils.

Bernie Nicholls: "He's the greatest clutch player in the game. Gretzky and Mario get a lot of credit, but when the chips are down, I want Messier. He's their leader. He leads, they follow. He can't say 'We have to win tonight,' he has to say, 'I guarantee it.'"

Steve Larmer: "To predict a win when we were on the ropes like that, then to back it up, was incredible. To put yourself on the line like that . . . but then that might be normal for him. That seems to be the way he plays. He's always putting stuff on the line."

Mike Richter: "It really was the stuff that myths are made of."

The Rangers and Devils would play a seventh game for the right to go to the finals.

"When you're this near to death and you don't die," Richter said, "you're tougher to kill."

The Rangers were very much alive.

■ ■ ■

The next day, Messier didn't issue any predictions or guarantees, just warnings. He wanted the Rangers to come down from their Game Six cloud, lest they float right into an ambush by the Devils in the deciding game at the Garden.

"Game Six is over with," Messier said. "The moment we walked off the ice it was over with and we had to start preparing for Game Seven. We need to play the best game we've played this year, and we're playing a great team as well. I think only a fool would look ahead at this point. We have to treat this as we have all year. We know what's at stake, and what we have to do. We're not going to get too wound up.

"It's an opportunity. You start in September with a goal in mind, to win the Stanley Cup. You have to take it step by step. This is the next step. It all gives us an opportunity to take the next step."

One of the greatest playoff series ever played deserved a dramatic, emotional finish. That's what it got.

The Garden shook and quaked as these two exhausted, injured teams finished their heavyweight brawl. Leetch, cementing his MVP credentials, scored a breathtaking goal for a 1-0 lead. The lead held up until the final minute, when the Devils again pulled Brodeur for an extra skater.

As time wound down, the Rangers scrambled to protect their lead. Stephane Richer's shot from the left corner bounced off Richter's pads. Lemieux, who had scored in the final moments of Game One, slipped the puck across the crease to Valeri Zelepukin. Richter did a split, and amazingly kicked his left leg all the way across the crease to stop Zelepukin's shot. But there was no Ranger to prevent Zelepukin from pushing in the rebound. The Garden crowd, which had already started a massive celebration, went into stunned silence. With only 7.7 seconds remaining in the third period, the game was tied at one.

The Rangers' coaches weren't sure what to say during the intermission, but when they went to the locker room to talk to the players, they saw they didn't have to say a thing. At first, the locker room was quiet. No one said a word. Then, one by one, the former Edmonton Oilers players got up and spoke.

"Maybe this is destiny," Kevin Lowe told his teammates. "Maybe this is the way it's supposed to be." Lowe, the five-time Stanley Cup champ, screamed that if it weren't so difficult, so gut-wrenching, it wouldn't be so satisfying to win. He hammered the idea into his teammates' heads that this would be the sweetest victory, to battle such adversity and win.

"The guys were just very stunned," Richter recalled. "We thought we were going to the finals and suddenly it was gone."

Often during Messier's career, Lowe had come up with a perfect message for the moment. At those times, Messier knew to defer to Lowe. This was one of those times. Messier said some things, but he basically backed up what Lowe had been hollering. Lowe was speaking from the heart and his sermon needed to be heard.

The Rangers attacked the Devils in the first overtime. They didn't look like a team that had just blown its shot at the Cup. They looked even hungrier than before. But Brodeur was solid. He couldn't be beaten. The Rangers and Devils returned to their locker rooms to prepare for a second overtime.

Stephane Matteau had broken his skate lace and was back in the Rangers' locker room when his teammates went onto the ice for the start of the second overtime. Matteau ran into scratched teammate Ed Olczyk, who was wearing his suit jacket inside out for good luck. Olczyk decided the Rangers needed more luck, so he kissed Matteau's stick.

Before returning to the ice, Matteau found an obstacle in the corridor outside the locker room: The Prince of Wales Trophy. League

The Messiers are an extremely close family. Doug, a former player, is Mark's agent, and Mary-Jean drove Mark to his games when he was young. In 1984, Mark celebrated his first Stanley Cup and the Conn Smythe Trophy as playoff MVP with his parents.

Even on a team with superstars such as Messier, Wayne Gretzky, Paul Coffey, Jari Kurri, Grant Fuhr, and Glenn Anderson, coach Glen Sather ran a tight ship and kept his finger on the pulse of the team.

Off the ice, Gretzky and Messier knew how to have a little fun.

They were one of the greatest duos in hockey history: Mess and Gretz. They dominated with their skills and their personalities, and celebrated hundreds of goals together with the Oilers.

Messier and coach Mike Keenan, who were together in 1991 with Team Canada in the Canada Cup, were another great duo.

Messier was on the golf course when he learned that Gretzky had been traded to Los Angeles, and he was on the golf course again when he learned that he had been traded to the Rangers.

Messier, a celebrity in the sports world, was a busy man off the ice, but found time to pal around with movie stars Goldie Hawn and Burt Reynolds.

The New York Rangers hadn't won the Stanley Cup in 41 years when Messier joined them in Montreal in 1991 and pulled on their jersey for the first time.

With Messier's arrival, the Rangers finally had a great duo of their own: Messier, who in 1992 won his second Hart Trophy, and defense-man Brian Leetch, who that same year won his first Norris Trophy.

A career milestone: Messier scored his 500th career goal on November 6, 1995, against goalie Rick Tabaracci of the Calgary Flames.

Messier was working toward a more important goal in 1994 when the Rangers tried to end their Stanley Cup jinx, but he had to spend a lot of time undoing the damage caused by coach Mike Keenan.

"Mark Messier, come get the Stanley Cup!" Messier delivered what he had been brought to New York for when NHL Commissioner Gary Bettman handed him the Cup after the Rangers won Game Seven of the 1994 Stanley Cup finals.

Back in Canada: After an acrimonious divorce from the Rangers during the summer of 1997, Messier signed with the Vancouver Canucks. That ended his one-year reunion with Gretzky in New York.

Gretzky and Messier were together again in April 1999 when The Great One played his final game.

officials, thinking the room had been vacated, had placed the trophy in the hallway. Matteau couldn't get around it, so he asked the officials if he could touch it for luck. He did.

He couldn't have been luckier. With over four minutes gone in the period, a back pass into the corner by Slava Fetisov hit Tikkanen in the seat of his pants. Matteau scooped up the puck in the left corner, then skated behind the net. He tried to come out in front, but couldn't, so he tried to stuff the puck. Brodeur came across the crease. The puck glanced off of his leg pads and into the net.

Suddenly, Matteau had become a part of Rangers folklore.

The goal touched off a giant celebration in the stands and on the ice. Fans hugged other fans and chanted "We want the Cup!" The Rangers hugged each other. Keenan hugged everybody he saw. "Matteau! Matteau! Matteau!" screamed Rangers radio play-by-play man Howie Rose.

And poor Brodeur. An hour after the game, he was in his street-clothes, standing at the Zamboni entrance to the left of the net, with his face pressed up against the glass, and staring straight at the spot where Matteau had scored the winner.

"It was great hockey," Messier said. "It was like two boxers that have styles that make for a good fight. The styles seemed to mix. It was one of the better series I've ever played in."

But, as Howie Rose had also said, the Rangers still had one more hill to climb: the Stanley Cup finals and a date with the Vancouver Canucks.

11

Dragonslayer

Madison Square Garden had become a magical place in June 1994. New York fans were ecstatic over the two Garden teams, the Rangers and the Knicks of the National Basketball Association, who were both in the finals.

New York City as a hockey town was an unusual concept. Because of this new fascination with the Rangers, Messier became as big a celebrity as there was in the biggest city in the world. But the Vancouver Canucks weren't concerned with the attention he was getting and with what Messier was saying. They were concerned with stopping Messier from beating them singlehandedly.

"I don't know if anybody can match up with Messier physically," said Pat Quinn, Vancouver's general manager and coach. "There are not many like him. And I'm not sure if a matchup we'd like would be allowed anyway. We could probably diddle around and try to get it. But whatever center or line we have against him is going to have to deal with his skills."

In Games One, Two, Five, and Seven, in New York, Keenan would get the final line change and, therefore, favorable matchups for Messier and for dealing with Vancouver's own dynamo, Pavel Bure. In Games Three, Four, and Six, at Vancouver's Pacific Coliseum, the Canucks would get the final change, and would try to rough Messier up. But Messier's speed and skill would be too much for the Canucks' strongmen unless they wore him down. This would be one of the main sidebars of the series.

The Canucks had reason to dread Messier, who had terrorized them throughout his career. In eighty-five games against Vancouver, roughly the equivalent of a full season, he had 56 goals, 70 assists, and 126 points. One of the reasons Messier had so much success against the Canucks was that most of those games were played in Edmonton and Vancouver, where the ice was in perfect condition and favored good skaters and high-tempo, high-skill teams. Madison Square Garden's ice was possibly the worst in the league.

Messier couldn't wait to start the series. As Game One neared, he became agitated by the media attention and the questions reporters were asking.

"What will you tell your teammates before Game One?" a reporter asked.

"Let's go," Messier said dryly. "That's it. That's my Knute Rockne."

Whatever he actually said didn't matter. The Rangers soundly out-played the Canucks but were beaten in overtime, 3-2. The heroics of Canucks goalie Kirk McLean, who stopped 17 shots in overtime, enabled Greg Adams to score the winner with 33.1 seconds remaining in the extra session. The winner came moments after Brian Leetch had hit the crossbar.

In Game Two, the Rangers evened the series with a 3-1 victory. The win wasn't sealed until Leetch slid the puck the length of the ice and into an empty net. The posts and crossbars were as important as either goalie in this game. Pucks clanged off of iron all night.

Messier was in the middle of the winning goal. With the Canucks on a power play, he stole a Trevor Linden pass and skated in on a break-away. With Jeff Brown in pursuit, Messier pushed the puck ahead and lost control. McLean stepped out of his crease to poke the puck away, but he knocked it right into Messier's skates. Messier chased down the loose puck at the side of the net and passed it into the crease to Glenn Anderson for an empty-net dunk.

When the series shifted to Vancouver, Quinn had the final line changes and the chance to dictate matchups. The matchup he chose was unusual and one the Rangers almost welcomed. Quinn, who had ignited a brawl by putting his tough guys on the ice in the last regu-lar-season meeting between the Canucks and Rangers, chose ruffians Shawn Antoski and Tim Hunter, and checking center John McIntyre, to harass and hammer Messier. Quinn had seen enough of Trevor Linden's offensive line playing against Messier's line in the two fast-paced games at the Garden. He didn't like the way the two lines had traded scoring chances.

There was nothing new or wrong with Quinn's strategy of playing his tough guys against Messier. Since the beginning of hockey, teams have tried to rough up their opponents' top players in an attempt to wear them down, aggravate them, and lure them into retaliation penalties. That's what the Rangers tried to do to Bure, and it paid off when Bure retaliated against Jay Wells in Game Three. Bure was kicked out of the game for swinging his stick at Wells and cutting his eyelid. The Rangers went on to win, 5-1.

"For a few shifts, things worked out fairly well for them," said Colin Campbell, referring to the matchup. "One shift [Quinn] got what he wanted."

That was the shift when Antoski punched Messier, who punched him back. Each player received a minor penalty. But the Rangers felt that, for most of Game Three, the matchup of Messier's line against McIntyre's was working in their favor. If Messier and Graves played nearly thirty minutes, then for thirty minutes Vancouver's best offensive players were on the bench. The Rangers knew Hunter and Antoski weren't going to beat them.

Early in the first period, the Canucks were outshooting the Rangers and the Antoski-Hunter pairing was causing the Rangers some problems. Then Keenan, who had alternated Anderson, Larmer, and Kovalev on Messier's right, decided to use Joey Kocur in that spot. Kocur got in Antoski's face, but couldn't draw him into a fight. The Rangers, however, finally started getting some shots and grabbed control of the game.

"I guess you'd have to say trying to wear down Mess with size and strength, at the expense of everyone else's ice time . . . I don't know," Campbell said. "As long as they don't do damage to Messier, Leetch, or Graves, I guess we don't mind it. Mess is strong enough and fit enough, and so is Graves. I guess the other way to go is to throw Linden against him and try to outchance them."

In other words, Quinn was choosing his poison.

"Simply, we're out to hit Mark Messier, and to hit him often," Quinn said. "I don't just want three guys hitting him, I want twenty-five guys hitting him. They won't let me dress the extra five guys I want to hit him."

By the end of Game Three, Quinn had joined the legion of Leetch fans. Quinn again admired him in Game Four, when Leetch's brilliance, and Richter's series-turning save on a penalty shot by Bure, allowed the Rangers to fly back across the continent with a three games to one lead. The Rangers won, 4-2. Their first Stanley Cup in fifty-four years was only one win away.

Leetch had a hand in each Rangers goal. He weaved his way through three of the four Canucks on the ice and set up Kovalev's power-play goal with 4:55 remaining in the third period, snapping a 2-2 tie. Leetch had been slashed so badly skating into the Vancouver zone that he couldn't raise his arms to celebrate the goal. He was in pain. But he completed his four-point night with an assist on Larmer's bouncing 75-footer that clinched the win.

He also caused the series' most memorable moment, a penalty shot awarded when he tripped Bure from behind on a breakaway. Richter's body exploded across the goalmouth to rob Bure and turn the momentum of the game in the Rangers' favor. The save was remarkably similar to the one Richter had made on Bure at the All-Star Game in January.

"He's done it for us all year long, and in the playoffs he's done it even more so," Leetch said of Richter. "He did the same thing against the Devils in Game Six. We got down 2-0 and we couldn't afford to give them another one and he shut them down and gave us a chance. Without that we might not even be in the finals."

The Rangers were on a high. Madison Square Garden would be electric for Game Five and the potential Cup clincher. But, as was always the case for the Rangers, winning wouldn't come easily, or without controversy.

A few days earlier, the Detroit Red Wings had fired general manager Bryan Murray and his assistant, Doug MacLean. Immediately, the media speculated that Keenan would be in line for the job, especially since his relationship with Neil Smith had deteriorated and Detroit had been interested in him the year before.

The speculation became more than rumor and innuendo when the series returned to New York. Informed talk out of Detroit had Keenan negotiating with the Red Wings about the job . . . even with his team one win away from the Stanley Cup and four years remaining on his contract.

When asked about the Detroit situation, Keenan replied: "No comment. I'll talk about it after the season."

The truth of the situation was that Smith and Keenan couldn't work together much longer even if the Rangers won the Cup. Smith, in off-the-record, half-joking moments, would say things about Keenan such as: "Escape clause? No, he doesn't have an escape clause, but if he wants to go I'll drive him to the airport." And: "If we win the Cup and he leaves, it will be like winning two Cups."

Smith wouldn't joke much longer. The situation was about to reach crisis proportions for the Rangers.

■ ■ ■

Game Five, Madison Square Garden: With the Cup in the house, ready to be raised by Messier, this was the biggest hockey night ever in New York. The Rangers knew how close they were to living a dream and to ending those annoying chants of "1940." Messier knew how close he was to bringing the Cup to New York and fulfilling his goal. But he refused to look ahead.

"We're not going to fall into that trap at all," he said.

But when the night ended, the still-corked bottles of champagne were packed and put on a west-bound plane, along with the Rangers and their equipment. The Rangers blew a chance to clinch the Cup in front of a raucous crowd at the Garden. They rallied to score three goals in the third period and tie the game, then allowed three straight Canucks goals in a sloppy 6-3 loss.

Keenan blamed the loss on the party atmosphere, the stories in the newspapers, and the talk on radio proclaiming this as the ultimate hockey night in New York. Before the game, the Rangers had been steely-eyed. They were cordial, but unsmiling. They went about their business in a workmanlike manner. Messier was stoic, uptight. He tried to put on his "just another game" face to calm down his teammates.

Yet, the victory party had already been planned. There was no question in anybody's mind that this was the night the Rangers' curses would die. They didn't.

"We can be seduced by success," said Keenan. "Certainly the media was seduced in this case, which I think was picked up by our club. I don't think we were tight or over-excited, but it certainly had something to do with looking into the future."

Meanwhile, speculation about Keenan increased. He knew the answers to all of the reporters' questions regarding the Detroit situation, but he wasn't supplying any, so that led to more speculation.

"There's a lot of speculation," Keenan said. "But I haven't had any time to spend time thinking about it. Those things happen in this game and I certainly realize it. My focus is on winning the game."

Rob Campbell, Keenan's agent, said: "There's absolutely no truth to it. I handle all Michael's business affairs and I haven't spoken to anybody. I think the whole thing is really inappropriate. It's probably wishful thinking by Detroit. I have had no discussions with the Detroit Red Wings. In fact, I haven't spoken to [owner] Mike Ilitch in about two years."

The demons would not release their hold on the Rangers. The dragons that cursed them would not purge their fire. The score of Game Six in Vancouver was Canucks 4, Rangers 1. The series would return to New York for Game Seven.

"Before the season, if you said we'd be going home with a chance to win the Stanley Cup in Game Seven, we would have been pretty happy with that," said Messier, forcing a smile. "This is a situation where we don't have anything to be down or disappointed about. This is an opportunity to go home and win the Stanley Cup."

But the Rangers had problems. For most of the series, Messier hadn't been able to come through when the Rangers needed him most. His lack of performance affected the rest of his line. Graves hadn't scored a goal since Game Three of the Conference finals. Defenseman Sergei Zubov, who had led the team in scoring during the regular season, had been hurt and played poorly. The Canucks loved to hit him.

"What they're doing, I don't really know," Messier said. "But they're playing well. We've got to come up with our best game."

That wouldn't be easy. The craziness that had surrounded Keenan became crazier after Game Six. Keenan had felt the media distractions were responsible for the loss in Game Five, and he didn't want a repeat of that situation during the two days before Game Seven. His proposed solution was to fly the team to Lake Placid in upstate New York and practice there. There, Keenan felt, the Rangers could avoid most of the media crush, he could avoid answering questions about going to Detroit, and the entire team could avoid talking about the 3-1 series lead they had lost.

The players and the rest of the coaching staff knew what the Rangers really needed: Rest and some strategic tinkering. Campbell stepped in, as did Messier and Lowe.

"Mike was worried about reporters," Campbell said. "I said, 'Forget about the reporters. They're dead tired, too. They've been traveling back and forth, and they've had it. There are no more stories anyway, no more Mike-going-to-Detroit stories. The only story is the last game. It has nothing to do with what's happening at the rink.'

"I said, 'Boy, we've got to get him off this thing. That's just going to make us more tired. We're all whipped. We've got to get home, get rested, get work done on the video and plan for Game Seven. I've got to get Mark and Kevin.'"

Lowe and Messier got to Keenan first. By the time Campbell spoke to Keenan, Keenan had already decided not to take the team to Lake Placid.

During the two days between games, Campbell and assistant coach Dick Todd devised a strategy to combat the Canucks' defensemen, who were joining the play on every rush and creating problems for the Rangers. They also wanted to show the players some clips from the first four games to reinstill some of their eroded confidence.

The problem was, Keenan didn't like video.

So, in one of the most unbelievable stories of the season, Campbell called Rob Campbell, who was his agent as well as Keenan's. He told Rob Campbell to phone Keenan to discuss the Detroit job. The agent came through. He called Keenan and tied him up on his office phone for more than twenty minutes while Colin Campbell met with the players.

Before the team meeting, Lowe told Colin Campbell: "You've got to give everybody shit. Even Moose." Moose was Messier.

"Even Moose?" Campbell asked.

Nobody likes to be criticized in front of his teammates, especially the great players. There was no way Campbell was going to yell at Messier, especially since Keenan hadn't done it all season. But, while Keenan was occupied with his agent, Campbell and Todd showed their video and had their meeting.

■ ■ ■

Messier had lifted the Stanley Cup five times. He was brought to New York in 1991-92 to lift it once more, on the world's biggest stage. Now he had the chance to deliver or fall flat on his face. He was asked whether Game Seven was the biggest game of his career.

"Yup, just like Game Six was the biggest game of my career, Game Seven is the biggest game of my career, no doubt about it," Messier said with more than a touch of sarcasm. "This team's been through a lot and we trust each other. We've been through everything together and I know we'll bring our best game."

But would Messier? And if he didn't, could the Rangers still win?

Messier had not been a major factor since the last biggest game of his career, Game Six of the Eastern Conference finals. Now, for the first time since Game Seven against the Devils, elimination loomed just as boldly as celebration. But the Rangers, and Messier, had played poorly in the last two games.

"When you play this kind of hockey for this long, you're going to have some games where you don't play well," Messier said. "But we played well enough to give ourselves enough cushion in case we did have a couple of off games."

Although the pressure was on, Messier downplayed any talk about all of the pressure being on the Rangers.

"If both teams are genuinely serious about winning it, then there's just as much pressure on them," he said.

He also admitted that, if the Rangers lost, it would be hard to evaluate the season as anything but a failure.

The excitement of Game Seven would be mixed with equal parts anxiety and fear, the elements that had plagued this franchise and its fans: The ghosts of 1940.

"We've tried to take care of that," Messier said. "But all the things that have happened, all the burdens, it would be too much for anybody to tackle. We felt the best way to tackle it would be for us to be sure that the 1993-94 team was successful. The 1940 thing is too much. If we had let it, it would have destroyed us a long time ago."

Messier made no guarantees this time. He simply issued a warning about what was ahead.

"It's no time for the faint of heart," he said.

■ ■ ■

One day before the most important hockey game ever in New York City, the most important game of his life, and the most important game of many of his players' lives, Keenan decided to address the Detroit rumors. The night before the game, Keenan gathered the Rangers and told them he was not leaving to take a job with the Red Wings. Then he said the same thing to the media.

"I can deny that rumor one more time," Keenan said after practice. "It's getting to the point of being ridiculous. I am not going to Detroit. I am the coach of the Rangers, I signed a five-year contract, and there is no escape clause, nor am I looking for an escape clause. I came here to coach the Rangers for five years. I don't know where these things are coming from, nor do I care at this point. I said two or three days ago I'm staying here to coach the Rangers, and I will say the same thing. If people don't want to believe me, that's beyond my control. The fact that this has come up is just another distraction we have to deal with. I will be coaching the New York Rangers next year, unless my bosses don't want me to."

Keenan claimed he hadn't thought about another scenario, in which Smith left and he became the Rangers' general manager and coach. He described his relationship with Smith as strictly business and limited only to decisions on personnel. But Keenan couldn't explain why he had waited so long to deny the rumors.

"I did deny it," Keenan insisted. "I said they're erroneous. Things happen all the time. Somebody said, 'Does it make sense?' I said, 'Sure it makes sense. I was a manager and a coach, there's an opening, sure it makes sense.' But I've got a hockey club preparing to win the Stanley Cup. That's my job. I'm focusing on winning the Stanley Cup. People who know me know that is my purpose here. That is my focus. My mission here is not to win the Stanley Cup, but to win the Stanley Cup a number of times."

He told the players the same thing. They apparently believed him.

"One of the things we talked about all during the season was the distractions and about trust," Messier said. "When you're playing in a city where there's as much attention as we get, there are going to be rumors and a lot of things trying to drive wedges between you. The only way you can overcome it is to be able to rely on and trust the guy sitting next to you. When the story came out about Mike, it was another thing we knew we had to put aside. Someone was trying to put a wedge between us and Mike. Around here, molehills turn into mountains in a hurry. There are so many bigger things around this team right now."

The players knew Keenan was selling his house in Greenwich, Connecticut. He told them he was selling it to buy a smaller house in the same area.

But Keenan had more on his agenda than simply telling the players he planned on sticking around. He also delivered an intense, emotional speech that Messier later said was one of the best he had ever heard.

"Go out and win it for each other, and if you do, you will walk together for the rest of your lives," Keenan told the Rangers.

"He seized the moment," Messier said. "He took control of the situation. We needed it at the time. Mike came through when we needed him most, Everything he said hit home, to everybody. It was incredible. It got us back on track."

The Rangers were much more relaxed for Game Seven than they had been for Game Five. Prior to Game Five, most of the players had worn scowls. Before Game Seven, the players acted as if they were about to play just another big game.

Less than an hour and a half before game time, Keenan, who usually didn't like videos, showed the team two videos. One was a highlight film set to music, the other was the collage of ticker-tape parades he had shown them in September.

"When Mike showed us the image of the parade in training camp, when you could see it visually, then when all the things we went through happened, that was the one thing that got us back on track," Messier said. "When the season got long, when it got tough, that one image stuck in my head."

Keenan should have shown that tape to the fans, whose gloom and doom attitudes belied the fact that their team was one win away from the Stanley Cup. Hours before Game Seven, backup goalie Glenn Healy said: "There are twenty-three million people in New York today who have already dialed the 9 and the 1, and they're waiting to see if they have to dial the last 1."

■ ■ ■

The game was played recklessly and at high speed. There were dirty hits, trash talk, face-to-face confrontations, and not a backward step taken by either side. The Rangers' leaders led. Their best players played like they were the best. Keenan was at the top of his game.

The Rangers took the lead, 1-0, with 11:02 gone in the first period. Leetch struggled out of John McIntyre's bear hug, was slashed by Antoski, and led the rush. Messier got past Bure inside the blue line, drew two Canucks, and dropped the puck to Zubov. McLean came out to cut down Zubov's angle, so Zubov held the puck, then found Leetch all alone at the left of the net, thanks to a pick by Adam Graves. Leetch accepted the pass and, with plenty of time, calmly angled his shot into the vacated side of the net.

Just 3:01 later, the MacTavish line's work low in the Canucks' zone drew a penalty. On the power play, Zubov carried the puck into the offensive zone and fed Kovalev, who was skating down the left wing. Kovalev found Graves wide open in the slot, and Graves' snap shot beat McLean for his first goal in eleven games.

The Canucks got back into the game in the second period when Linden scored a shorthanded goal. The Rangers answered back. On a scramble in front of the net, Graves, Noonan, and Messier all took pokes at the loose puck. The sticks of Messier and Graves arrived simultaneously and the puck flipped off the inside of McLean's right pad and into the net. The Rangers had a 3-1 lead. Messier was credited with the goal that would become the Cup winner. For years afterward, any time Graves was asked if he had scored that goal, he'd answer: "No, no, no, no, no, no, no, no, no. Is that plain enough?"

The Rangers took the 3-1 lead into the third period, but when Linden scored a power play goal to cut the lead to one, the fans got nervous. Then, late in the period, Nathan Lafayette of the Canucks beat Richter with a shot, but the puck hit the goalpost. Luck, it seemed, was finally on the Rangers' side.

Helmet-clad policemen ringed the arena as time wound down. In the final seconds, Larmer sent the puck out of the Rangers' zone. The Rangers' bench vibrated from fans jumping up and down. Nick Kypreos jumped onto the ice and hugged Richter.

But Larmer had been called for icing. There were still 1.1 seconds remaining in the game.

"I was so excited, I couldn't wait," Kypreos said later.

Then the officials added another half-second onto the clock.

"When it was 1.1 seconds left, and they said they were going to add more time, I said, 'Not again, no, no, no, not again,'" Graves recalled. "Remember what happened last time they put more time on the clock?"

That was in Game Seven against the Devils, when the Devils tied the game with 7.7 seconds remaining in regulation. This time, MacTavish won the faceoff back to the defensive corner, Messier knocked down Bure, Larmer sealed off his man, and Doug Lidster made sure he had his man. The buzzer sounded. Messier leapt for joy.

June 14, 1994: The date would live with the Rangers and Messier for the rest of their lives. On that night, with one mighty hoist of the shiny Stanley Cup, and a thrust toward the Garden's shaking ceiling, Messier cleared out the ghosts. With one triumphant yelp, the gleeful Rangers' captain freed the world's most frustrated and ridiculed fans from fifty-four years worth of disasters and hexes.

"It's the biggest challenge in sports," Messier said. "It's one thing to win the Cup. After fifty-four years, all you heard was about the ghosts and dragons and everything else. But I said to Mike Keenan, 'You can't be afraid to slay the dragons.'"

"We started out as underdogs but contenders, then turned to favorites," Keenan said. "To be favorites in New York City, people don't realize how difficult that is. It takes every ounce of energy you have, all your physical energy, your psychological energy, everything you can think of has to be put into it in order to accomplish this."

Unlike their predecessors, these Rangers never let the seemingly inevitable happen. Richter made every key save in all the biggest games during the playoffs, including one on Bure with 13.2 seconds left in Game Seven. Leetch had another big game, despite enduring more physical punishment from the Canucks. Messier had been absolutely correct when he said Game Seven would not be for the faint of heart.

"Nineteen-forty!" the fans chanted in mockery when the game ended. That taunt, like the curse, was dead, and immediately replaced by a chant of "Nineteen-ninety-four!" Fans cried. A massive party broke out. The Rangers had won the Stanley Cup. "Now I Can Die in Peace," read one banner.

"We got a lot of bounces along the way," Graves said, "but we also had a lot of hard work and a lot of bumps and bruises. In the end, it was all worth it. We didn't do anything the easy way all year, and it wasn't any different, I'll tell you that. Game Seven wasn't the ideal thing, either."

Messier's smile filled his face. A baseball-style hat that proclaimed the Rangers as Stanley Cup champions covered his bald head. For a moment, he looked like the kid in Edmonton who had lifted the Cup for the first time in 1984.

NHL commissioner Gary Bettman walked onto the ice, congratulated both teams, and introduced Leetch as the winner of the Conn Smythe Trophy. He was the first American-born playoff MVP. Then two men wearing white gloves carried the brilliant, glowing Cup to center ice.

"Ladies and gentlemen," the P.A. announcer intoned, "the Stanley Cup!"

When Bettman said, "New York, your long wait is over," the fans roared. The Garden shook. Throughout the building, fans cried.

"Captain Mark Messier," Bettman announced, "come get the Stanley Cup."

Messier waved to the fans. He shook Bettman's hand. He looked at the Cup and began trembling. And laughing. He bobbed his head up and down as he grabbed the trophy. He opened his mouth as wide as he possibly could and let out a deep, hearty laugh, a joyous laugh. His face seemed to disappear behind his smile. His eyes were dark slits underneath the black, white, and orange cap. He excitedly shook the Stanley Cup, even while Bettman held it for photographers. He let out a loud, "Yeaaah!" Then he grabbed the trophy. The Garden wanted him to lift it high above his head. This was the moment they had waited for.

Messier called over his teammates, then, with many of them crying for joy, he lifted the Cup straight over his head. The fans roared louder.

This was the moment Neil Smith had dreamed about when he first pictured Messier in the Rangers uniform: No. 11 on the back and sleeves, the big "C" over his heart, and the Cup in his hands.

Messier didn't have a great final series, partly because of his aching body. But make no mistake: He had been as important to the Rangers as he had ever been to any team.

Messier brought the Cup over to Lowe, the man he referred to as his alter ego. This was a tradition for the two teammates. He and Lowe had lifted the Cup six times in the past eleven seasons. Then he made sure everybody got to lift the Cup, every player, even those who didn't play, every coach, Smith, every member of the support staff, and then Garden president Bob Gutkowski, and Rudy Giuliani, the mayor of New York.

"I feel privileged to be part of this with Mark Messier," Keenan said. "He is the greatest leader in pro sport today."

"I wanted to win it so bad for so many people," Lowe said, "but first and foremost for Mark Messier because he wanted to win it so badly."

The Cup was passed to Leetch, who had carried the team on a bad shoulder for so many games. The Cup felt light by comparison. Then it went to Jay Wells, a first-time lifter at age thirty-five. Wells planted a big kiss on the Cup. The scene summed up his joy: the grizzled, rugged Wells, in absolute rhapsody, his toothless face defining the moment.

"I honestly didn't know what to do with it," Wells said. "Fifteen years and I've never even looked at it. I'd seen pictures, but I never saw it up close. When I got it in my hands, I didn't know what to do but scream."

He was nearly in tears. This is what the Cup meant to people, so Messier made certain everybody got to enjoy the moment.

"I didn't know whether to laugh or cry," Greg Gilbert said. "I was watching the older guys, like Steve Larmer and Jay Wells, guys who had played a lot of years and never had the chance. I was so happy for them."

Messier delivered the Cup to Keenan.

"We did it!" Messier told Keenan, who hoisted the Cup for the first time in his career.

Finally, the Cup was passed to Smith, the man who had brought Messier to New York and engineered this very moment. Without Messier, and therefore without Smith, the Rangers wouldn't have won the Cup.

"You're sort of in a trance when you get it," Smith said. "I could have just cried. I wanted this, we collectively wanted this, so badly. I wanted it for so long, from the day I got here. I can't believe it. I don't know what happens now. This is all I'm living for. Of course, a month from now I'm going to try to do it again. But for now, who cares?"

Finally, the Cup was returned to Messier, who skated to the corner glass and looked up to where his family was standing.

"I don't fuckin' believe it," Messier repeated over and over.

Messier skated the Cup around the rink and let dozens of fans fulfill their dreams by reaching out and touching the Cup. On his way off the ice, in the runway between the benches, Messier paused again, allowing more fans to touch the Cup. They slapped it and tried to kiss it. Most of them had tears in their eyes.

Keenan was soaked with champagne and emotionally drained after the game. Back in the players' lounge, Messier told Keenan, recalling the coach's emotional speech, "That was the best fuckin' speech I ever heard."

"We just had to restore that belief and confidence they had in each other," Keenan later explained. "Because of the work of Vancouver, that was eroded a little bit."

The players credited Keenan's speech as the impetus for their victory in Game Seven. The part about winning and walking together for the rest of their lives truly hit home.

"To know you've secured something, slayed the demons and the dragons, to be able to do it together, we will walk together forever as a group of players," Messier said.

Messier compared Keenan's emotional talk to the one made by college basketball coach Jim Valvano in which Valvano said: "Don't give up. Don't ever give up." Valvano, who was terminally ill, was less than a year away from dying.

"And it's so true," he said. "There's not a guy that I've been together with for one of those Cups that I couldn't go out for a drink with, or to dinner with, or do something, maybe just to talk with. You need special players to win, but you also need special people."

Keenan had the speech ready to go. It was similar to the one used by coach Fred Shero with the champion Philadelphia Flyers of the mid-1970s. Keenan had almost used it on his Flyers before Game Seven against Messier's Oilers in 1987.

"I've only had two chances to tell that story, to make that speech," Keenan said. "One was in 1987. I didn't make it then. I learned from that. I didn't know enough. I didn't have the experience. It was just instinctive this time. I was staring out my office window at the water, collecting my thoughts, and I didn't think it was anything striking. But it was what I felt needed to be said."

Keenan's reputation had been eroded, too. Once again, he denied he was leaving.

"I'll be back, if they'll have me back," he insisted.

That remained to be seen. For now, he was coach of the Stanley Cup champions.

"It's a feeling of pride and accomplishment," Keenan said. "There's a calm feeling, a sense of pride that comes from working with people like Mark Messier, and these guys, with players who are committed from Day One. The day prior to our departure to London, we set our goal to win the Stanley Cup. It's a tremendous sense of pride and accomplishment to deal with the aspects of New York City that make it difficult to win a Cup. People don't know how difficult it is to win a Cup anywhere. To win it in New York took every bit of energy we had."

Before the night ended, Messier shook about five thousand hands, hugged about two thousand people, drank champagne out of the Stanley Cup, and said something special about everyone who had anything to do with the Rangers' victory. Then he made one more guarantee after coming through on the biggest promise of his career.

"We're going to celebrate this like we've never celebrated anything in our entire lives," he said.

And he was true to his word.

■ ■ ■

During the post-game celebration, a TV reporter asked Neil Smith if the flurry of trades at the deadline had won the Cup for the Rangers.

"No," Smith said. "The trade that won the Cup was the one that brought Mark Messier here."

12

Late Night with Stanley

The stretch limousine pulled up on East 89th Street at about four a.m. In the front seat was a chauffeur—and the Stanley Cup.

Messier and his family were in the back. Messier climbed out of the limo and a crowd of a few thousand people cheered him wildly. The captain of the Stanley Cup champions grabbed the Cup and handed it to a bouncer, who carried it into The Auction House, the upper East Side bar where the Rangers were having a party.

For a square city block, police cars and barricades kept the street party under control. A bagpipe band played. Chants of "Let's Go Rangers" and "We got the Cup" lasted until daylight.

The entire block was closed to traffic because people had crowded the intersection from one curb to the next. While the Rangers' family partied inside, the people who couldn't get in partied outside as New York showed the world how to celebrate a championship.

There were no riots. New York didn't want to fight, loot, start fires, or overturn cars. The city had waited too long for this moment. Thousands of fans stayed outside The Auction House and sang, danced, and chanted all night. Esa Tikkanen, the wild-eyed five-time champion, emerged from the bar a couple of times with the Cup and handed it to the crowd. The big, beautiful trophy was passed from one raised arm to another. Delirious people kissed the Cup, drank from it, raised it, and took pictures of it. Then the Cup was returned to Tikkanen, who was watching from the top of the stairway.

Inside The Auction House, Madison Square Garden office employees, former players such as Hall of Famer Rod Gilbert, and the players'

131

families and friends, took turns drinking champagne and beer from the big bowl. When the Cup was empty, they'd bring it to the bar, have it refilled, and pass it around again. Finally, the Cup was passed to the back room, where the players' families and friends had gathered.

Lord Stanley's Cup stayed at the Auction House past six a.m., went to Messier's place for another celebration, then went back to the Garden for pictures. The Cup was placed at center ice and hundreds of Garden employees, from security guards to kitchen help, lined up in single file for the chance to have their photo taken with the Cup.

That night, the Cup was on display at a dinner in the Rangers' honor. The next morning, it was at a TV talk show, and that night it was the guest of honor at a reception at Gracie Mansion, the home of Mayor Rudy Giuliani. The next day, it was at a function for the Rangers' owners, Viacom/Paramount. It joined Messier and Co. for a host of parties. New York Yankees' owner George Steinbrenner invited the Rangers and the Cup to Yankee Stadium for a game. The Rangers, along with the Cup, would be the guests of honor at the White House.

"That's what's so great about that trophy," Messier said. "Everybody gets to have it, to get to see how it feels. It creates a real fan friendly atmosphere. It's something the fans can feel a part of."

Even the fans in not-always-friendly New York City.

"You'd better fasten your seatbelts when you go out with this baby," Messier said. "It's been in cabs, and a couple of the cab drivers have been scared to death to have that thing in the front seat."

The Cup does different things to different people. Glenn Anderson had been on every one of Messier's championship teams, but on the night the Rangers won, nobody carried the Cup longer or with more emotion that Anderson.

"I treated it like it was my last one," Anderson said. "I treated the whole playoffs like they were my last."

Anderson had a quiet playoff until he scored the game-winning goals in Games Two and Three of the finals. At age 33, Anderson's NHL days were winding down.

"Right now there aren't any goals," he said, "so there's no sense in me playing until I set some goals for myself. I accomplished all I wanted to do, to win a Stanley Cup with a team other than Edmonton. Now that I've done that, I don't see any light at the end of the tunnel. Been there. Done that. Got the T-shirt."

Anderson considered playing in Tokyo or Europe the following season. Or, he said, he may not play at all. He owned a marina three hours outside of his native Vancouver.

"Or I'll find a job, maybe on a beach somewhere, selling watermelons," he said.

Anderson didn't sell watermelons in 1994-95. He played in Germany, Finland, and for the Canadian National Team, before returning to the NHL with the St. Louis Blues.

■ ■ ■

Now that they had won one Cup, the Rangers figured, why couldn't they win more?

"Now the Rangers' five nucleus guys have done it," Lowe said. "It was a little disappointing to hear everyone say, 'You've got to win it now because you're getting too old.' But now that those guys have done it, they'll carry the torch."

Lowe was talking about the younger players, such as Graves, Leetch, Richter, Zubov, and Kovalev. Although nobody was painting the Rangers as a dynasty-in-the-making, Messier didn't know why they couldn't keep on winning.

"I was a little frustrated throughout the playoffs because I read some stories that we had to win it this year or we'd never be able win it next year," Messier said. "But I see a core group of players and it looks like we have a superstar at every position. We're going to hold onto this. And once you get a taste of it, you don't want to let it go, believe me."

■ ■ ■

On June 15, the day after the Rangers won, the Cup made two important stops: One was at the Ed Sullivan Theater for *The Late Show with David Letterman,* the other was at half-time of Game Four of the NBA finals between the Knicks and the Houston Rockets. When Messier carried the Cup onto the court at half-time, the Garden fans cheered almost as loudly as they had the night before.

The Letterman show was memorable, too. At first, the entire team was going to be on the show. Then Messier found out that the skit involving the team might not be entirely complementary. He was concerned that the show would make a mockery of the team or the sport. Until four o'clock that afternoon, Letterman wasn't sure if Rangers were coming. Messier finally agreed to show up with Leetch, Richter, and the Cup, as long as the team, the sport, and the Cup weren't mocked. They weren't.

Before the taping, Letterman had Leetch parade around the crowd with the Stanley Cup. People reached and stretched across one another into the aisles to touch the trophy. They patted Leetch on the shoulders. Before bringing out Messier, Richter, and Leetch for the show, Letterman walked over to a wall unit offstage and said that unusual things are sometimes discovered in the cabinet.

"Let's see what we have there tonight," Letterman said.

The camera panned down to the bottom shelf. Letterman reacted as if something had caught his eye. There was shiny Stanley. The Ed Sullivan Theater sounded like Madison Square Garden after the Rangers won the Cup.

Leetch was excited about being on the show. He had watched Letterman all through high school and college. But after performing so heroically in the playoffs, he choked when Letterman asked him questions. He realized, "I'm on Letterman." Messier, the smooth veteran, bailed out his buddy and answered all of Letterman's questions. Some of the show's production people said it was one of the greatest moments they had ever had.

Messier, Leetch, and Kypreos wore Yankees pinstripes and brought the Cup to the mound at Yankee Stadium, where they threw out the first pitch. Unfortunately for Leetch, rain prevented him from carrying out his fantasy of taking batting practice at Yankee Stadium. So, the players went under the stands to the indoor batting cages.

Steve Howe, one of the Yankees' pitchers, threw to Messier in the bullpen. Messier did pretty well, according to Leetch, although he hadn't caught more than a softball once or twice in fifteen years. Howe loaded up and threw pitches in the high eighties.

"Try to catch this," Howe challenge Messier.

Messier caught every one, even the sliders, which he scooped out of the dirt.

"I don't think he was real happy about that," Leetch said. "I don't think he had a cup on, either."

■ ■ ■

New York's Canyon of Heroes is a row of skyscrapers on both sides of Broadway in downtown Manhattan. It's called a canyon because the tall buildings on both sides block out the sun. Sometimes it's dark in the middle of the afternoon.

The Canyon of Heroes is where America's finest have been honored, from Charles Lindbergh to war heroes, from astronauts to the Iran hostages. And, of course, New York's championship teams. Years ago, people watching the parade from the windows overhead tossed ticker-tape. Now they throw computer printouts, confetti, and toilet paper.

The parade route is always the same, commencing at Battery Park and moving ever-so-slowly through a sea of humanity and a sky filled with floating paper up to City Hall for another reception and a ceremony. The Canyon of Heroes had never been noisier than it was the day the Stanley Cup arrived on one of several floats carrying every member of the Rangers' organization.

Some 1.5 million New Yorkers poured out their hearts to the Rangers. By six a.m., people wearing Rangers jerseys were already lining the parade route. At eight a.m. the first "Let's go Rangers" chant was heard in Battery Park. Around eleven a.m., the Rangers' bus, surrounded by fans, left the Garden. At 11:30, Messier placed the Cup on a float and the noise started. The crowd didn't quiet down until long after a ceremony in which mayor Giuliani gave every team member a key to the city.

"Unbelievable," Messier said of the noise. "It didn't stop. And it kept getting louder. New York fans outdid themselves today."

"You can't even imagine how overwhelmed you are when you're in a setting like that," Keenan said. "A parade of that magnitude we probably didn't really expect, and we probably won't totally deal with what we just went through for some time."

The roar made Madison Square Garden's game night din sound like a squeak. The players were breathless . . . and they loved it.

"I could never imagine anything like that," said Russian Sergei Nemchinov.

"Let's keep going around," said Eddie Olczyk.

Richter took a deep breath, looked around, and tapped Messier on the shoulder. Richter, wide-eyed, told Messier, "I hope we get a flat tire so we can stay right here."

Fans wearing blue and white Rangers jerseys and T-shirts climbed walls to get a closer look at their heroes. They stood as deep as the eye could see. They chanted, "We got the Cup! We got the Cup!" Every time a player lifted the Cup, the volume rose another few notches.

The fans held up posters. One said: "My grandfather thanks you, my father thanks you and I thank you." Another read: "Free at last." Still another: "Dreams do come true." Some of the posters simply said, "Thank you." "Now I can die in peace" made a return appearance. Many of the posters read, "Messiah." Another read, "Mess is God."

Former New York mayors Abe Beame, Ed Koch, and David Dinkins attended the ceremony. Mayor Giuliani said: "This team has taken on an entire city, and taken its heart."

When Keenan stepped up to the microphone, the fans chanted "Don't leave Mike! Don't leave Mike!" followed by "Four more years! Four more years!"

Olczyk got his key to the city, grabbed the microphone, and made the only unscheduled speech of the day. He led the crowd in a chant of "Heave ho! Heave ho! Heave ho!" just as he had with his teammates in practices during the season. Then he added, "Heave ho, two in a row!"

"Like Eddie said," Messier told the crowd, "we're having so much fun here this year, we might as well come back next year."

Messier's speech was barely audible. His voice was gone from the week of celebrations. He wore sunglasses, had a rose sticking out from the neck of his white Rangers jersey, and donned a Stanley Cup champions baseball hat. Even though Keenan had shown the Rangers video clips of past ticker-tape parades, they had had no idea their parade would be so huge.

"Every day there has been a set of events that drive home how enormous this is," Richter said. "You get so caught up in the games, I didn't really think about parades. Brian Leetch and I were talking about it, but it didn't really hit us until we were on the bus on the way over here. The fans always cheer us in the arena, but to bring them outdoors, en masse like that, it was unbelievable. We were saying thanks to them as much as they were saying thanks to us."

It was an incredible ending to an incredible season.

■ ■ ■

Years later, Colin Campbell discussed what Messier had meant to the Rangers.

"When you preach the discipline and the gameplan for a team you're going to play four to seven times in a period of eight to fourteen days, you have to have total acceptance by the team," Campbell said.

"Everyone has to buy into the program, and when you're selling the program you have to make sure it's bought in the dressing room. Having Mark helps sell it.

"The product is winning, and what Mark loves about this game is enjoying the win, celebrating the win. I really didn't understand that until I saw him celebrate the year we won the Cup here. You don't just get the Cup, carry it around, and that's it for the summer. You enjoy it. You celebrate it. When he raises the Cup and laughs and smiles, he really means it. There's a message to every kid that loves this game that you can read when Mark lifts the Cup. The message is why the game is played. It's not the six million dollar salary. It's not the products he endorses. The product he endorses to us all is it takes all of us to win, and when you win it's worth it."

Lowe agreed. "During the season, you're committed on and off the ice, but you have your life to live, too," he said. "But come playoff time, it's hockey and nothing else. No marketing, even family stuff. It's wake up, go to the rink, play, go home, lay around, get up and go to the rink."

Said Messier: "Having won before, that is what makes it, having the experience of winning before and how great it is to pull it all together and win a championship. Everything else derives off that. It's just a branch off the ultimate goal of winning. It's not so much a personal challenge or this or that, it's trying to bring it all together, all twenty-five guys and winning. That's what it's all about. Having experienced winning before makes you want to win it all that much more again, to experience those highs again. And after all, that's why we're here in the end. That's basically why we're playing."

Even though he had won the Cup five times before, Messier wanted this victory more than the others. The pressure of winning weighed on him from the day he arrived in New York until the night he won the Cup. MacTavish had seen this when he came to the Rangers.

"At the time, I remember saying to Mark, 'It's a high risk, high reward, the whole situation,' because if we didn't win there was going be a lot of scrutiny and criticism," MacTavish said. "And when we did win, it was just unbelievable, the parade, the adulation that came with it. It was wild. There was a lot of pressure on him. He put a lot of pressure on himself to win. He was under a lot of pressure the whole playoffs. I really noticed it more then than I'd ever had in any of the previous Stanley Cups that I've been with him, that he really felt the burden of having to do it, of bringing the Stanley Cup to New York. I had the impression he was as relieved as he was happy, he'd put so much pressure on himself. It was a testament to him, that Stanley Cup.

"It's all part and parcel of the expectations that go with Mark. Wherever he goes, he's expected to bring a championship. It's almost a prophecy when he gets there. He felt that burden to bring it here. He'd spoken about it, and he imagined himself winning it. He was totally focused on hockey, where before, in the other Stanley Cups where I'd been around, he was able to get away from the game and get out and golf and relax a little bit, get away from it physically and mentally. But this time he was totally consumed by it. He lived and breathed hockey totally, one hundred percent."

That's why Messier let loose when the playoffs were over. As Campbell said, Messier knows how to enjoy success.

"Enjoying it, living it, and talking about it," Messier said. "That's any game, even a regular-season win. If you go out and play sixty minutes in game fifty-four and you can't come in the dressing room and feel good about yourself, why are you playing? You should be happy when you win and you should be disappointed when you lose, and it's okay to celebrate. But then to win the Stanley Cup, if you can't experience that and enjoy everything it has to offer, I think it would be defeating the purpose of all the blood, sweat, and tears that go into it."

Later on, Messier would rank this Cup victory among his best ever.

"It was a lot like the first Cup I had won because so many people on the team were part of the Stanley Cup team for the first time," he said. "That innocence of winning, the drama, all the things that go along with it. Playing here the years I did, you kind of get to appreciate the history of the organization and the alumni that follow the team are here a lot so you kind of really become a Ranger in more ways than one. So when we finally did go on to win, all of that stuff came to the surface, and it really felt like a first time. That's why there was such an incredible celebration."

■ ■ ■

While Rangers fans chanted, "Four more years!" to Keenan, Neil Smith stood a few feet away and tried to smile. Smith and Keenan had embraced briefly and privately after Game Seven, and they sat together at the post-parade ceremony at City Hall. They didn't say much to each other. When asked by reporters about his relationship with the general manager, Keenan called it "professional." Smith's silence was deafening. From June 7, when the Keenan-to-Detroit rumors surfaced, he had never said, "Mike Keenan is going nowhere." He did nothing to squelch the rumors.

Hockey insiders everywhere insisted there had been contact between the Red Wings and Keenan during the finals. Indeed, massive evidence had mounted that Keenan and the Wings had spoken.

Messier stayed out of the affair. He had nothing to say, mostly because he was aware of the power he wielded not only in the organization, but with the entire city. Whatever Messier might have said would have the full, unconditional support of the fans. Messier was the man. And he wanted Keenan to stay.

Messier and Keenan had made a wonderful couple. Keenan gave Messier all the power and respect he deserved and needed to be a strong captain. Messier privately kept Keenan in line when necessary, and publicly treated him with the respect and power Keenan needed to be an effective coach.

"In a strange way, they almost think alike," said Steve Larmer, who had been coached by Keenan in Chicago and New York. "They're both highly motivated, very dedicated, almost win-at-any-price guys. I think Mark had a calming effect on Mike, and Mike had a lot of respect for Mark. Mike learned a lot from Mark, and vice versa. Yeah, there's always a lot of controversy, but there's controversy everywhere, not just around Mike. As a player, you can't worry about all the bullshit that goes on behind the scenes. You can't control that. You just worry about doing your job. Just go out and win. You can't change the stuff you can't control."

MacTavish credited Messier with helping to alleviate potential problems when the Keenan-to-Detroit rumors circulated during the finals.

"Mark really had a way of capsulizing everything that Mike said," MacTavish said. "In a way, more was made of the whole Keenan thing externally than it was internally. Everybody perceived, externally, all this irrevocable damage that was being done to the core of the team, and I think Mark puts those things in perspective very well, and he did that very well for the team at that point. It's not about the coach totally. It's about the team and the organization. And so much was being made of the distractions that Mike was creating.

"Mark really put those things behind us very quickly. You know, it was a very experienced team as well. Then the Detroit thing came up, and they made another big deal about Mike: Was he going to be here next year? Well, nobody really cared. At that point, nobody cared who'd be there next year. It's a very fleeting role we all play on different teams. Who knows who's going to be here next year? Mark was like, 'We're not going to be worried about what's going to happen next year. Let's just get through this.' He really put those things in perspective very quickly, in a way we all understood.

"Mike took a lot of criticism, but he brought the Stanley Cup. Any coach who does that is doing something right, and he obviously was. Mark and Mike worked very well together because Mike would come in and he'd do more damage than he thought he was doing. He'd be a little more vindictive, or berate the team a little more than he himself would have thought. That's my impression of Mike. But Mark would quickly put those things in perspective and if there was any damage control that needed to be done, he did it very quickly. They worked very well together in that respect.

"And he didn't have to address it often. I don't want to make it like Mike was a raving lunatic every day. That wasn't the case. By and large, Mike is the type of coach, when you're winning he's a great guy to play for. He treats his players very well. When you're losing, maybe he does overreact at times and can become a little irrational. But Mark put those things in perspective quickly. There aren't a lot of coaches who do everything perfectly. There aren't any. There's no perfect coach and there's no perfect player out there. Everybody has their skeletons, and everybody has their weaknesses, but when you put it all together, we won the Stanley Cup."

■ ■ ■

The Rangers' party continued through the summer. The Cup traveled 61,400 miles with members of the Rangers. Parties were held for the Cup wherever it went, through New York City and across Canada. Olczyk, a horse racing fanatic, took the Cup to Belmont Park, where a horse stuck his snout in the Cup. When the photograph appeared in newspapers, Olczyk insisted the horse was only looking inside the Cup, not eating out of it. Messier spent a lot of time with the Cup and let others spend time with it, too.

"He didn't have it that long," Richter said. "He only had it that first day, then he made sure everybody got it in a hurry."

The old Cup took a beating. It needed repairs several times and appeared to be dented when it was placed on display at the NHL Draft.

This Cup abuse resulted in stricter NHL rules regarding how the championship team was allowed to treat the trophy, but it also emphasized how much fun the Rangers and New York were having with their new toy. Everybody wanted a piece of Stanley, and almost everybody got a piece.

Stephane Matteau returned to his tiny hometown of Rouyn-Noranda, Quebec, during the summer and found himself in the middle of a Stanley Cup parade.

"The whole town was in the parade," Matteau said.

Graves said: "I remember taking it back to my house, and my dad spent about forty-five minutes polishing it up, taking care of it. Nothing can compare to it. I mean it was unbelievable to win my first Cup in Edmonton. I just remember the last ten seconds, thinking 'I can't believe this is going to come true. I can't believe I'm here.' In '94, it was just absolutely pride, that fifty-four years. It was just like, 'Yeah!' The parade and the way the city celebrated, it was just incredible. Whether I stay here for a long time, and regardless of what happens in the future, it'll always have a special place. This will be the place I remember. These memories last a lifetime. And that goes for everything, from having the pleasure of playing with Mark and Brian and Ricky [Richter] to winning the Cup. These are opportunities to kill for."

Said Campbell: "Adam Graves used to tell me what it was like once you've won it, how you never want to let it go. I know when Mike Hudson dropped it off at my house in Ontario, he handed the Cup off to me and said, 'The Cup does some strange things to you.' He's right. As an individual, as a player or a coach, you have to win it again."

■ ■ ■

The summer-long party was only half-over when, on July 15, Keenan left the celebration. Keenan terminated his employment with the Rangers, claiming they had breached his contract by being a day late on a $620,000 bonus for winning the Cup. This was the first blow in what would be an ugly public battle between Keenan and the Rangers.

Garden president Bob Gutkowski said he had learned of Keenan's intentions only twenty minutes before the announcement was made in a Toronto TV studio. He called Rob Campbell's car phone, only to have Campbell hang up on him.

"Mr. Campbell disconnected the call when he learned it was Mr. Gutkowski," read a statement issued by the Garden. "Madison Square

Garden is stunned at the capricious actions of Mr. Keenan and his agent Mr. Campbell and will take all necessary actions to preserve all of its rights."

There would be lawsuits and countersuits. The mailbox at Keenan's house in Greenwich, Connecticut, which was already for sale, was blown up.

"I am going to seek opportunities and hopefully I'll have opportunities to seek in the next little while," Keenan declared. "I hope there will be opportunities in the NHL. I guess for all intents and purposes, I'm a free agent."

He wasn't a free agent for long. Keenan quickly found a job, not with the Detroit Red Wings, but as general manager and coach of the St. Louis Blues.

The contemptuous battle between Keenan and Smith lasted several weeks. Keenan claimed Smith had purposely been late on the payment so as to force his hand. Smith claimed Keenan was merely looking for a way out; if Keenan hadn't found that loophole, Smith said, he would have found another. Insiders claimed Smith and Keenan had conspired to create the situation: Keenan wanted out, Smith wanted Keenan out, the thinking went. Keenan and Smith had merely aided each other's cause.

NHL Commissioner Gary Bettman stepped in to resolve the situation. The 1994 Stanley Cup champion Rangers were a team without a coach, and beset by the kinds of controversies and problems that had plagued them for fifty-four years.

13

Locked Out

There was still some celebrating to do, but it would have to wait through the tumultuous summer, a labor lockout that lasted 103 days, and a messy renegotiation of Messier's contract. The players' names would be engraved on the Stanley Cup, their championship rings would be presented, the Stanley Cup banner would be raised at Madison Square Garden, and the team would visit the White House. But all that would happen later . . . much later.

Colin Campbell, the Rangers' assistant coach since 1990-91, was named to replace Mike Keenan as head coach five weeks before training camp opened. Campbell knew he was inheriting problems: A possible Stanley Cup hangover and the Messier situation. Campbell was smart enough to know that his relationship with Messier would be the key to his success or failure. He had been through the Messier-Roger Neilson fiasco in 1992-93, and through the Keenan-Messier marriage that worked in 1993-94.

"Mark is a strong-willed individual and he has to have done something right to have won six Stanley Cups, and to be the only player to captain two different Stanley Cup teams," Campbell said. "I have no problem with Mark. He's a great leader and he can obviously be a help to any coach. Mark's at the point in his career where he has to have an impact with the coaching staff and the management of the organization. Some teams have success using the trap. But you can't ask an Adam Graves or a Mark Messier to hang around in the neutral zone and wait for the other team to come at them."

Despite his positive feelings about Keenan, Messier had nothing but praise for the new coach.

"We all learned a lot last year as players and as coaches," Messier said. "The experience of going all the way and winning is a huge advantage. And I think that as an apprentice, as an assistant coach, topping it off with a Stanley Cup will make the transition a little easier. Soupy [Campbell] developed a good rapport with the players here over the years, and he's paid his dues, I think he's ready, and he deserves this. I'm really happy for him. This is the situation you want, to have somebody in-house come in. From that standpoint, it's great. I wouldn't foresee him changing a lot from last year, and I say that because of the type of team we have. You don't take a ballerina and turn him into a blacksmith."

Campbell, 41, had spent eleven seasons as a tough defenseman for Pittsburgh, Colorado, Edmonton, Vancouver, and Detroit. For one year, he was a teammate of Messier and Lowe in Edmonton. His nose has been broken many times, and if you needed to be reminded that his listed height of 5'9" might be an exaggeration, Neil Smith would gladly provide a "short" joke.

"He was always the fiercest of competitors," said Smith, who worked with Campbell in the Detroit organization. "The only way he got where he was going was through sheer determination. He didn't get there by being five-foot-nine. He got there by having a big heart. He is, in reality, the toughest guy I know. That's how he lived his hockey career."

Training camp opened ominously and with a labor dispute looming in the short distance. Riding the coattails of the Rangers' championship, the NHL was poised for a breakthrough season in 1994-95. The NHL had the opportunity to attract the young people who were supposedly turning away from baseball, basketball, and other pro sports and turning to hockey. National TV, magazines, and advertisers had finally started paying attention to hockey, which was selling itself aggressively and properly. Yet, the owners and players couldn't agree on a new collective bargaining agreement, and the owners had already threatened to lockout the players.

The owners wanted a plan for revenue sharing. The players wanted to retain the free-market system that had resulted in such a windfall for them. The clock was ticking down to the deadline.

On a nice September day, the Rangers underwent physical exams, then boarded a bus that would take them to training camp in Glens Falls, New York. Messier was absent, away without leave. A clause in his contract allowed him to request a renegotiation of his contract if the Rangers won the Cup. He couldn't demand it. He could only request it. Messier had made the request.

Nobody knew how long Messier's holdout would last, but everybody knew how disastrous it would be if the Rangers raised their Stanley Cup banner without the man who delivered the victory. In dispute was Messier's salary, which was scheduled to be $2.682 million for the 1994-95 season and $2.75 million for the 1995-96 season. Smith and Garden president Bob Gutkowski made offers in negotiations with Doug Messier, including an extra $1 million for each of the next two years, elevating Messier's salary to around $3 million a year, and a one-year contract extension worth $4 million. Messier would be thirty-six years old when the 1996-97 season ended.

Messier, though, wanted a contract similar to the ones that had been signed by Lemieux and Gretzky, who had combined for as many Cups as Messier had won. He wanted a three-year deal worth $6 million per year.

The gap was significant. The negotiations were one-sided. They sounded like this:

Rangers' offer: "$3 million per year."

Messier's: "$6 million per."

Rangers': "$4 million per."

Messier's: "$6 million per."

Rangers': "$4.5 million per."

Messier's: "$6 million per."

And so on, and so on, and so on.

■ ■ ■

Missing training camp was no big deal to Messier. He hated the pre-season. The negotiations provided him with an excuse to stay away. He had missed a few other training camps over the past fifteen years because of contract holdouts, injuries, and participation in the Canada Cup. During a televised interview, Gretzky joked that Messier was holding out "to get out of training camp."

Messier had proved in 1991-92 that he didn't need training camp. He had held out from Edmonton, was dealt to the Rangers the day after the season opened, and went on to win the league's MVP award.

But there was an unavoidably darker side to Messier's holdout. He was unhappy about Keenan's departure. He had never commented on the Keenan debacle, partly because he was extremely annoyed that Keenan had been allowed to leave a month after the Rangers won the Cup.

Smith spent all of training camp saying things like, "It's not bothering me, to be honest, that he's not here because I know we're going to work it out. It's absolutely inconceivable to me that the Rangers and Mark won't agree on a new contract, and in relatively short order." But Messier, after making a presentation at the MTV Music Awards in New York, boarded a flight back home to Hilton Head, South Carolina.

On one hand, Messier was silly to argue that he deserved as much money as Gretzky. After all, Gretzky was widely recognized as the greatest player in hockey history. Messier's argument, however, was that while Gretzky and Messier had won four Stanley Cups together, Gretzky had never won one without him. Messier had won two without Gretzky, one in Edmonton and one in New York. Also, Messier said, he was holding out because he didn't hold out in 1991, when he reported to the Rangers without a contract and lost all of his bargaining leverage.

"When I came to the Rangers without any leverage, a few things were left out of the contract," Messier said. "What we wanted and what we ended up with were pretty different."

What Messier got in 1991 was a series of clauses that would kick in if he accomplished certain things in certain years. The Rangers' Stanley Cup victory earned him bonuses, but not the right to demand a renegotiation of his contract.

"The understanding was that if I played to my ability and the Rangers were successful, we both agreed I'd be taken care of with the top three players in the game, which is obviously Lemieux and Gretzky," Messier said. "What Wayne's done, and done for the game, is why he's where he is. I feel I fit in right behind him."

Gretzky's official salary for 1994-95 was $6.531 million. Lemieux's contract, which included complicated bonuses and about $30 million in deferred money and marketing rights, wasn't filed with the league because it was a personal services contract with the Pittsburgh ownership. Lemieux's contract was for six or seven playing years and a total of twenty years. His annual income fell somewhere between $6 and $8 million for his playing years. Messier's contract placed him fifteenth on the league's salary list.

Garden president Bob Gutkowski's direct involvement indicated the seriousness of the Messier negotiations.

"This is our most important issue, and Mark is our most important player," Smith confirmed. "Bob was very supportive of that and he is dealing with his superiors and getting direction from that level of management. We're working together in this. I think it is something that will get resolved very soon."

Messier emphatically denied that he wanted to be traded, saying New York was his last stop no matter how long his contract lasted. But he wanted the deal done quickly.

"Let's face it," he said. "I want to be in uniform when they raise the banner at the first home game."

Messier's picture was shown on the Garden scoreboard during the Rangers' first home exhibition game. The fans cheered loud enough to let Smith and the rest of the Garden higher-ups know how they felt about Messier's holdout. Fans almost always take the player's side when the player is a hero, and New York at that time had no bigger hero than Messier. He was as big as former heroes Willis Reed of the Knicks, Joe Namath of the football Jets, or Reggie Jackson of the Yankees, ever were. Maybe bigger.

But when the Garden was sold, Gutkowski was forced to resign and the Messier negotiations took a step backward.

"We were very, very close to completing something," Doug Messier said. "I guess where it goes from here and how it affects us depends on where we start from. I was told, and I don't know why, that it's like we're starting over."

Smith, who had handed off the negotiations to Gutkowski a week earlier, took over the talks. The question was whether the Garden's new owners would understand Messier's value to the team, or force Smith to play hardball with the Messiers. Smith insisted that no new salary ceiling had been imposed by either the current owners or the owners-to-be, Cablevision/ITT, and that the change in ownership "has not changed our negotiating power." He insisted that he had not considered trading Messier.

A few days later, and a week before the scheduled opener, Messier, his father, and his accountant arrived in New York for a ten-hour session with Smith and new Garden president Dave Checketts. During a break in the talks, Messier watched the Rangers-Islanders preseason game on TV. Inside the Garden, the fans chanted, "We want Messier."

The fans didn't get Messier. And they stopped getting hockey. On October 1, opening day of the regular season, with the negotiations over the new collective bargaining agreement at a stalemate, the owners locked out the players. All games were off.

Messier, who had union blood in his veins, had been very involved in the 1992 strike, even though he wasn't a player representative or a member of the union's negotiating team. During the current labor war, however, he had kept a low profile.

"I don't necessarily think it's a kids' fight, it's all the players' fight," Messier said. "I think it's going to affect the younger generation more, the kids who have ten years left in their careers, and the kids still in juniors. What we're going through now is going to have an effect on the future of the game. So for guys like myself, who have two or three years left, the only way it affects us is we're not playing. I'm itching to play. It's the first time in about thirty years I'm not playing hockey at this time of the year. You realize how much you miss the game. I only can hope to get back to it soon, so we can get on with the chance to defend the Cup."

Messier had skated only a few times since the Cup-winning game. He had been working out at his own gym, but mostly he had been flying back and forth between Hilton Head and Manhattan for promotional and charitable appearances.

The lockout dragged on and carried into January. On Day 100 of the lockout, during a conference call involving 125 players, Messier and Gretzky urged the players to reject the owners' latest proposal. The players did, by a 26-0 vote of team player representatives. The deadline for canceling the season was fast approaching.

"The last proposal we gave them was far and above what we wanted to give," Messier said from Hilton Head. "We felt we went a long way. We felt if they modified it a little bit, we could have gotten the season started. But to completely redo it with so little time left was a disappointment to everybody. The bridge between the two sides was a long way apart with the proposal they gave back to us, so I don't think there's any real middle ground."

Yet, almost miraculously, the lockout ended three days later. The players successfully resisted payroll-controlling devices such as salary caps and luxury taxes, but the owners appeared to have won every other aspect of the agreement. The NHL would play an abbreviated 48-game schedule, beginning in mid-January. The Rangers would finally get to raise their banner. The championship rings would finally come out of their boxes. The Rangers, for the first time since 1941, would be defending champions.

148

But now they had the Messier contract renegotiation to worry about.

"We were close at the time of the lockout and I expect the progress to continue," Smith said. "Mark's going to be out there opening night."

Messier agreed to attend the Rangers' mini-training camp that preceded the short season, but nobody knew if he'd play on opening night. There was speculation in newspapers that Messier had been issued an ultimatum to show up for training camp.

"I was planning on coming to camp," Messier insisted. "I'm not showing up because they're giving an ultimatum. I'm coming because I feel it's the best way to finish off the negotiations. Threats at this point in my career—I've played sixteen seasons—aren't going to make me make a decision one way or another. I expect it to be finished before the opening game. The Rangers have given me no reason to believe it's not going to be done, so I would have to say I would be there."

Messier arrived for a skate and a physical exam before scooting off to Manhattan for another appearance on *The Late Show with David Letterman*.

■ ■ ■

Messier's thirty-fourth birthday celebration was low-key but memorable and sentimental. On January 18, 1995, the Rangers received their Stanley Cup rings. Messier had been keeping his five Edmonton rings in a safe deposit box, but this one would go on his finger, at least for a while.

"I'll wear it for a while, then put it away," he said. "You don't want to get complacent."

Messier used the occasion to take a shot at Oilers owner Peter Pocklington, the man who had sold the members of one of the greatest teams in NHL history.

"We had to talk Mr. Pocklington into putting diamonds in the rings instead of zirconia," Messier cracked.

The next day, Messier summoned his teammates into a room at the Rangers' practice rink. Once the door slammed shut, the players talked quietly before breaking into a loud chant of "Benny! Benny! Benny!" Then Benny Petrizzi, an eighty-one-year-old man from Harrison, New York, who worked at the practice facility, was given his Stanley Cup ring. Petrizzi broke into tears. Messier cried, too.

"I don't think Mark was ready for Benny's reaction," Leetch said.

"I loved it," said Petrizzi, who considered the players his sons. "I didn't want to cry, but I've waited for this for seventeen years. I can't wait to get home and show my wife."

Petrizzi did the team's laundry, shined the players' shoes, and carried out other errands for the Rangers. Although all of the Rangers' support employees received their rings that day, none were prouder than Petrizzi, an Italian immigrant who had settled in Rye in 1926, and worked at Rye Playland, the Rangers' practice rink, before joining the Rangers in the early 1980s. Messier left the room with tears running down his cheeks.

Petrizzi quickly put away his ring. After all, there was laundry to be done, and he didn't want to lose his new jewelry in a washing machine.

■ ■ ■

An hour and a half before the Rangers' home opener and the raising of the Stanley Cup banner, the players and coaches were still unsure whether Messier would be in uniform. He hadn't signed a new contract. The Rangers insisted that Messier had a valid contract and had to play.

"It'll be a distraction if Mark's not signed," Leetch said sternly. "We shouldn't have this night if he's not there. I guess it's too late to put it off now, so they should just sign him so there is no problem."

Said Kevin Lowe: "You can't ever overstate his value to this hockey club. To me, if he only had 10 goals, or 20 assists, what he does for a hockey team, no other guy can do. And I don't know if you can put a price tag on that."

Most of the Rangers didn't know that the price tag had been settled upon the night before the opener. Doug Messier had talked throughout the day, via phone, with Checketts and Smith while his son's accountant juggled the numbers. Mark tried to sound optimistic. The sticking point in the deal had been the length of the contract. Messier would be thirty-six in its final season, and the Rangers wanted that to be an option year—their option.

"I would never compare myself to Gordie Howe, but I wonder how many times he's been through this: 'Gordie, you're going to be thirty-six. Gordie, you're going to be forty. Gordie, jeez, you're fifty-two years old,'" Messier said.

Messier wanted to be in uniform for the raising of the banner. He considered it important.

"It's a reminder of all the things that happened, all the hardships we endured to be champions," he said. "It's a reminder that this year we won't be able to accept less. The banner will go up for the rest of history, and we'll be part of it forever. But once that banner goes up, we've got to do it again. You've got to be prepared to go through the same things, unselfishness, commitment, and a willingness to compete at that level again.

"When you go through a championship season, a lot of things happen, not all good things. There are a lot of dark moments when the team has to rally around, but there are also great moments. There's nothing more beautiful in sports, when you can get all twenty-five guys thinking and playing the same way. When you think about all those things that happened, you realize that banner is only a couple hundred feet up there, it's about something won, but it's also a whole new list of challenges now up there."

Of course, there was a simpler reason to be excited about opening night.

"It's just time," Leetch said. "It's just a long time since we played."

Over seven months, in fact. The opener would be played on January 20, 1995.

■ ■ ■

The banner went up, and Messier played. While all of the other parties claimed work still had to be done, Messier declared, "A deal is imminent. The contract is about done, except for a handshake." In reality, Messier had never dreamed of missing the banner raising.

At 6:13 p.m., Messier walked down from the Madison Square Garden executive offices, through a corridor, and into the Rangers' locker room to get ready for the game. Out on the ice, he and his teammates watched an elaborate lasers, lights, fireworks, and smoke show during which the Cup was lowered from the scoreboard. A hand-picked group of long-time Rangers fans raised the banner.

There had been considerable doubt earlier in the day about whether Messier would be signed before the opener. After the morning skate, Messier had shrugged when asked about his contract status.

"It's a business decision," he said. "They have to make a decision they're comfortable with, one way or the other."

Messier decided to get involved in the negotiations. Late in the afternoon, he walked into the Garden and had to get directions from the locker room area to the executive offices.

Paul and Doug Messier said Mark was playing because he owed it to his teammates, and that he was going to play regardless of his contract status. Smith said he never doubted that Messier would play.

151

A loud ovation erupted from the Garden crowd when Messier skated onto the ice for the pregame warmups. The ovation got louder during the ceremony.

"I'm here for good, so those other issues can be put aside now," Messier said. "The banner's up. Now we can get on with the rest of the year and defending the Cup."

The Rangers lost their opener to Buffalo, 2-1. Campbell had waited from August 9, when he was named coach, to January 20 for his first game. Then he had to wait another night for his first win. Messier knew the defending champs couldn't afford a bad start, especially under a new coach, so he delivered a message to the team. He told them the second game of the season against Montreal was a must-win. Then he went out and scored his first goal of the season to break a 2-2 tie with 6:27 remaining in the third period. The Rangers went on to win, 5-2.

After the game, Messier presented the game puck to Campbell. "It was a long time coming," he told his new coach, "and it's the first of many."

■ ■ ■

Messier broke down and cried when his contract was officially completed, signed, and announced after the fourth game of the season.

"Are you happy?" Smith asked him.

"I'd be happier if we were 3-1," Messier replied. The Rangers were 1-3.

"That's what Mark is all about," Checketts said. "We search the world over in this business and it's hard to find people who are all about winning. Mark Messier is all about winning."

His new deal was worth about $6 million a year. The Rangers retained the option for the 1996-97 season, although it would have to be exercised halfway through the previous season. Otherwise, the Rangers would owe him a $1 million buyout.

At the contract announcement, Messier looked around a room crowded with reporters, Rangers' management, and members of his own family, and tried to talk about how much his New York experience had meant to him. But he choked up when he said, "It's been three amazing years." Several times he stopped talking as tears streamed down his face. Smith cut in and gave Messier a moment to compose himself.

"He's going to be a Ranger for life," Smith said before turning nostalgic. "It seems like yesterday we were in the Montreal Forum, when the Rangers made what maybe was the biggest trade in the history of the franchise."

Patrick Ewing, the Knicks center who was getting ready to warm up for the Knicks' game that night, walked in to congratulate Messier. Checketts introduced Ewing to Messier's father.

"Doug Messier; stay away from him," Checketts cracked.

Messier had gotten what he wanted: $6 million a year, and a place among the top three highest paid players in the league.

■ ■ ■

The next big event for the Rangers was a visit to the White House. The Rangers had a game with the Washington Capitals on March 5, so that afternoon they stopped in to see President Clinton in the Rose Garden. They were late.

The Rangers had flown in on the day of the game so the players could attend the funeral for Joe Murphy Jr., the son of the team trainer. At the wake, most of the Rangers took turns consoling the Murphy family in small groups. After Messier expressed his sympathy, he took a Rangers jersey and draped it neatly and discretely in a remote corner at the front of the room.

"It was just perfect," Leetch said.

Unfortunately, the Rangers had their 10:30 a.m. flight canceled because of fog. They finally got out on a 12:30 flight, so their one o'clock appointment at the White House had to be pushed back a few hours. Of course, the president didn't have much to do while waiting for the Rangers to show up—nothing besides meeting with Irish Prime Minister John Bruton and dealing with a few dozen issues, from Affirmative Action to Bosnia to House budget cuts to a new surgeon general.

"After waiting fifty-four years for the Stanley Cup, I'm not surprised LaGuardia was fogged in and we were an hour and a half late," said NHL commissioner Gary Bettman.

The Stanley Cup arrived on time. It had been placed on a morning flight from Toronto and would spend the night at the White House.

Smith presented the president with a small silver replica of the Cup with the engraving: "President Clinton, From one Madison Square Garden winner to another, The New York Rangers." The allusion was to the 1992 Democratic National Convention at Madison Square Garden, where Clinton had won the nomination for president. Messier presented Clinton with a Rangers jersey with No. 1 on the back and sleeves. The

President said he had watched the Rangers during the 1994 playoffs and particularly enjoyed Messier's guarantee of victory and performance in Game Six of the Eastern Conference finals.

Even at the White House, Messier ran the show.

"We were all trying to get settled for a picture with the president and Mark's directing traffic," Richter said. "He was going, 'Bill you come down here, Eddie you're over there, Secret Service down in front. Everybody was kind of bumbling around, including the president, and Mark's putting everybody in their spots, then he sits down. All of a sudden there was a sigh, kind of an appreciation that he had just rearranged the White House furniture. It was hilarious. But it was actually necessary, because everybody was bumping into each other, trying to be polite and not knowing where to go."

Nick Kypreos came up with the best line at the White House visit.

"I want to find this FICA guy," he said, "and find out where all my money's going."

■ ■ ■

Messier rarely avoided the press after games. Sometimes he steered the conversation in the direction he wanted or brought up a topic that took the reporters by surprise. He was an expert at dealing with the fawning media. Sometimes he was brutally honest. Sometimes he'd convincingly give an answer he knew wasn't true. He was very much at ease.

One night in Boston Garden's filthy visitors' locker room, a cockroach dove off the ceiling and onto the shirt collar of John Dellapina of the *Daily News*. The pest scurried around Dellapina's neck and shoulders, and Messier, in the middle of a lengthy answer, didn't miss a beat. He calmly reached over the pack of journalists and flicked the cockroach across the room.

Another Messier moment came late in the season at Nassau Coliseum in a game against the Islanders. With the Rangers trailing the Islanders after two periods and their playoff hopes hanging in the balance, Campbell walked to the locker room with the intention of charging up the team. He was too late. The door was closed. Messier had already taken over. The Rangers responded and rallied to win, 3-2.

"One guy spoke, and it was from the heart," Lowe said. "It was sort of the state of the union. It was kind of about where we had come, and where we were going. It was, we're out of excuses, and we just had to go out and win the hockey game if we want to continue on.

It was very controlled, very much from the heart, and very emotional, which is typical of him."

Messier, who was playing with a bad thumb, strained his back and had to miss the next-to-last game of the season in Philadelphia. The Rangers needed the game to clinch the final spot in the Eastern Conference. Eric Lindros, the Flyers' star, got hurt early in the game, and the Rangers won, 2-0.

The defending champions finished the season with a losing record, 22-23-3, but slipped into the eighth spot for the playoffs. They would play Quebec, the No. 1 seed, but they didn't know if Messier would be ready.

"In Mark's past, it's been muscle tears," Campbell said. "He's got a lot of scar tissue in there. He's lost a lot of battles to win the wars."

Leetch simply summed up the situation: "We aren't going to win a Stanley Cup without Mark Messier," he said.

■ ■ ■

Putting pressure on himself and his team and issuing the challenge to win another championship had become an annual event for Messier.

"Anything short of winning the Stanley Cup this year isn't going to be a successful year," he said. "Anything short of the Cup can't be considered a good year. You say that all the time, but it's especially true this year. Winning the Stanley Cup is like going to the moon. You have to come back to earth, then try to get back to the moon again."

The Rangers' opponents were the Quebec Nordiques, a young, fast team, which had finished first in the Eastern Conference, eighteen points ahead of the Rangers. The Rangers split the first two games at Le Colisée in Quebec City. They blew a late lead and lost Game One on Joe Sakic's goal. They won Game Two, in which Messier scored his 100th playoff goal. Messier didn't know he had reached a milestone, so a trainer had to retrieve the puck for him. Nor did he know that only he, Gretzky, and Jari Kurri were members of the playoff 100-goal club.

"I guess it's kind of interesting that two guys I played with are the other two with 100," he said with a wide, proud smile. "It says we've been doing this for a long time."

The Rangers won Game Three at Madison Square Garden. Then the series got bizarre. The Rangers were trailing, 2-0, in Game Four and had lost Jeff Beukeboom to a concussion. Then Craig Wolanin laid a one-handed slash across Alexei Kovalev's back. Referee Andy van

Hellemond saw Kovalev, who had the puck along the left wing boards, go down in a heap. Van Hellemond refused to blow the whistle as Sakic skated in on Glenn Healy and scored. Van Hellemond, who kept looking back at Kovalev writhing in pain, had a problem. He waved his arms as if to indicate he didn't know what to call, or whether he would allow the goal to stand. Eventually, van Hellemond claimed he had blown the whistle, even though he hadn't. The goal was disallowed. The Rangers went on to win the game, 3-2, and take a three games to one lead in the series. The next day, the league admonished and fined van Hellemond.

The Nordiques won Game Five, but the Rangers clinched the series in Game Six at the Garden. Messier paid the price for the victory. He was hit in the face by a puck and chipped several teeth. Nine stitches were required to close a cut on his chin. He couldn't talk after the game.

"I felt like I got shot," he said the next day. "I can imagine what it feels like to get hit by a Mike Tyson uppercut. Everything went black for a moment; the lights went out."

For the next two days, Messier ate nothing but soup and milkshakes.

■ ■ ■

Next up for the Rangers were Eric Lindros and the Philadelphia Flyers. The media made a big deal out of the battle between Lindros and his boyhood idol, Messier.

"He's the best player in the league this year," Messier said. "But I don't think I need this as a motivational tool. The Stanley Cup is enough. Philadelphia presents a big challenge. That's enough motivation. The further you go along in the playoffs, the better the teams you have to play and the bigger the challenges."

Messier vs. the much bigger Lindros was a mismatch. The Flyers won Games One and Two in less than twenty-four hours. The Legion of Doom line of Lindros, John LeClair, and Mikael Renberg scored 13 points in two games.

"Mark did a heckuva job," said Campbell. "He went out right from the beginning and said, 'I'm going to battle Lindros.' For a guy who's thirty-four and played as much hockey as he has, he did a pretty good job against a young guy who's six-four, 230 pounds. Mark is our leader. He got right in Lindros' face."

Messier refused to go down without a fight. He renewed his rivalry with Kevin Haller, whom he had pummeled in a fight during the season.

In the first period of Game Four, Messier steamrolled Haller in open ice. In the second period, Messier retaliated for a butt-end by Haller and was penalized.

If only the rest of the Rangers had played with such emotion. They ended up getting swept in four games. The defense of their Stanley Cup championship had ended without much of a fight. Watching Game Four at the Garden, Doug and Paul Messier bemoaned the fact that "too few were asked to do the work of too many."

They were absolutely right. Most of the Rangers made no contribution. The few who did their jobs couldn't hold off the bigger Flyers. The Cup, which had required so much effort to acquire, was given back with little resistance.

"We just broke down," Messier said. "We didn't have anything left to give. There wasn't a lack of trying, or a lack or effort, or a lack of want. But there was nothing left in the tank."

The Rangers had no choice but to watch as another team won the Cup.

"There will be just about every emotion going," Messier predicted. "The guys will all feel that. When they see somebody skating with the Cup in late June, they're going to feel it. It's not going to be a feeling that's easy. There's pain. And I'm anxious for all of the guys to feel that so they'll fight back."

That the new Cup champion was the New Jersey Devils, their cross-river rivals, only made the Rangers' summer more painful.

14

Still the Man

People who have played with Mark Messier have, more accurately, played for him. His teams aren't teams he's on. His teams are his teams, under his power and leadership. The people who have played with Messier always say the same thing: That if he scored only a handful of goals and a handful of assists, he'd still be the most valuable guy on the team because of all the other things he brings to the table.

All that is good and correct to an inarguable degree, but it also diminishes Messier as a player. Because of what Messier has done off the ice, on the bench, and everywhere else for a team, at times people forget what a tremendous athlete he is. Because of all the attributes that set him apart from most other players, we forget that he is still a player. We tend to overlook his basic ability. While everybody tells us that Messier minus the statistics would still be a great leader, the reverse is also true: Messier, minus any leadership skills whatsoever, would still be a Hall of Famer. He wouldn't be a legend, and he wouldn't be a six-time Stanley Cup champion, but he would still be one of the greatest players who ever lived.

As Messier reached old age in terms of his playing career—a columnist once made Messier laugh by writing that thirty-two was like ninety-six in hockey player years—he was once again proving that he still had plenty of games left in his tank. Not that his leadership had slipped. Not one bit.

Rangers coach Colin Campbell told the story about how the team's braintrust had huddled in Florida over the summer of 1995 and mapped out its needs for the 1995-96 season.

"We blueprinted it out, and one thing we knew we needed was goals," Campbell said. So the members of the coaching staff and management penciled in how many goals they thought each player would score. They wrote 17 next to Messier's name.

"He was trying to take the pressure off me, or something," Messier said later. "Jeez, I'm not that old."

What the Rangers got from Messier was 47 goals and 52 assists. He was three goals short of scoring 50 when he suffered a bad tear in his ribcage cartilage, costing him the final six games of the season. Had he scored 50, Messier would have gone fourteen years between 50-goal seasons. No other player had ever gone more than five years between 50-goal seasons.

He was showing no signs of slowing down.

■ ■ ■

If you have Messier on your team, you have to go for the Stanley Cup. Nothing else makes sense. So even though the Rangers had gone through a disappointing season after winning the Cup, they continued to swing away at Lord Stanley.

After getting pushed around by the Flyers, the Rangers knew they had to get bigger. They added ultra-tough defenseman Ulf Samuelsson and perennial 40-goal left winger Luc Robitaille in a trade with Pittsburgh for skilled defenseman Sergei Zubov and skilled-but-soft center Petr Nedved.

The trade posed potential problems. Messier loved Zubov. He was a sucker for defensemen who could move the puck, skate, pass, and join the play, much like Coffey used to do in Edmonton. There was also the potential for conflict between Messier and Robitaille, who had blamed Wayne Gretzky when he was traded from Los Angeles to Pittsburgh. And Messier had an ongoing feud with Samuelsson. In 1993, both players were suspended for an incident in which Messier knocked out Samuelsson's teeth.

Fortunately for the Rangers, Messier had no problems with Robitaille and quickly developed respect for the warrior-like Samuelsson.

■ ■ ■

When Messier showed up for 1995 training camp in Burlington, Vermont, tests taken showed that he was in possibly the best shape of his NHL career.

"I've come up with a lot of little excuses," Messier kidded about his usual truancy from training camp. "That's why I've been able to play eighteen years."

But this year he was at camp and ready to go. He claimed his presence had nothing to do with the mid-season deadline for the Rangers to pick up the option on his contract for $6 million or buy him out for $1 million and make him a free agent in July 1996.

Messier would give the Rangers no choice but to keep him. On November 6, 1995, Messier had felt horrible before the game against the Calgary Flames. Then he went out and padded his legend and his Hall of Fame statistics. Messier scored three goals, including the 500th of his career, in a 4-2 victory over the Flames. He did it with his parents, grandmother, sister, and friends watching from the stands, and with his former general manager and coach, Glen Sather, watching from a skybox.

"There's no question there was karma in the building tonight," Messier said. "You can never put your finger on why, but you certainly feel it. That's what makes great theater. I really understand that side of the game, seeing how a crowd reacts, not only to the game, but to the theater within the game. It was really perfect."

The crowd reacted with the loudest, longest Garden ovation since January 20, 1995, the night the Stanley Cup banner was raised to the Garden roof.

Doug Messier was just about the only person in the arena who wasn't sure if he had actually seen No. 500. Three nights earlier, Messier didn't receive credit for a goal against Anaheim until a few hours after the game ended. The next day, newspapers didn't have the corrected box score, so Doug thought Mark had gone into the Calgary game with 496 goals, not 497. When Mark scored his second goal of the game, Doug shrugged when asked whether he thought his son could score No. 500. He thought scoring four goals was asking too much.

"He's a master of being able to grab the moment," said Neil Smith, who watched the game with Sather. "What he did in Game Six two years ago, not many players would have the intestinal fortitude to guarantee victory and carry it out. Tonight was another one of those rare performances, not only to get the 500th goal but to get it like that."

No. 498 came on the rebound of a shot by Bruce Driver. No. 499 came off of an uncharacteristic full-windup slapshot from the left circle that squeezed between the pads of goalie Rick Tabaracci. After

Calgary cut the Rangers' lead to 3-2, Messier scored No. 500 with a signature wrong-footed snapshot from the off wing.

"I was well aware of 500," Messier said. "I was well aware that not many people have done it, and that the people who have done it have been great and had great careers. And longevity is something you can't underestimate. But I've never really, in my own heart, put a lot of emphasis on goals and assists. I more or less put more emphasis on doing what was necessary in each particular game, and doing what it takes to win. If that meant scoring a goal or setting up a goal or making a hit or blocking a shot or killing a penalty, or setting somebody up . . . anything that that particular game called for."

Messier, who had felt so lousy before the game, triumphantly walked out of the building with his arms wrapped around his family. But first, he made the rounds with the media. When Messier left one TV studio and headed for another, he was intercepted by well wishers, including Garden President Dave Checketts.

"Hopefully, there'll be a lot more goals," Messier said to Checketts.

Checketts knew without being told that he had to make sure Messier wasn't running out of Rangers goals. The team had until December 28 to exercise its option or buy out Messier for $1 million and turn him into an unrestricted free agent after the season.

"It's not a factor," Doug Messier said. "We made a deal, and now he's just playing. I would imagine as an organization, they wanted to make sure they had some protection. It's not an issue."

Two nights later, Messier had a goal and an assist to cap a come-from-behind victory over the Tampa Bay Lightning.

"We can't constantly say, 'Mark, do something heroic,'" Colin Campbell said.

Yet they were, and he was coming through.

Prior to the Tampa Bay game, the Rangers had a surprise ceremony to honor Messier for his 500th goal. Messier's entire family was brought out, including his son, Lyon, who lived outside of Washington, D.C. with his mother, and Glen Sather. Messier broke down and cried.

Another night brought another major milestone. On December 4, Messier notched three points, giving him 1,400 in his career. He was the seventh player to reach 1,400 points and trailed No. 6, Bryan Trottier, by 23 points.

Two nights later, something far more significant happened. On a night when Messier needed six stitches to close a cut on the bridge of his nose, the captain received an envelope from Neil Smith. Inside was notification that the Rangers would exercise the option on his contract for the 1996-97 season.

"It was nice," Messier said. "It was nice that it didn't become a distraction. It had to come at the 40-game mark, and I was concerned it might be a distraction."

Messier, who would turn thirty-five on January 18, had been playing great hockey and was talking about playing beyond the 1996-97 season. But neither Messier nor the Rangers were ready to sit down and discuss a contract extension.

"At this age," said Messier, "we can afford to take it one year at a time. I feel great right now, and I want to play a couple more years at least. I'm happy those seasons are going to be here."

To Smith, the Rangers' investment in Messier had been worth every penny.

"So far, the whole time he's been here, he's exceeded expectations," Smith said. "Particularly when, at the time we made that deal, there were people saying this could be another Marcel Dionne or another Blaine Stoughton, another guy past his prime. Mark's really been a godsend for the franchise."

So much for the 17 goals the Rangers had expected from Messier. By December 11, he had 19 with fifty games remaining.

"You wonder when he's going to slow down," Campbell said.

■ ■ ■

Messier prides himself on doing whatever it takes to win, so there was plenty of laughter when, while his Eastern Conference all-star teammates were competing in a puck-control relay race during the SuperSkills competition, Messier noticed a puddle on the ice. Messier went to FleetCenter maintenance, got a broom, and swept the puddle off the ice. Then he went out and knocked down four targets with four shots to easily win the shooting accuracy competition.

The next day, Messier was robbed by goalie Felix Potvin of what would have been the game-winning goal late in the All-Star Game, then assisted on Ray Bourque's winner with 37.3 seconds remaining.

■ ■ ■

Meanwhile, on the West Coast, the Los Angeles Kings were talking about trading Wayne Gretzky. The Rangers wanted to make sure they were a contender, even though Smith wouldn't trade for Gretzky unless he was certain The Great One would sign a new contract. Gretzky was scheduled to become an unrestricted free agent after the season. Not signing him to a new contract opened the possibility of giving up players to get him, then losing him for nothing at the end of the season.

Messier, Gretzky's closest friend in hockey, said he would understand if the Rangers didn't get Gretzky.

"It all depends on what the price is," Messier said. "There's twenty-six teams interested. I'd understand perfectly. It's not that easy to do something like that. You never know what they want."

The first game after the all-star break pitted Messier against Gretzky in a game that was excruciatingly difficult for both players. After the game, Gretzky was brought to an interview room at the Garden. The MSG Network televised Gretzky's question-and-answer session, at which Gretzky appeared uneasy, sad, and emotional, as he talked about the potential trade.

Down the hallway in the players' lounge, Messier sat in a leather chair, his back straight, his chin stuck out, the muscles in his temples twitching, his dark eyes staring at the large TV screen and squinting intently, while Gretzky endured the discomfort of answering reporters' questions. Messier felt his friend's pain and was suffering, too. Messier looked like he was about to break down. As Gretzky's press conference ended, Messier quickly stood up and walked to a private room where he could be alone with his thoughts.

■ ■ ■

The Rangers did get involved in the Gretzky Derby. Smith received permission to talk to Mike Barnett, Gretzky's agent, about a new contract. If the Rangers could work out a deal with Barnett before the trade deadline, Gretzky would be a Ranger. If not, he wouldn't be.

At the same time, Messier was encouraging the Rangers to get long-time Gretzky bodyguard Marty McSorley, who not only had been traded with Gretzky from Edmonton to Los Angeles, but who had also had several fights with Eric Lindros of the Flyers.

The Rangers, however, needed to get bigger players, and they did it by acquiring McSorley, Shane Churla, and former Oiler Jari Kurri from the Kings.

But the Rangers' bid for Gretzky never materialized. Instead, the Blues and Mike Keenan ended up getting him.

Messier expressed no regret over the lost possibility of a reunion with Gretzky in New York.

"I don't even know how close he was to coming here, what was true, what was false," Messier said. "That's why I wasn't even going to get involved in it. Trade rumors are something we live with, so as players, we don't get involved. I don't think we ever really expected our paths to cross anyway."

■ ■ ■

Late in the season, Neil Smith sat behind his big desk in an office that had become something of a Rangers Hall of Fame and Museum. He talked about his legacy, which is and always will be Mark Messier. Smith was the man responsible for bringing Messier to New York, and therefore he was equally responsible with Messier for all that had happened since October 4, 1991.

"It's the way we wanted it to be," Smith said. "It couldn't have turned out any better than it turned out. The day we made that decision, if somebody said, 'This is what you'll have in the next five years: You'll win the Presidents' Trophy, you'll miss the playoffs, you'll win the Stanley Cup, you'll have a lockout and a very, very mediocre season, then you'll be headed for first place again the fifth year,' I'd be delighted.

"More than that, we needed to have a symbol, a leader, a lead horse, and he became that icon for the club and the organization, and we really needed that. I don't think in hockey that person can be a coach, and I know for sure it can't be a GM. Mess was the chosen one. He's the one who was offered the chalice and took it and did this with it. In some ways, I look at this whole thing like a Broadway show or a movie. Everyone needs the star, the leading man, the best actor. Mess was ours. Thank God we got one.

"And really, the whole thing really revolves around that star, and it should. A lot of people wouldn't have had the courage to grab the ring like he did all these years. Geez, it's scary to grab that ring in New York. So whatever he's gotten out of it—the money, the lifelong fame now—he deserves it because he was given a great opportunity. But he did with it the most that you could do, and I really think he did it in a pretty selfless manner. I think he did it in his belief that he was doing the right thing for the team. A lot of people would grab the ring thinking, 'Well there's a lot of money in it at the end of this and I'll have a life of fame in New York if I can do this.' And I don't think that ever came into his mind. I think that was all byproducts of it."

Smith admitted that he hadn't obtained Messier without some trepidation.

"There was some, but there always is, on every trade I make," Smith said. "You're always nervous, and that was one I was extremely nervous about. At that point in time, you have to remember, the Rangers had a history of making trades for superstars well past their prime that didn't work out. They gave up their future and ended up with a player retiring. The Doubting Thomases all thought this was another of those situations, 'Here they go again getting this aging superstar who's all banged up and has played a million playoff games, and what will the Rangers get out of him? Instead of developing their own young players, here they are going after an old washed-up guy again.'

"Although I was sure they were wrong, or I wouldn't have made the trade, there was a fear that, 'What if I'm wrong and they're all right? What if? What if that one-percent is true, that he does have a bad knee and a bad wrist and isn't the type of player Glen Sather said he is, isn't the type of person? What if he is less than what he turned out to be?' To say you had no fear would be absolutely lying. But he proved pretty quickly that first year that there was no need to worry about that."

As Messier aged, the many aspects of his personality became more pronounced, particularly as he became the biggest sports celebrity in the biggest city on the biggest stage. He was friends with Madonna. The two were seen together around New York City, admitted to having talked to each other a few times, and were an item on the gossip page of *The New York Post*. He dated model Frederique van der Wal. He was a regular guest on David Letterman's show and appeared on ESPN's *ESPY Awards* and the *MTV Music Video Awards*.

He did a considerable amount of charity work for Tomorrow's Children, whose annual fund-raising dinner always brought Messier to tears. His emotions often got away from him when he visited children in hospitals.

One night, while working on his stick outside the Rangers locker room, Messier related a sad story about a man who had made a huge, but phony, donation, at the charity dinner. The problem was, the charity never got the money. The man stole millions of dollars from his wife, ostensibly to make the donation, then kept the money for himself. Messier's temples twitched and his Adam's apple danced in anger as he told the story. He would have loved to get his stick on that guy.

Another time, Messier got a call from a woman whose husband was dying of cancer. The man, a lifelong Rangers fan, wanted to meet

Messier before he died, but the Rangers were on the road and Messier couldn't visit the hospital. Instead, he phoned the man a few times. The man was on painkillers and couldn't speak, so the woman's wife relayed Messier's messages. It meant so much to the man, who died before Messier could visit him. As a show of gratitude, the man dedicated his considerable collection of memorabilia to the Tomorrow's Children fund. Before the next home game a reporter approached Messier, who was choked up.

"That was really a great thing you did for him," the reporter said.

Messier nodded, then set his chin outward and swallowed deeply. He said nothing.

"How do you do it?" the reporter asked. "I mean, it's got to be really hard to visit these people, to do these things all the time."

Again, Messier only nodded. He couldn't speak.

One day, Richter, Leetch, and Graves sat around talking about Messier. Their admiration for him couldn't have been clearer. They sounded like the Mark Messier Fan Club.

"I've heard the way people describe him who don't know him, guys from other teams and what not," Richter said. "I think it's very easy to get the wrong impression of who he is. He's amazingly gracious in so many ways. I mean, that guy is one of the most giving people you'd ever meet."

"It is unbelievable," Leetch said.

Richter: "It's like someone taught him how to make somebody feel comfortable, or not make somebody feel uncomfortable. He defines that in so many ways. During that year we won the Cup, I was out with my family and a bottle of champagne comes over. It's from Mark. Always that stuff. Always making you feel you're family, so everybody's included. The guy would give you the shirt off his back at any time. At the end of every year it's, 'Look, if anybody wants to come down to my house . . . you guys gotta come down here.' Whether he's there or not. Even if he happens to be away, he's going to make sure you feel like you're welcome one way or another."

Leetch: "His family's the same way. It's incredible."

Richter: "They're like, 'What do you mean you're not going to come down? Get down here.' Just like he always made sure you had somewhere to go for Thanksgiving. That year of the lockout, he invited a couple of us down. Gravy, Leetchie, and I were down there, Dougie Weight, too. His grandmother was making that big-ass honey ham, making sure the place was stocked for us. It's like going to summer camp there. It just seems to come natural to them."

Leetch: "They all care about anything they get involved with."

Graves: "I think there are a lot of common misconceptions, especially among people away from the game, this idea that he takes his teammates and throws them against the dressing room wall all the time. He's fearsome on the ice, but he cares about all his teammates. He's really an amazing, caring guy, and a lot of people don't know that. They think he's mean, and he is mean when he plays. But in the dressing room, he's very emotional and he doesn't forget anyone. He tries to include everyone, and it doesn't matter who you are or what role you play on the hockey club. He's concerned about everyone, and he tries to lead the way he lives.

"When he came to New York, not everyone knew quite what to expect. I don't think it took a while for anybody to accept him. I think that was right away. It was great getting him. But it took a while to understand and to appreciate what a great human being he is and what a great player he is."

Leetch: "He's just a unique individual."

Richter: "All through those playoffs, you're winning, and you're not numb to everything else that's going on, but you're pretty damn focused on playing. It's a game every other day, often going late, in overtime, and especially playing Vancouver, you play a game, soar across the country, and go back and forth. Yet when we won, Mark had his checklist of people you don't forget, things you have to do, things you don't want to do. He knew it all."

"He'd won the Cup a few times before that," Leetch said with a laugh.

"But it was amazing," Richter said. "He was saying things like, 'Make sure you take a cab or a limo. We can set that all up so you don't get stranded.' Just little things you don't screw around with. They sound funny, but he just wants to make sure everything remains good and everybody has a great time. He was talking about the trainers and locker room attendants, how they're every bit as important as anybody on this team, and don't forget them. Make sure they're taken care of. Most people, I don't think that's the first thing that comes to their mind when they win a championship.

"If you read any book, or ask anybody who's got experience, how you should approach a given situation or the game, or what kind of attitude you should have, he embodies that so much it's unbelievable," Richter continued. "Maybe you look at someone like Paul Coffey and say, 'He's got the perfect stride.' You look at Mark, and I don't know if perfect is the right adjective, but he's one of the most mentally disciplined and strongest people I've ever met. That's why he's so successful. He has that very rare combination of being very strong mentally, and physically he has the capability of putting into action and delivering all the things he demands of himself.

"I remember one time, that whole year with all that crap going on with Roger, and that year we didn't make the playoffs in '93, I remember him muttering to himself, 'I'm so disappointed. I've let myself get too negative through all this and it's affected my play.' It almost came as a shock. It was like, 'Wow, it's not automatic for him.' It doesn't happen for free. He has to work at it like anybody else does. You meet strong people, or somebody who's in shape like Leetchie, and he's got an amazing gift. But he has to work his ass off. Brian does, and that's why he's in shape. And Mark, he works. He's disciplined mentally. That's why he doesn't let himself get too negative. That's why he doesn't doubt himself. I don't know if it was a relief or rather sobering to see he is human. It doesn't just happen all the time."

Although he was a little rough around the edges at first, Messier had become a connoisseur of the finer things in life since arriving in New York. In his first season, he was playing in a charity golf tournament. When he walked off the eighteenth green at an exclusive club in Westchester County in upstate New York, he removed his shirt. Some of the club members were mortified. People just didn't do that at an exclusive club.

But Messier quickly became sophisticated in his own way.

"One of the assistant coaches, Billy Moores, when he first came here, and Dick Todd [another assistant coach] were taking their wives downtown," Richter recalled. "Billy said, 'Geez, where should we go?' Mark said, 'Go around Central Park, that's really nice, and look, I know a nice restaurant on the East Side. After the theater, stop in here and I know the guy.' They go to the restaurant, have a great meal, finish up, and the maître d' says, 'The check's been taken care of.' It's those things. Mark doesn't make an ordeal out of it at all. He always made you feel you're part of something pretty unique. If he was having somebody over, he'd invite everybody over."

Leetch: "It wasn't hard for him to act like that. It was all part of being successful to him. Those are all ingredients to him. It's not something that he starts to look around for, out of his way, like 'How can

I do this?' He knows what it takes to be successful. He knows what made him a successful person, and it's so easy for him to spread that around and share it with everybody. It's very unusual."

Richter: "There would be one person at the arena who would be more excited than you if you scored a goal, or won a game, or had a great game, and that would be Mark. He'd just be ecstatic. Look at any picture or watch any film of anybody else scoring. Mark's over there hitting him and hugging him, having a big group hug with that big grin. I mean, is there anybody who's having more fun, or is more excited for you than him? It makes you feel great.

"I remember his parents came up to me after the 1994 All-Star Game and said, 'Gee, we wanted Mark to win that MVP, but if it had to be somebody else, we were so happy for you.' They're a family, and it wasn't just Mark. You could see where Mark gets it. Everybody's in the same boat here, everybody's pulling in the same direction.

"A nice characteristic is, you always knew he was the leader, and he'd always put himself in the position to be the guy to stand up and say something or lead the team on and off the ice, and he wanted that responsibility and did it well."

Leetch: "But every time there's success, boom, he would share it. There was no insecurity or jealousy about him. He knew that, when you win, when you're successful, praise and acknowledgment are automatic. You don't have to do anything more than that. And he wants everybody to share in that. There's nothing that hurts him worse than not being successful except not having things done the way he thinks they could be done. That hurts him just as much as not being successful—not getting an honest shot at it."

Richter: "I think people misinterpret him. He's a pretty stubborn man when it comes to that stuff, in a good way. You've got to be if you're not going to settle for being mediocre. I remember one time we were heading to Philly on a train, and Mark always does everything this way: Have the best equipment, have the best locker room, have the best personnel, have the best system, work the hardest, win the most. You know, he was just amazed if someone else wasn't holding up their end of the bargain. So we were taking a train down to Philly, and his mouth just dropped open and he goes, 'How the fuck can we not be in first class?' I just laughed. I didn't know if he was serious. But it's not an arrogant thing at all. People may take it that way. It's just in his eyes, everything he does, he tries to do it top-notch. That's just the way he approaches things. If you don't know him, or don't see where he's coming from, it can rub someone the wrong way. But he just has no time to be cutting corners or doing something halfway, because he doesn't feel that's the most direct way to be successful.

"He has unbelievable people skills in terms of making sure you get the most out of people. He knows one of the best ways of doing that is being supportive, making someone feel you support then, kind of creating that environment in our own locker room of absolute support. You don't put up with a half-ass effort, but you also reward those guys for working hard and make everybody knows they're important no matter what they're doing, whether they're sitting or playing twenty-five minutes a game. He really looks to get everybody pulling the same rope."

But even at age thirty-five, Messier was among the meanest men in the NHL—and getting away with it. In a game against Edmonton, he smacked the Oilers' David Roberts across the face with his stick. Roberts suffered several broken facial bones and a concussion. Messier got a minor penalty for roughing, but he wasn't suspended.

Messier's distaste for certain players, such as former teammate Petr Nedved, was obvious. In an 8-2 loss to the Penguins, Messier repeatedly slashed and speared Nedved. Referee Kerry Fraser never called a penalty on him.

After the reporters were done asking him about the incidents, Messier made the type of face one might make when struck by a sudden odor. He complained about Nedved "fuckin' laying there like a fuckin' lapdog." To Messier, nothing was worse than a player lying down and faking an injury. That's exactly what he thought Nedved had done.

The Rangers were doing some lying down of their own at one stretch during the 1995-96 season. They were playing poorly, so the following day at practice, Campbell had the pucks pushed aside, sent the goalies to the locker room, and had the rest of the players line up for sprints. For fifteen minutes, the Rangers' forwards and defensemen skated. Some of them looked as if they were on the verge of collapsing or vomiting. But Messier was ahead of them all and smiling throughout the drills.

When the session ended, Messier skated to one end of the rink, took passes from assistant coach Dick Todd, and fired pucks into an empty net. Messier's message: If I can stay on the ice and work extra hard, so can everybody else. Few players had the gumption to leave the ice while Messier was out there.

That's how Messier treated most of the punishment practices during his Rangers career. He would take it like a man, almost appearing to enjoy it, like he was making a statement to his teammates and his coach.

"Sometimes you need a bit of a rude awakening to get yourselves snapped out of it," Messier said.

He was mean when he had to be. In a game against the Islanders, he dropped Kenny Jonsson to the ice with an elbow. Jonsson suffered a concussion, but Messier was not suspended.

"The league doesn't believe in reprimanding certain players," Islanders general manager/coach Mike Milbury said. "And he's certainly in that category."

He was, in fact, in a category all his own.

■ ■ ■

On April 4, Messier had 47 goals and the Rangers got to test their new size in a game against the Flyers at the Spectrum in Philadelphia. Not only did the Rangers get beaten, 4-1, but Messier had a fight with Joel Otto, his old nemesis from the Calgary-Edmonton wars of the 1980s. Otto jumped Messier, who left the game with torn ribcage cartilage that would rob him of his chance at scoring fifty goals. Messier clearly remembered his previous rib injury.

"I had one on the other side three years ago, when a rib popped out against Edmonton," he said. "This isn't as painful. The other one, it popped right out of the socket there."

Messier played that season with the rib protruding. He had also suffered a back and ribcage injury in the 1992 playoff series against the Devils, and, although he never admitted to it, he had an injured ribcage during the 1994 playoffs.

Without Messier, the Rangers won only once in their last six games, costing them a 100-point season. They would end up with 96 points, despite the awful finish. Down the stretch, they also lost feisty Pat Verbeek, Messier's right winger, who was having a career year with 41 goals before suffering a knee injury.

The Rangers went into the playoffs banged up. Messier was questionable right up to the start of Game One against Montreal. Verbeek and Kevin Lowe had just come back from injuries. And, in the final game of the season, Colin Campbell had wanted to rest Leetch, but Leetch played, blocked a shot, and broke a bone in his foot.

Messier, suffering from a torn rib muscle, skated in practice on the day of Game One, but didn't shoot or take face-offs. He had done nothing in more than a week since being hurt.

"Getting in and out of bed to go and eat, that's been my exercise," Messier said. "Going up and down the stairs to get to the kitchen and back."

Messier didn't think the Canadiens would target him because of his injury, but he also wondered how it would feel to get into heavy contact again.

"I don't know," he said with a laugh. "Getting out of bed isn't quite the same thing as running into Lyle Odelein."

The Rangers lost Game One at the Garden, 3-2 in overtime, on two goals by Vincent Damphousse, who dominated the head-to-head matchup with Messier. Messier was on the ice for all of Montreal's goals. In Game Two, also at the Garden, the Rangers allowed two shorthanded goals in a 5-3 loss.

The Rangers were in trouble. They headed back to Montreal down two games to none with Campbell's job on the line. The Rangers had won only once in Montreal since 1983, going 1-20-3 in their last twenty-four visits. They were 0-6-1 in seven visits since their lone victory in Messier's Rangers debut on October 5, 1991.

"It's just another set of hurdles you have to knock down," Messier said. "We've probably been faced with one a bit earlier than we thought we would, but there is always a set of obstructions you have to overcome in the playoffs. There are times when you have to look down the barrel of a gun and pull the trigger. This one's a little earlier than usual this year, but we have to look down the barrel of the gun and pull the trigger."

Messier made a miraculous recovery for Game Three. He dominated on face-offs, killed penalties, and intimidated the Canadiens with his speed. Although he had a goal disallowed, the Rangers beat the Canadiens, 2-1, and Messier assisted on both goals. At one point, Messier returned to the bench aching. He applied an ice pack to his ribs until he was called to go back on the ice.

"They were just cooling him off," said a smiling Graves, who scored both goals for the Rangers.

The win sparked an incredible turnaround. The Rangers won four in a row, including three in Montreal, to win the series. Campbell's job was no longer in danger. When asked about the Rangers' system, Campbell replied: "My system is Mess, Leetchie. Mess, Leetchie. Mess, Leetchie."

■ ■ ■

In an ironic twist, the Rangers' next opponent was the Pittsburgh Penguins. They had spent an entire year bulking up and getting ready for big, tough teams like New Jersey and Philadelphia, and here they were about to face their second consecutive finesse team. The Penguins, however, were speedier and more talented than the Canadiens. They also had Mario Lemieux and Jaromir Jagr.

Messier was awful in Game One. He spent the entire game chasing and whacking at Nedved and Jagr. He played well in Game Two, but the Rangers could not cope with Jagr and Lemieux, who would combine for fifteen goals in a five-game victory over the Rangers.

Once again, the Rangers' season had ended in the second round.

Nobody knew what the offseason would bring. Lowe, still a warrior at age 37, had played the end of the Pittsburgh series with a broken wrist. He and many other Rangers were not expected to return for the 1996-97 season. Indeed, during the offseason, Jari Kurri fled to Anaheim, Pat Verbeek went to Dallas, and Marty McSorley's salary was dumped on San Jose. Lowe signed with Edmonton.

The playoff loss was a crusher because it was starting to become apparent that these Rangers and Messier might not get another shot at the Cup.

"The worst thing you can do is start analyzing right after a series ends," said Messier, who had done just that the previous year. He went on to congratulate and praise the Penguins, before closing with, "Other than that, I don't have much to say right now."

On breakup day, however, he had plenty to say. Some of the things he said would be used against him later on. Messier reiterated that he wanted to finish his career with the Rangers and that he wanted to play beyond 1996-97, when his contract expired. Messier also said he would accept less money on his next contract.

"I'm not at all worried about an extension or getting another deal signed," he said. "I have no hidden agenda about playing somewhere else. My main thing is to stay here. I had my time being paid well, being the highest paid, and probably at the end of next year I won't be deserving of that and I'll turn that over to Brian Leetch or Mike Richter. I'll take what I deserve in terms of what I can produce."

Smith said lengthening Messier's contract was something to consider down the road, not now. Nevertheless, even at thirty-five, Messier was one of the three finalists for the Hart Trophy as NHL MVP. Smith didn't have the need or the time to worry about Messier.

Besides, he had more important matters to think about. Like bringing Wayne Gretzky to New York.

15

Mess and Gretz: The Sequel

A private jet streaked westbound across North America in late July 1996. Aboard were Neil Smith and his wife, Katia. Smith was on an exhausting mission that started in New York City, stopped at a small airport near Los Angeles for a brief pickup, then turned right around and headed back to New York. Smith didn't even step off of the ITT-owned jet to stretch. He was so excited, he didn't care how exhausting the coast-to-coast round trip would be.

The cargo on the return trip was precious: An agent, a friend, a son, a wife, a mother-in-law, and Wayne Gretzky. When Madison Square Garden president and CEO Dave Checketts announced that the Rangers had signed Gretzky as a free agent, he said that when you have the chance to get the Babe Ruth of hockey, you do it. This was an opportunity to reunite the Babe Ruth of hockey with the Lou Gehrig of hockey. Messier and Gretzky were together again.

Gretzky had become available when Mike Keenan, the St. Louis Blues general manager and coach, cut off contract negotiations during the playoffs. Before one of the Blues' games, Keenan yelled at Gretzky in front of his teammates. Right then, Gretzky decided he was done in St. Louis. He became an unrestricted free agent, and Rangers ownership freed up enough money so that Smith could bring Gretzky to Broadway.

Messier had spoken with Gretzky about a possible reunion and both players were thrilled by the prospect. The allure of playing in New York, and of playing again with Messier, was enough to attract Gretzky, even though the Rangers' offer wasn't the highest. The Vancouver Canucks had actually outbid them.

The signing turned the Rangers into the biggest story in hockey. They had the greatest player in history, Gretzky, and one of the greatest players in history, Messier, two thirty-five-year-old hockey icons who were certain Hall of Famers. The pairing had been seen once before, with the Edmonton Oilers, and now it was going to be seen again.

Messier beamed at the press conference during which Gretzky and his wife, Janet, were introduced to New York. Smith and Checketts looked like they had just pulled off the steal of the century. Sure, Gretzky wasn't as great as he had been during the 1980s, but he was still a great player, capable of scoring over 100 points in a season. He was a major drawing card and a sensational performer, too. And now the Rangers had two legends who, they thought, would finish their careers together on Broadway.

"I'm probably one of the first free agents ever to come to New York that came for less money," said Gretzky, who signed for a base salary of $4 million. "It was a tough decision, but it just came back to my gut feeling. I guess what tipped the scale was the chance to play with Mark and the opportunity to get a chance to play with a team that is really focused on trying to win a championship."

Gretzky was asked if he would have a hard time sharing the spotlight with Messier. After all, Gretzky had always been the main man wherever he played. Now he'd be 1A to Messier's 1.

"Mark and I have been best friends since we were eightteen years old," Gretzky said. "I don't care if I'm 3B. Mark has handled all the pressure and deserves all the credit he's received on this team and all of the accolades. The only reason I'm here is to fill the Cup one more time."

Messier made sure he said all the right things, particularly regarding his contract, which had only one season remaining. Gretzky's contract was for two years.

"I assured the Garden, Neil, and Mr. Checketts, that a contract extension wasn't an issue," Messier said. "But getting a guy like Wayne was."

Messier talked about how Gretzky would elevate the Rangers' level of play "to a place where they haven't been before."

"Selfishly, this is great because he's a friend of mine and all that," Messier said. "But more importantly was whether he was filling a void. You can take it further than him being the greatest hockey player who ever lived. I think if you look at Wayne's numbers, comparing what he did in his sport to what people did before, he has to be considered one of the best athletes who ever graced the earth."

Smith insisted he wanted to work on Messier's contract extension.

"I don't want him to go anywhere else, and I think he can play beyond this season," Smith said.

■ ■ ■

Fox Television seized upon the Gretzky-Messier reunion by creating two clever promos for its "NHL on Fox" telecasts. In one, Messier and Gretzky play chess. The spot opens with soft violin music. The word "STRATEGY" fills the screen. Gretzky and Messier, wearing their white Rangers uniforms, sit in an enormous, luxurious living room.

"There are two distinct approaches to hockey," a narrator says. "One is the thinking man's approach."

Gretzky makes a move and thinks, "Bishop to King's Knight four. He'll have to sacrifice his Queen."

Then the narrator says: "The other is the physical game."

And Messier viciously backhands all the pieces off the board and onto the floor.

"Oops," Messier says. "I slipped."

The other spot drew ovations when shown on the video boards at NHL arenas. It was a take-off on the opening of *The Odd Couple* television show. With *The Odd Couple* theme playing in the background, a narrator intones, "On June 13, Wayne Gretzky left his place of residence . . . never to return."

A door with a St. Louis Blues logo is shown. The door closes. Gretzky is dressed like Felix Unger in a blazer, vest, and tie. He sits on a suitcase on the curb, just like Felix did in the opening scene of *The Odd Couple,* and hails a cab while holding a hockey stick.

"Not knowing exactly where to go," the narrator says, "he found himself on the team of his friend Mark Messier."

Messier, wearing a Rangers uniform, is shown throwing out the garbage, à la Oscar Madison. He wipes his hand on his Rangers jersey and offers the hand to Gretzky. Both players, wearing their Rangers uniforms, step out in front of a Manhattan apartment building that looks like the building where Oscar and Felix lived in *The Odd Couple*. Messier is wearing a baseball hat backwards, just like Oscar. Unlike Oscar, however, Messier is chewing on an apple. The producers wanted him to use a cigar, as Oscar did, but Messier refused on principle. So they settled on the apple.

As Messier and Gretzky step outside, Messier tosses the apple core onto the sidewalk. Gretzky, with his stick, backhands it into a trash basket.

"Can two men with different styles play together without driving each other insane?" asks the announcer. "Stay tuned."

■ ■ ■

The reunion was a big deal everywhere. A *Sports Illustrated* cover photo showed Gretzky and Messier on the west side of Manhattan. The story inside had the headline, "West Side Story." Gretzky and Messier appeared together on *The Late Show with David Letterman*. Their smiling faces were on all of the Rangers' promotional material, including the media guide, yearbook, and pocket schedules. They were on just about every media outlet's wish list.

The actual on-ice reunion of Messier and Gretzky took place during the World Cup of Hockey in August and September 1996. This best vs. best tournament, similar to the Canada Cup, featured the greatest players on the planet playing for their countries. Gretzky and Messier played for Team Canada, along with Adam Graves. Brian Leetch and Mike Richter played for Team USA.

Sure enough, the United States and Canada met in the best-of-three games championship. Canada had to survive some scares to get there, losing to the United States early in the tournament and barely getting past Sweden in the semifinals. In the Canada vs. Sweden game, the Rangers' Niklas Sundstrom took a run at Messier. Messier respected Sundstrom because he was good in all areas of the ice, but he didn't at all enjoy banging heads with his teammates.

Messier's body was battered by the time the finals started. He had a strained groin, stomach flu, and a headache that wouldn't go away. Gretzky had a bad back. After playing five periods against Sweden and four in Canada's overtime win over the United States in Game One of the finals, Messier was wincing. He was told about a newspaper story that made it sound as if he were dying.

"Sometimes that's how it feels," Messier said in a rare moment of candor regarding an injury.

Messier skipped Game Two, a victory by the United States, and returned for Game Three, in which the United States won the series thanks to the play of Richter. It was a devastating loss for Canada.

After congratulating Richter and Leetch, Messier started looking toward the season. He was suffering from headaches and blurred vision, so he went for a CAT scan. At one point during the finals, Messier couldn't see at all. The test results were negative and Messier eventually began to feel better. He was scared, though. Messier never went for X-rays unless he was certain something was wrong.

Rangers training camp had already started when the World Cup finished. Gretzky finally walked through the doors of the Rangers' locker room for the first time. Messier's first appearance five years earlier had caused a sensation. Gretzky's first appearance didn't cause a sensation, partly because Messier eased his friend's introduction.

"Sometimes the thing is to sit back and watch a little bit," said Messier, who smiled, joked, and skated hard through a brisk practice. "It always seems to take a while for everybody to find where they're going to fit, but I sense good chemistry here already."

"It was special," said Richter. "I think guys are still feeling their way around and getting used to the fact that two of the greatest players in the history of the game are in this locker room, which is pretty eye-opening for everybody here. A player with as much personality and impact as Wayne Gretzky, it'll be a little bit of an adjustment. But it will happen and it will be great. I mean, if Babe Ruth walks into your clubhouse, it shakes things up a little bit. It's an adjustment, and a great one, too."

Messier giggled when asked if he felt he had to show Gretzky around "his house," the Rangers' locker room.

"When I came here, I never really expected that he'd ever end up here," Messier said. "I think we both know we can't rely on our past to make anything happen here. I think we both have a lot to offer and contribute in a lot of different ways to try to take a run at it. To try to put it all together and take a serious run at the Cup."

Colin Campbell issued a warning: "Expectations are something you always have to stickhandle around," he said. "Wayne and Mark bring great expectations. I hope it doesn't bring any of the negative."

■ ■ ■

With Gretzky, the Rangers would have even more leadership in their locker room. Yet, nobody ever questioned which player would be the team's captain. Gretzky was offered an "A" as one of the alternate captains, but scored points with his teammates by turning it down so Graves could retain his "A."

Gretzky knew when he arrived that Messier would be the captain. The Rangers were Messier's team.

"Wayne doesn't need an 'A' to be shown respect by anybody," Campbell said. "There never was any question that Mark is our captain. Adam represents the young players and the youth on our team, and Brian Leetch, we don't have to make a statement there. He made his own statement during the World Cup as the captain of the U.S. team. Adam had already spoken to Wayne during the World Cup, and he'd already come to us and wanted to hand it back in so Wayne could be the assistant captain. Wayne said, 'No, you've done a great job. I don't need an "A" to show my leadership,' which is right. He doesn't need the letter for respect, and there's no lack of it by not giving it to him."

■ ■ ■

The Rangers were the story of two countries and the center of attention of the entire NHL. Yet, they weren't winning.

Gretzky made his Garden debut on October 6, 1996. Prior to the game against Florida, the Rangers put on a light, smoke, and laser show during which they introduced the players, including their new legend. The crowd roared for Gretzky, the next-to-last player introduced.

Remarkably, however, the crowd got louder when Messier was introduced.

"It was more than I expected," Gretzky said. "It was very flattering, and then when Mess got his share I got even more excited about it. Mark's always been a good friend, and always been a very unselfish person with his teammates. All the accolades he got he deserves. They love him here, and that's the way it should be."

The Rangers lost, 5-2, and Messier was suspended for checking Florida's Mike Hough from behind. Two days later, Messier walked through the lobby of a Miami hotel hours before a rematch with the Panthers.

"They fuckin' got me for two," he complained.

He meant a two-game suspension for the dangerous hit from behind. That night, when Gretzky showed up at Miami Arena, a "C" had been sewn onto his jersey.

"I have no idea how it happened," Gretzky said. "I put my sweater on for warm-ups and saw the 'C.' I was probably more surprised than anybody. I'll hold the fort until Mark gets back. Then he can have it back."

■ ■ ■

179

Rookies always looked up to Messier, and in 1996-97 two of the Rangers' rookies were Daniel Goneau, a cocky kid, and Christian Dube, who was shy, unassuming, and polite.

A custom at the Rangers' preseason fan club dinner was for the rookies to stand up at the podium and introduce themselves. Eric Cairns, an enormous defenseman with a baby face and an "aw shucks" personality, went first and stumbled through his speech.

Goneau went next. He sped through his speech in French so nobody could understand him. The fans and players laughed.

Then Messier introduced Dube and noted that Dube's father had played in the WHA during Gretzky's career.

"Wayne played with him," Messier said, taking a jab at Gretzky's age . . . which was the same age as Messier's.

Gretzky came right back at Messier.

"Yeah, Mess played with him, too," Gretzky said. "I'm pretty sure Mess ran him."

The rookies quickly made their marks. Goneau's first NHL goal was set up by Messier, Dube's first NHL goal was set up by Gretzky.

After a home game early in the season, Messier took the two rookies aside and told them about a Rangers' tradition. Goneau and Dube, with their eyes bulging, stood and listened to every word, their heads nodding in agreement.

"Tomorrow," Messier said, "before fuckin' practice, go down to a fuckin' cigar store and pick up a bunch of fuckin' cigars for everybody. You have to when you score your first fuckin' NHL goal. They don't have to be the fuckin' big ones. Just the fuckin' nice little ones. Get enough for the fuckin' players, the fuckin' coaches, the fuckin' trainers."

One of the rookies asked Messier where to buy the cigars. Messier told him to go to a store on Purchase Street in downtown Rye, a short drive from the practice rink.

"Right on that fuckin' main fuckin' street," Messier continued. "Right as you fuckin' go through fuckin' Rye there. Pick up a couple fuckin' boxes each, enough for fuckin' everybody, and hand 'em out right out after fuckin' practice tomorrow."

Dube and Goneau grabbed their coats and went out to buy the cigars.

Messier's varied vocabulary was amazing. Among teammates and male friends, he was an old school, salty man's man with a rugged, profanity-laced vocabulary. But, remarkably, when he was in mixed company or in a situation where the slightest off-color word would be inappropriate, he cleaned up his language. If he was talking to a couple of men and a woman showed up, he'd change the way he was talking in mid-sentence.

■ ■ ■

The Gretzky-Messier reunion didn't make an on-ice impact until the sixth game of the season, a 5-4 victory over Calgary. The win came with controversy for the Rangers, who were 1-3-2 and off to their worst start since the 1980-81 season.

The Flames were leading, 2-0, in the second period and the Rangers were on their second consecutive power play. Messier and Leetch were exhausted from long shifts. The fans were booing Messier for taking a couple of gambles that failed. That's when Messier called a time-out.

Coaches, not players, usually usually call time-outs in hockey. After the game, Campbell claimed he had told Messier to call the time-out. Gretzky claimed the time-out was called because, after skating over to the bench to confer with Campbell, Messier would have been forced to leave the ice if the Rangers hadn't called time-out. Many members of the media didn't buy into either version. They thought Messier was coaching the team and Campbell had bowed to Messier's power. That the Rangers scored on the power play, and went on to win the game, didn't lessen the speculation.

Campbell's job was already on the line. The first twenty games of the season felt like sixty. The Rangers were 6-10-4 when they left on a pivotal six-game road trip through Pittsburgh, Western Canada, Phoenix, and Colorado. Fans called radio talk shows asking for Campbell's neck. Messier was asked if this was the team's worst slump since he had joined the Rangers.

"If it's not," he said, "It sure feels like it."

Was confidence a problem?

"You name it, it's a problem," he said.

"Perhaps playing on the road would help?"

"It doesn't matter where we're playing," he said. "Playing in Timbuktu isn't going to help. We're in a huge downward spiral right now."

Messier was concerned.

"I think the guys are playing hard for Colie, there's no doubt about it," he said. "As a coach, you can only do so much. He can't put his skates on and do it himself. He's a tremendous competitor and nobody takes a loss harder than Colie. That certainly isn't our problem."

Campbell hit a low point when a fan in Edmonton greeted the Rangers' team bus with a sign that read, "Colin Cancer." Campbell's father had died of cancer.

But Messier saved both his coach and the season with a remarkable streak of play. On the six-game trip, Messier scored nine goals, two of them game-winners, and the Rangers won three games. Campbell had survived what he called "the trip I wasn't supposed to come back from." The Rangers closed the trip with victories over Phoenix and the defending Stanley Cup champion Colorado Avalanche, starting an 11-1-1 roll.

Messier had already cost one coach his job during his Rangers tenure. Now he had rescued one.

Messier, however, was suffering from a number of nagging injuries. He had several bouts with the flu, his semi-annual wrist injury, and a hyperextended elbow that left him, as he said, "pretty useless."

■ ■ ■

Around Christmas, Doug Messier, during one of his many visits to New York, made a rare appearance at the Rangers' practice rink. Doug was wearing his agent's hat when he spoke to reporters. He painted a scenario in which the Philadelphia Flyers didn't win the Stanley Cup, then made a big offer to his son, who would become an unrestricted free agent after the season. The scenario made sense: Messier could form a lethal one-two punch at center with Eric Lindros, who idolized Messier.

Nonetheless, the scenario was difficult to visualize. Messier insisted he wanted to play nowhere but New York, and the Rangers said they had every intention of making sure he retired as a Ranger.

The two sides weren't talking. Every time Neil Smith spoke to Doug Messier, Smith would say, "Whenever you're ready to start talking . . ." And Doug would say, "No hurry."

And nothing ever got done.

■ ■ ■

Messier wasn't happy with the Rangers' makeup. During a game against the Hartford Whalers on December 16 at the Garden, Messier watched Gretzky throw a wild punch at Hartford's Kevin Haller, who had been abusing him all night. He watched Leetch go down after Haller cross-checked him from behind. Graves fought two Whalers at once, while all of the teammates he regularly protected offered no help. Mark Janssens of the Whalers slashed Richter. Messier watched the sickening scene as Stu Grimson of Hartford rained punches on the bleeding, injured left orbital bone of Shane Churla, who probably shouldn't have been playing.

"They started taking liberties on us," said Messier, who had just returned from an elbow injury. "Why wouldn't they? It's a long season and you've got to be able to protect players, otherwise the injury list is going to grow. They didn't have enough respect for us physically and started to take liberties. You've got to be able to cover all the bases, and right now we're not solid in that area."

Neil Smith called Messier's comment an "emotional reaction. When you see, right in front of your bench, a fight with a player who's injured, you wish you had a robocop to go over the bench right at that moment. Having said that, it's a decision we'll have to make. Can the players we have do what needs to be done? Or do we have to trade somebody on our team to get that?"

Messier thought the Rangers lacked muscle. He thought they needed to beef up before the playoffs started.

Perhaps he was frustrated. His big nights had been coming fewer and further between. He mixed awful games with average games, while sticking in a big game here and there. One of his best performances was in a 7-3 win against Florida on December 22. Messier, who had struggled in Montreal the previous night, scored two goals, two assists, and achieved two major milestones. His first assist made him the fifth player in history with 1,500 points, joining Gretzky (2,660), Gordie Howe (1,850), Marcel Dionne (1,771), and Phil Esposito (1,590). The two goals pushed him past John Bucyk for twelfth on the NHL's all-time goal-scoring list with 557.

His frustration was often obvious. Messier's anger boiled over a week later in a game against the Islanders. Messier and the Rangers felt that referee Don Van Massenhoven's calls were one-sided in favor of the Islanders. Messier, who set up the tying and winning goals after making shoddy defensive plays, was fined $1,000 for verbal abuse of Van Massenhoven after the game.

Messier called Van Massenhoven's performance "a disgrace" and "an embarrassment to the league." He said Van Massenhoven had "brought a personal vendetta" into the game. "He decided, for some reason, he wasn't going to call any penalties in the third period when, obviously, there were six or seven blatant infractions right in front of him," Messier said. "He missed a call on Ulfie [Samuelsson] in the first period, and it got worse from there. To me, when that's happening, then he's bringing in his own personal feelings and to me that's wrong. The good of the game is the most important thing."

He was particularly angry about a check from behind by Travis Green that sent Samuelsson out of the game with back spasms. Earlier in the season, Messier had received a five-minute penalty, a game misconduct, and a two-game suspension for a similar hit on Mike Hough. Green received only a minor penalty.

"There has to be some repercussions," Messier said. "Nobody's supposed to talk about the officials. Everybody's supposed to just get up tomorrow morning and forget about it and nobody notices. Then it never gets better. Nothing's ever done about it. For some reason, it became personal. I don't know why he was the way he was, you know, antagonizing. It was not right. It was wrong for the league and for everything else. He should have to answer to that. He should have to answer to his superiors."

Messier, who claimed he didn't curse at Van Massenhoven, had several run-ins with Van Massenhoven during the game, including a face-to-face conversation after he received a slashing penalty.

Finally, when he was asked one more question about Van Massenhoven, Messier turned coy.

"You're not supposed to talk about the referees," he said with a sly laugh. "So I'm not going to."

Messier wasn't exactly truthful in his insistence that he hadn't sworn at Van Massenhoven. Messier's curse-laden verbal assault on the referee had been clearly picked up by the MSG Network's rinkside microphones.

"Uh, Mark," a reporter said. "I don't know about Canada, but here in the U.S., the word fuck is considered a swear word."

Replied Messier: "I said fuck. I didn't call him a fuck."

Over the following days, Messier softened his accusations against Van Massenhoven. But Messier and the referee had a history together. Van Massenhoven was the ref when Messier was ejected for checking Hough. He was the referee in a Rangers vs. Detroit game the previous season, when Messier piled up sixteen penalty minutes against Red Wings defenseman Vladimir Konstantinov. During the lockout season,

Messier fought Kevin Kaminski of Washington in a game refereed by Van Massenhoven.

The repercussions of Messier's outburst lasted a while. In the Rangers' 2-2 tie with Colorado, the Avalanche were awarded eight of the last nine power plays by Terry Gregson, the president of the NHL officials union. Twenty-five of the next thirty-six power plays went to the Rangers' opponents. Against the Devils, the Rangers didn't get a single power play, the first time that had happened in thirteen years, a span of 1,065 regular-season games. In each of the twelve games after the Messier-Van Massenhoven incident, the Rangers' opponents had more power plays than the Rangers.

Ironically, the referee who broke the streak was Van Massenhoven, who had a brief conversation with Messier on the ice.

"Turn the page, go onto the next game," Messier said, describing the discussion. Van Massenhoven claimed he had not spoken to any other referee about Messier's remarks and that he wasn't aware Messier had been fined. He said the matter "was closed after the last game."

■ ■ ■

Alexei Kovalev, Messier's right wing, tore his anterior cruciate ligament in January and would miss the rest of the season. Kovalev's replacement was Vladimir Vorobiev, a rookie who didn't have Kovalev's skills, speed, or confidence. He walked hunched over, looking at the ground. Messier didn't like him; he thought he was tentative, a soft player.

In his first game, Vorobiev assisted on a goal by Messier. In his third game, Vorobiev had a goal and three assists. But Messier had light praise for Vorobiev: "It's only his third game, so he's still getting adjusted to the speed of the game and the style of play in the NHL. He's played pretty well. He's played three games, so we'll wait and see."

Vorobiev was only one of the Rangers that Messier didn't like. This disturbed the coaching staff. Messier had power in the locker room and power over management decisions. He had already helped get rid of Petr Nedved and Ray Ferraro.

"But he'd never turn on a player in front of other players," Leetch said, defending Messier. "He'd never treat that person differently, no matter what his opinion of that person. He knew we needed everybody that was there to be successful, and we needed to get the most out of them, even if it was like banging your head against a wall. It was never a point where it was like, 'I cut you out of this locker room. You're useless to me.' Certainly, he's got his beliefs about what kind of player he wants, who can help the team, but he would never show that because he knows the strength he has in the locker room, that if he does that all of a sudden you start to form divisiveness."

Off the ice, he was still the same old Messier. Mathew Loughran, the Rangers' director of operations, was a man the entire team counted on. He handled all of the team's travel arrangements, got the players tickets for Broadway shows and concerts, and was available to them, every day, via beeper, cellular phone or in person, for everything they wanted.

On Loughran's birthday, Messier called the Rangers out of the locker room a couple of hours before a home game. With Messier and Loughran leading the way, they walked down the corridor, past the visiting team's room at the Garden, and to the Zamboni entrance. There was parked a new black Mercedes that the players had leased for Loughran.

■ ■ ■

Despite the flu and his bumps and bruises, Messier went on a hot streak in February. On February 8, he scored three goals, including the winner, in a 5-2 victory over the Islanders. Messier's ten-game point streak gave him 27 goals and 51 points in thirty-three games and inspired public debate about his contract.

"Nothing surprises me," Gretzky said of Messier. "But more important than anything, he's unselfish. The best players who've ever played the game, the biggest thing among all of them is that they were unselfish."

Messier refused to join in the debate.

"The contract's a moot point," he said. "It's not an issue for me or the Rangers. There's been some talk, and some headlines in the papers, but as far as me and the people who are helping me out are concerned, it's a moot point until the end of the season. It hasn't been a distraction for me. I haven't even thought about it."

Richter said Messier might still be playing great hockey "when he's fifty-six. I mean, he's so consistent in his approach, in some ways he's a victim of his own success because you expect him, game in and game out, to be the guy we go to. Yet he does it so often."

Three days later, during a practice in Florida, Messier strained his upper back. He played through pain for five games, but was ineffective. The injury halted his fine statistical run. He'd score only four more goals the rest of the season and finish with 36.

The Rangers were a dreadful team without Messier, who missed eleven games during the 1996-97 season. They had mismatched lines and little speed. Even with Gretzky, Messier was still the Rangers' No. 1 center. Opposing teams usually assigned their checking lines and top defensemen to face Messier's line. When Messier couldn't play, or when he played injured, the Rangers were easily shut down. They were a boring, plodding team.

Were Smith and Co. paying attention?

Messier's back injury was even worse than he had let on. One day, he said the spasms in his upper back were preventing "the rib from popping back in."

The rib? What rib? When had Messier's rib popped out? He didn't say.

There was no such thing as the whole truth when it came to Messier's injuries. A typical answer when he was asked how he felt: "I'm alive and breathing. That's about it."

■ ■ ■

Messier knew the Rangers needed to get more grit in order to be serious contenders in the playoffs. But the Bruins were asking too much for rugged winger Rick Tocchet, and the Rangers ended up shipping popular forward Sergei Nemchinov and Brian Noonan to Vancouver for Esa Tikkanen and Russ Courtnall.

Messier was livid. He was a big fan of Nemchinov, as well as his friend. He didn't feel the trade made the Rangers more legitimate playoff contenders. When a reporter asked Messier if he felt the Rangers now had enough talent to contend, Messier looked puzzled. He rolled his eyes.

"Enough?" he asked, his voice going up an octave in exasperation. "Enough?" he said again. "Fuck."

He obviously didn't think they had enough.

Messier's play continued to deteriorate. The Rangers' management and coaches wondered if he was sulking. A popular theory was that Messier was worn out after starting the season in August in the World Cup and from all of the ice time he had logged early in the season.

Campbell called Messier into his office and asked what was bothering him. Was it the trade? Was it the contract? Was he having problems with his girlfriend, model Frederique van der Wal? Was he hurt worse than he was letting on? Could the organization do anything to help him?

Messier's answers were succinct: "Nope, nope, nope, nope, nope."

Another time, assistant coach Dick Todd thought the Rangers needed to make a minor strategic adjustment in their penalty kill or their forecheck. Campbell told Todd that Messier wouldn't go for it. When Todd broached the topic with Messier on the practice rink, the captain simply said, "If it ain't broke, don't fix it." And he skated away.

But the Rangers, who were barely over .500, were broken.

Messier's plea for toughness earlier in the season had also been a plea for his teammates to play tougher. He wanted the Rangers to stick together and have a one-for-all attitude. He wanted teammates to step in and help other teammates when they were in trouble.

That's why it was surprising when Messier was allowed to fight Marty McSorley of the Sharks. The fight started during a scrum behind the net during a Rangers power play. Graves wasn't on the ice. The Rangers had four finesse players surrounding Messier. Messier and McSorley came together. When Messier threw a left at McSorley's chin, no Ranger could stop McSorley. Nobody even tried. Messier was left on his own to go toe-to-toe with one of the toughest men in hockey.

He held his own, but that the fight was allowed to happen was shocking. Something like this would not have happened the year the Rangers won the Cup.

■ ■ ■

Behind the scenes, management decided to offer Messier a pay cut because of his declining performance, but not until after the season. They were concerned that he might stop playing hard if he knew he was about to be offered less money than he was making.

The season continued its downward spiral for both the team and for Messier. The Rangers seemed to have given up on the season. Campbell called the Rangers' effort "disgusting" after a 5-4 loss to the Canadiens.

"Someone's got to be accountable," he said. "I guess it's going to be me eventually. Someone should be accountable before that. I've been asked the question, 'What can you expect at this time of year?' I expect momentum and consistency. We did get momentum. We're going the wrong way fast. Where our heads are at, I have no idea."

Messier was right at the top of the list in the accountability department. Maybe he had given up on the team. Perhaps he was sulking about the lack of a contract offer from the Rangers. But he didn't stick around to say so. After one of his worst games as a Ranger, Messier left without speaking with reporters.

"I have no comment," Messier snapped.

A gang of reporters followed him down the winding hallway at Madison Square Garden. Messier stopped and posed for pictures with some kids from the March of Dimes. Then, with his family a few steps ahead of the media horde, he escaped through a door leading to the garage where his car was parked.

Messier rarely acted this way. Before the game, Messier had been asked whether he was comfortable with the Rangers' roster.

"We have to do the best we can with the players we've got," he said, "and that's something that's completely out of the players' control. You don't even think about that."

Messier's teammates tried to make excuses for his post-game behavior.

"He's been through everything in this game, and it probably got to a boiling point for him, just one of those nights for him," said Gretzky. "It was one of those games that was tough for everybody, and it gets to the point where you go from being mad to disappointed. He's human, and he does everything from his heart."

Said Campbell: "He's the quintessential leader in all of sports, maybe of all time. When he retires and goes into the Hall of Fame, at the induction ceremony that's what they're going to say. So we should look to Mark when something goes wrong, or after a loss. But I think it's time to look elsewhere in this room. We always look to Mark, ahead of the GM, ahead of the coaches, ahead of the other players. It's time other players lifted their games also, not only on the ice, but as leaders as well."

Messier was in a better mood a few days later. Concerning his behavior after the Montreal game, he explained: "My mother always said, 'If you don't have anything good to say, don't say anything at all.'"

Messier laughed, but his curt remark didn't explain his poor play or the poor play of the Rangers' other top players. So, Campbell treated the team to an unpleasant video presentation: a lowlight film of their many mistakes. Messier and Gretzky were the stars of the film. Campbell followed the video with a 35-minute punishment skate.

Messier couldn't explain why his game had bottomed out. Finally, a reporter asked him directly: "Why have you been so bad?"

"Actually," he said, laughing, "I thought I was playing pretty well until last night. Was I that bad?"

Emotions go up and down in hockey, and the Rangers felt a lot better after their next game, an impressive win over the top-notch Detroit Red Wings. Messier was superlative in the victory. He skated well and was conscientious in all three zones of the ice. Unfortunately, he didn't make it through the game. He suffered a deep thigh bruise after getting hip-checked by Viacheslav Fetisov. Blood would pool in Messier's leg and cause swelling, and the blood would later seep down to his knee, leaving it sore and stiff. His leg wouldn't be right for a while.

■ ■ ■

Messier got a kick out of himself for falling for one of the oldest tricks in hockey in a 4-0 loss to the Devils on March 27. The comic moment told the whole story: The Rangers had a three-on-two. Messier carried the puck down the left wing, but didn't shoot. Valeri Zelepukin of the Devils, who was trailing the play, tapped his stick on the ice and called for the puck. Without looking, Messier passed it to him.

"He yelled, 'Mark,'" Messier said. "He could have yelled. 'Mess.' It's getting a little personal to yell 'Mark.'"

In the final week of the season, the Rangers won a home-and-home series against the Flyers that was highlighted by Zamboni-gate.

The Rangers were taking team pictures on the afternoon of the first game at Madison Square Garden and the session went fifteen minutes over, into the time allotted for the Flyers' morning skate. The Flyers weren't happy. Three days later, when the Rangers showed up in Philadelphia for the rematch, the visiting team's entrance to the building was locked. They had to trudge around to the other side of the building. Then they found two Zambonis parked on the ice at the CoreStates Center. The Rangers didn't get onto the ice until half an hour after they had been scheduled to skate.

Messier recalled two similar incidents from the past. In the first, the visiting team's trainer cut the microphone cord to prevent the home team's lucky anthem singer from singing the national anthem. In another, the Oilers' bus broke down on the way to practice at a suburban Philadelphia arena.

"We figured Bobby Clarke did it," Messier said. "There we were, in our uniforms and equipment, hanging out on somebody's front lawn."

■ ■ ■

Before the playoffs began, Messier delivered his annual speech about how anything less than winning the Stanley Cup would be a failure for the Rangers.

"That's always been my feeling, going into any season," Messier said. "That's just the way I feel about it, and hopefully everybody else does. I'm not talking about just the players, I'm talking about everybody, because it takes everybody."

There was no reason to think the Rangers' 1997 playoff run would be successful. They had finished the season with a record of 38-34-10, fifth overall in the Eastern Conference. They would open the playoffs on the road against the Florida Panthers, who had finished three points ahead of them.

"I've never gone into a season saying, 'I hope we get to the finals,'" Messier said. "It's always been, 'I hope we win the Cup.' There's got to be some kind of goal and you might as well make it a big one, to have some kind of light at the end of the tunnel, something to shoot for. Especially this team. There are a lot of expectations on this team. We were a benchmark for the entire league two years ago. Now we have to find a way to get back."

Incredibly, they almost would.

■ ■ ■

Messier's performance in the playoffs was confounding. At times he was downright bad, making risky, forced passes, playing on the perimeter, taking shortcuts, and leaving the defensive zone early. At times he was a non-factor. And at times, he was pretty good. Those times, however, were few and far between.

He could still lead and make sure his teammates were ready to play. He could skate and win crucial face-offs. But the rest of his game was more inconsistent than it had ever been. Messier scoffed at the idea that he was hurting.

Campbell blamed the natural aging process for Messier's problems and spoke about it as delicately as he could. Others in the organization thought Messier's skills were eroding to the point where there was no way they could justify paying him anything close to the $6 million he had made the three previous seasons.

Messier was a high-maintenance player. He needed to be coddled and included in every personnel decision. He demanded large amounts of ice time. The team's style of play had to be tailored to his. He didn't

191

like the Nemchinov trade. When he didn't like certain players, he forced them out of town. He and Gretzky were against a deal that would have dealt Kovalev and others for power winger Brendan Shanahan. The deal never came off.

Besides, the Rangers knew Messier's playing days were numbered. He was thirty-six. Whether they kept him or let him leave, soon they would have to rebuild. But they felt rebuilding would be impossible with Messier around. And they knew Messier would never accept a lesser role, less ice time, or fewer responsibilities.

Messier had so much power that Campbell had difficulty coaching him. There were times when Campbell sent out Mike Eastwood, a reasonably good penalty killer who could win face-offs and skate well, and Messier would just go out onto the ice. Eastwood would skate back to the bench and Messier would take the face-off. There was no way to reduce Messier's ice time. Meanwhile, Campbell was trying to nurture the younger players in crucial situations.

In the playoffs, Campbell had introduced a defense-first system that was actually the neutral-zone trap. Of course, nobody dared use the words "neutral-zone trap" with Messier around. Roger Neilson, the last Rangers coach to use the trap, had been fired. This time, however, Messier bought into the idea of cutting down the risk-taking.

The simple truth of the whole season, and of most of the previous season, was that when Messier produced, the Rangers were a dangerous team. When he didn't produce, the Rangers weren't very good.

After losing Game One against the Florida Panthers, Campbell called on the other Rangers, besides Messier and Gretzky, to "carry the baton."

"With Mark, we want his leadership in every area, off and on the ice," Campbell said. "There are times during the year when we far too often looked to too few guys on our team, when we should have been looking to ourselves."

Messier hadn't changed his expectations for himself.

"I expect to play well and be a major factor, like every other year I've played," he said. "The team needs me to play well and produce offensively and play a solid game. Leadership is by example. That's always been the best way to lead, so what you do on the ice is what's important."

Messier and Gretzky, the Rangers' leading scorer during the regular season, made speeches to their teammates during a team dinner the night before Game Two. The next day, the Rangers tied the series with a 3-0 victory at Miami Arena. Messier and Gretzky, who had been portrayed by the media as washed-up superstars, had once again become forces capable of recapturing history.

"That's obviously what we're facing now at this stage of our careers," Messier said. "What our predecessors have done before, what someone could or couldn't do at this age, what you've done in the past and can you still do that? For us it's just about trying to find a way to win, and it doesn't matter how you win. You certainly want to be productive. Ten years ago is ten years ago, last year is last year. When we got into this stage of our careers, we didn't really realize we'd have to battle with the twenty years behind us and battle the comparisons we've made for ourselves."

The crucial moment of the series occurred in Game Three at Madison Square Garden. Trailing 3-2, Messier and Gretzky combined to set up Luc Robitaille's tying goal with 18.9 seconds remaining in regulation. Esa Tikkanen won it for the Rangers in overtime. The next night, Gretzky scored all three Rangers goals in a span of 6:23 of the second period and the Rangers won, 3-2.

Game Five belonged to Messier. He was in the mood to play and Gretzky noticed. He, Tikkanen, and Gretzky had shared a cab back to the team hotel after the morning skate and Messier refused to join in the conversation.

"I knew right there he had his game face on," Gretzky said.

Twenty seconds into his first shift, Messier hit Terry Carkner with a solid shoulder check. Moments later, Leetch broke up a play in front of Richter and passed the puck ahead to Tikkanen, who made a touchdown pass down the middle. Messier gathered the pass, sped in on goalie John Vanbiesbrouck, and deposited a backhander between his pads.

As the second period wound down, Messier took a pass from Ulf Samuelsson and rifled a one-footed wrist shot under the crossbar. Then, with the game tied 2-2 in overtime, Messier made a cross-crease pass to Tikkanen, who scored the series-winner.

For the first time since 1988, Messier and Gretzky were on the ice together as winning playoff teammates. After Tikkanen's goal, they hugged for a few minutes, then went off to join the celebration with their other teammates. After a long season, Messier and Gretzky were winners again.

■ ■ ■

The Rangers' next opponent was the New Jersey Devils, who had the best record in the Eastern Conference during the regular season. The Devils showed why they were favored by winning Game One, 2-0, in New Jersey.

Messier set another record when he took his first shift in Game Two. He was playing in his 228th career playoff game. In the four major sports, baseball, hockey, basketball, and football, only NBA standout Kareem Abdul-Jabaar had played in more playoff games, 237.

"It's been an interesting journey, to say the least, from the time I started, to standing here today," Messier said. "But I feel I have a lot more to accomplish. I feel as good as I ever have playing, and I don't need to set any other standards or goals. I can just relax and play year-to-year and enjoy the game while I'm playing."

Although Messier wasn't a major factor in the game, he got the Devils' attention by whacking Doug Gilmour across the forehead with his stick in front of the New Jersey bench.

"He just surprised me," said Messier, who wasn't called for a penalty. "I didn't even know it was Gilmour at the time. I was at the end of a shift, shot the puck in, looked up and somebody was there. I just tried to protect myself."

The Devils were livid. "The worst things are like the cross-check Messier did on Gilmour in front of our bench," Devils coach Jacques Lemaire complained. "That was big time. I feel the referee should take care of the game. You're capable of taking a cheap shot to get the other guy in the box, but when he doesn't get in the box, then you get frustrated and usually you get in the box."

Messier's check turned the series in the Rangers' favor and rendered Gilmour, the Devils' top forward, ineffective the rest of the way.

Although Messier didn't score much in the series, he made his presence known in other ways: In two consecutive games, the Devils had the tying goal disallowed because one of their players was in the goal crease. In the second instance, Lemaire claimed that referee Kerry Fraser wasn't going to ask for assistance from the video replay judge until Messier told him to. NHL rules prohibited teams from requesting video reviews.

"The ref was going to put the puck down for the face-off, and after seeing it on the video screen, everyone was yelling and Messier jumped on the ice," Lemaire said.

Lemaire complained that Messier and Gretzky got preferential treatment. Messier responded that he and Gretzky had been hearing the same stuff "pretty much every year."

Said Campbell of Messier and Gretzky: "They're old, too. They need some help. Other than the linesmen holding their canes when they complain, I think that's absurd to think they get preferential treatment."

The Rangers won both games at the Garden to take a three games to one lead. Messier then helped clinch the series in Game Five in New Jersey. Shortly after hitting the crossbar and being denied what could have been the first playoff overtime goal of his career, Messier withstood a huge check from Randy McKay in order to feed the puck ahead to Graves. Graves carried the puck around the net and stuffed a wraparound shot past goalie Martin Brodeur. The Rangers were headed to the conference finals.

■ ■ ■

The matchup in the Eastern Conference finals was Rangers vs. Flyers, but the focus was on Messier vs. Eric Lindros. Asked if Lindros was meaner than him, Messier laughed and said, "There are many guys a lot meaner than me." Asked whether he saw a lot of himself in Lindros, Messier quipped, "Yeah, except for about five inches and thirty pounds." Actually, Lindros was three inches taller and thirty-one pounds heavier than Messier. He was also twelve years younger.

As they had in the first two rounds, the Rangers lost Game One. Campbell reunited Messier with Gretzky and Tikkanen, so that Graves could play on another line and check Lindros. In Game Two, Gretzky scored three goals in a 5-4 Rangers' win that evened the series. But the win had its price. The Rangers, who had already lost Kovalev, Niklas Sundstrom, Bill Berg, and Pat Flatley to injuries, and were without defenseman Alexander Karpovtsev, lost their best defensemen. Leetch badly jammed his right wrist and suffered ligament damage when he was checked hard by Trent Klatt.

The Rangers tried to hide the injury to Leetch, but they couldn't hide their inability to deal with the much larger Flyers. Messier was a nonfactor in Game Three as Lindros scored three goals in a 6-3 Flyers win.

Messier was grouchy prior to Game Four. The official word on Leetch was that he wasn't hurting badly, but Messier knew otherwise. Leetch was in bad shape, and Messier knew the Rangers had no chance of winning without him. As he worked on his stick outside the locker room, a TV cameraman pointed his camera in Messier's direction. Messier doesn't like being photographed in candid situations and hates having his picture taken when he's not fully dressed. He was wearing only his underwear.

"Hey," Messier hollered to the cameraman, "turn that camera off."

Messier talked about the severity of Leetch's injury and Leetch's toughness.

"You can't intimidate that fuckin' kid," Messier said. "He's got that fuckin' military mentality."

Before Messier went back into the locker room, he noticed that the camera was still pointed at him.

"Hey, I told you to turn that fuckin' camera off," Messier screamed. "I'll shove that fuckin' thing up your fuckin' ass."

Messier wasn't in a better mood after the game. Lindros scored a power play goal with 6.8 seconds remaining in regulation to give the Flyers a 3-2 victory. Two days later, the Flyers closed out the series with a 4-2 victory in Philadelphia.

Campbell had tears in his eyes after the last game. He told the players he was proud of them for their gallant effort in an unexpected playoff run.

Campbell suspected an era was coming to an end. He told the Rangers this was the last time they would be together. Many of the players wouldn't be back for the 1997-98 season.

Messier believed Campbell was talking about him.

■ ■ ■

Messier has a black and white theory about hockey: There's winning and misery. You either win, or you're miserable.

Messier had won in 1994. He was a lot less effective in a 1997 playoff run by the Rangers that, despite his strict standards, was a surprising success.

The worst, however, was to come. The real misery.

16

Back to Canada

For weeks after the Rangers were eliminated by the Flyers, there was no reason to believe Messier had played his final game as a Ranger. He would sign a new contract. He would never become an unrestricted free agent. He and Gretzky would play together for at least another year.

"I really don't think it's going to be a problem," Gretzky said. "Mark and the Rangers will sit down and somehow find a way to make it work. I know they want him, and I know Mark loves New York, so I don't think it will be a problem."

Neil Smith agreed.

"I don't think it's a difficult decision, whether we want to bring him back," he said "It should be a question that answers itself. As a hockey player, there is no decision. We'd love to have him back."

But at what price?

"You have to determine your ceiling for each and every player and at what point you're going to have a stalemate," Smith said, "It's still a business."

On team breakup day, when the players cleaned out their lockers and left for the summer, Messier said the same things he had been saying for the past two years: He reiterated that he didn't need to be the highest-paid Ranger. All he wanted was a fair contract. And he wasn't worried about getting one. He absolutely wanted to remain with the Rangers.

"I'll take a couple weeks or a month off now, and everything will get straightened out," he said. "After a long season, it's no time to make any decision. But I don't see any problem getting something worked out with the Garden and coming back and trying again. I'll just stand by and wait my turn. There are a lot of people to be addressed, not only with hockey but with basketball. I'll just wait my turn."

The owners of the Rangers were also the owners of the Knicks, and Patrick Ewing, the Knicks' star center, was about to become a free agent, too. His contract would be astronomical.

"I haven't even thought about playing anywhere else," Messier continued. "I've had a great relationship through the six years I've been here and I don't see any problem getting it worked out. It really doesn't matter to me if it's worked out before July 1 or after. I know how the Garden works, and you have to be patient. When your number's up, you'll take care of business. That's the way it's been since I've been here. That's good news, that it's just a matter of time and being patient.

"I don't think it's a pressing issue, that I'm demanding this or that," Messier added. "Both sides have to feel good about it, you know? They have a budget and they have to work within it, and their job is to win and to ice the best possible team. All those things, you have to think of their side, too, and what they're trying to accomplish. That's what negotiating is, just trying to find a happy medium, where everybody's comfortable.

"I'm playing now for the enjoyment and the winning. I don't need a three-year deal. I don't need the security. I'm secure enough financially. Loyalty, for me, is important."

Rand Araskog, the chief executive officer of ITT, which owned the Garden, took notice when Messier said he didn't need a multi-year deal and didn't have to be the highest-paid player on the Rangers. Araskog ordered Garden president Dave Checketts and Smith to offer Messier $4 million for one year. That's what the Rangers were paying Gretzky, and Araskog couldn't see paying anybody more than the greatest player in hockey history.

"Why would we offer him more than Gretzky?" Araskog asked Smith. "That should be the deal. He's thirty-six years old."

Smith knew the offer would anger Doug Messier. Both Smith and Checketts felt Doug Messier had bullied them in the 1994 contract negotiations, when the Messiers asserted their right to renegotiate the contract, even though the contract merely gave them the right to request a renegotiation. Smith also felt he had been fair when Messier first arrived in 1991 by giving him a big new contract. Both times, Doug had made a long list of extra demands for the contract: limousine service, club seats, and a luxury suite. Doug's demands and hard-nosed bargaining had angered management in 1994.

The Rangers felt they had rewarded Messier handsomely for delivering the Cup even though they were under no obligation to do so. Now they were hoping for some appreciation in return. They were hoping that Messier would accept a pay cut that kept him at the same salary Gretzky was making.

Doug Messier had other ideas. He refused to negotiate with the Rangers from May 25, when the Rangers were eliminated by the Flyers, until after July 1, when Mark became a free agent.

Shortly after July 1, Smith called Doug Messier and offered $4 million for one year. Doug responded by calling the offer insulting and disrespectful. He threatened to talk to other teams.

But threatening Smith wasn't in Doug Messier's best interests. Smith had been Mark's biggest ally since 1994, when Bob Gutkowski was forced to resign as MSG president and replaced by Checketts.

Meanwhile, the Knicks signed Ewing to a four-year contract worth $68 million. Mark understood that the NBA was different from the NHL, and that the Knicks and basketball generated far more revenue than the Rangers and hockey. Besides, thanks to the NBA's complex salary cap rules, the Knicks had to choose between paying Ewing $17 million a year or replacing him with a lesser player. They really had no choice but to meet Ewing's demands.

But it wasn't the size of Ewing's contract that bothered Messier. What hurt the most was that Checketts signed Ewing within hours of becoming a free agent. The Rangers hadn't made their lowball contract offer to Messier until days after he became a free agent.

On July 7, Messier was far out in the Atlantic Ocean off of Hilton Head, fishing with Richter and Leetch, when he learned that the Rangers had signed free agent forwards Mike Keane and Brian Skrudland. Richter, Leetch, and Messier exchanged high fives, feeling the Rangers had beefed up their roster. Messier figured he'd be next.

But the situation worsened. On July 14, Messier was angered by a report in the *Daily News* that claimed progress was being made in his contract negotiations. Messier thought the story had been planted by the Rangers. He arranged a conference call to reporters in which he announced that he would begin entertaining offers from other teams. He estimated that at least fifteen other teams were interested in his services, including the Islanders, Flyers, Canadiens, Canucks, Red Wings, and Capitals.

In reality, none of those teams had made an actual offer because they felt it was a waste of time. They simply assumed Messier was going to re-sign with the Rangers.

"We never even talked," Messier said, summing up his contact with Smith between May 27 and July 14. "Neil was down here [in Hilton Head] and never even visited. You know, come over for a beer. I mean, we put six good years in. I mean, show a little bit of respect."

Retorted Smith: "I don't think that it's disrespectful. I wasn't invited over. I mean, does [New Jersey general manager] Lou Lamoriello go to Scott Stevens' condo for a beer? I like the guy, and I'd love to have dinner with him. I think it's flattering, actually, that he wanted me to come over."

Smith felt he would be uncomfortable going to Messier's house, knowing how unhappy Mark and Doug had been with the Rangers' contract offer.

"I said at the end of the year that the Rangers are the team I want to finish my career with, or at least next year," Messier said. "But there doesn't seem to be any interest with the Rangers. To have to become a free agent and not have any interest from the Rangers is a little bit disappointing to us. So it's time to see what interest there is throughout the league. The Rangers don't seem to be part of the equation at this time. I thought we'd sit down and talk like men and professionals. That hasn't been the case."

Asked how far down the Garden's totem pole of priorities he had fallen, Messier said: "I don't even think I'm on the totem pole. The Rangers have shown zero interest." He hadn't heard from Checketts. "I don't know what they're thinking. Now, when I start talking to teams, I'll find out what my value should be. Obviously, the market is going to dictate where my value is. The Rangers and I could have set that. I didn't think we'd have to get into all this posturing.

"I'm a big boy. If I'm not in their plans, all they've got to do is let me know. I know I've got a lot of hockey left. I know I'm going to be playing somewhere next season."

Messier had delivered his message loud and clear.

Eight days later, with no progress being made, Messier sounded as if he was preparing for life after the Rangers. He called his first experience in free agency a "nightmare."

"We've gotten quite a few offers," Messier said. "We're trying to decipher through them all and see what comes up. I think there have been some really strong offers. Like I said before, I didn't expect to be in this position, so I've had to sit back and take them all in. Once we sit down and look at the offers and see what's going on, I'll have a better idea what's going to happen, in New York or wherever.

"The offers have been very strong, to say the least. Obviously there are some teams that feel I can help them and do a lot of things for them. That's where we are right now."

Despite what Messier was saying, the offers from the Islanders, Capitals, and Red Wings were for the same or less money than the Rangers had offered.

Meanwhile, a rumor came out of Canada that the Vancouver Canucks were about to offer Messier a long-term deal, perhaps worth $6 million or more for three guaranteed years. Vancouver had been burned by the Rangers in the previous year's bidding for Gretzky. The Canucks' offer had been for more money than the Rangers', but Gretzky chose New York nonetheless. This time, the Canucks and owner John McCaw Jr. had no intention of losing.

The Rangers upped their offer to $4.6 million for one year, with an option for a second year. Messier told his friends that had the Rangers made the same offer during the season, he would have signed a contract on the spot.

By now, however, everything had changed. The damage had been done. Messier recalled the organization's subtle remarks about his age, the $2 million pay cut the Rangers had offered, and that they wanted to give him only a one-year contract. He remembered Smith's snub in Hilton Head and lack of interest the Rangers had shown in signing him since he became a free agent.

He came to a difficult conclusion.

"They don't want me," he told Richter and Leetch.

Messier was stunned and hurt. He wondered if the Rangers were merely making offers as a public relations ploy, to make it appear as if they wanted to keep him when they really didn't. Certainly, although Smith, Checketts, and Campbell insisted they wanted Messier to return, they also sounded as if they didn't think he could help them for more than another year. At times, they sounded as if his presence on the team would be detrimental. The only reason Smith wanted Messier back was because it would be wrong for him to finish his career anywhere else.

Messier knew how to take a hint. He wasn't staying where he wasn't wanted for any price. He told Leetch: "All they've got to say to me is, 'Mark, thank you very much, we're just going to go in a different direction.' I can understand that. This is a business."

Said Leetch: "We talk about him being very respectful. That's what hurt me, and it hurt me to see his reaction. The way he treated everybody, and the way he approached things with a lot of respect, that's all he needed."

Orca Bay, which owned the Canucks, turned up the pressure. CEO John Chapple and Canucks general manager Pat Quinn visited Hilton Head, where they wined and dined Messier. They told him they would stay on the island for as long as it took to get a deal done. They flew Mark, Doug, and Paul Messier to San Francisco on a private jet. They took him out on John McCaw's yacht.

Mark was impressed. His accountant, Barry Klarberg, told him: "These guys make deals bigger than you every day."

Vancouver's offer was staggering: Three guaranteed years at $6 million per year, plus options for two more years. If the Canucks wanted out after three years, they would have to pay Messier another $2 million. That meant their offer was for a minimum of three years and $20 million, or a maximum of five years and $30 million.

The Canucks had blown the Rangers, and every other competitor, out of the water. There was no way the Rangers were going to pay Messier that kind of money. There was no way they were going to offer a third year.

The Canucks told Messier that they didn't want to get involved in a bidding war with the Rangers, as they had the previous year in the Gretzky negotiations. They didn't want him taking their offer back to the Rangers.

But Doug Messier placed one last call to Smith from San Francisco. He asked Smith if the Rangers were willing to offer $10 million over two years, as newspapers had reported, or whether their offer was for one year at $4.6 million. Money, Doug Messier told Smith, wasn't the issue. The issue was the length of the contract.

"Is $4.6 million your offer?" Doug Messier asked.

"Yes," Smith said. "Four point six."

"Thank you very much," Doug replied.

He hung up the phone. The next thing Smith heard was a click and a dial tone. Messier was no longer a Ranger. He was a Canuck. His six years in New York were over.

Messier officially signed with the Canucks on July 28, 1997. He spent the rest of the summer at home in Hilton Head, trying to understand how everything had gone so wrong. For a guy who was about to make at least $20 million, he wasn't very happy. A month later, a reporter called him at his Hilton Head home.

"How ya doing?" the reporter asked.

"I'll be all right," Messier answered.

He was, in fact, absolutely miserable.

■ ■ ■

Having lost the most popular player in franchise history, the Rangers went into damage control mode. Checketts said the Rangers were prepared to go higher if Messier had given them a chance to make their final offer.

"For some reason, the owner in Vancouver decided they would pay whatever it took to get the deal done," Checketts said. "Twenty million shocked twenty-six teams, I'm sure. He hit the Lotto, so it's time for him to move on now."

Said Smith: "Obviously, we didn't throw enough money at him to make him stay. I mean, if we threw the same money at him that Vancouver did, he would have stayed. He wanted to stay. He also wanted a huge contract. I can't tell you how disappointed I am that Mark's not going to be on our team. Even if Mark's heart is in New York, how does an individual turn down something that substantial? Boy, that's a chance of a lifetime. To be honest I would never have imagined that number coming from a Canadian team, and there were twenty-four other teams that felt similarly, because nobody else was in that kind of competition. But it only takes one."

Checketts accused Messier of being disloyal to the Rangers.

"Respect is a two-way street," he said. "After we won the Cup in '94, we only had an obligation to talk about a new contract, and we did one for $18 million for three years. Through the whole process, we listened to him in terms of the players he wanted around him. We felt we earned respect from him. I didn't offer him $20 million for three years. Everything short of financial lunacy, I think we did offer him. And we wanted him back, But he made a different decision. It was done, and he's on his way.

"This is crazy money, that's all I can say, and I believe in crazy money. In some circles, I'm known for paying it but, man alive, I don't believe this one."

Checketts appeared on a talk radio show in New York and was asked why Ewing, who had never won a championship, was worth $68 million, while Messier, who had won a championship, was allowed to get away.

"How long do I have to keep paying for that Stanley Cup?" Checketts snapped.

The *New York Daily News* was squarely on management's side. The day after Messier signed, the *News'* back page headline read: "NOT WORTH THE MONEY!" When the Canucks' offer became public, influential columnist Mike Lupica wrote: "Messier, who has always seemed so different, began to look exactly like everybody else. He also began to look like a phony . . . This is about money, always was."

Leetch, who would succeed Messier as captain of the Rangers, was heartbroken over his friend's departure.

"The amount of money Vancouver ended up offering Mark is a huge amount," he said. "My only opinion on the subject is I don't think it had to get to that point. Mark wanted to stay a Ranger. It could have been done sooner. The Rangers were put in a tough position as far as Vancouver being able to put their offer on the table."

Messier finally decided that moving on without hard feelings was best for everyone.

"I lived out a dream come true," he said. "Those six years are years I'll never forget. I'll never forget the cheers I got my first game there, or the Stanley Cup, the friends I met throughout the city. All those things made it tough to make the decision I had to make. It's never easy. I have nothing derogatory to say about the whole situation there. Things change. What can you say?"

Gretzky couldn't believe that Messier was gone and that their reunion had lasted only one year.

"I never thought we'd separate the first time," Gretzky said. "And I never, ever, ever thought we'd separate the second time. It was devastating when Mark left. If I had known he would leave, I never would have signed here."

■ ■ ■

Messier found himself in the middle of two minor controversies when he arrived in Vancouver. Trevor Linden, a respected, popular player, was the captain of the Canucks. Did Messier expect Linden to give up the "C?"

"No," he said.

Then there was the matter of Messier's No. 11, which had been worn by only one player in Canucks history: Wayne Maki, who died of a brain tumor shortly after retiring in 1973. Maki's number was never retired, but no Vancouver player had worn it since.

Messier said he would speak with the Maki family in the hope of getting their blessing to wear No. 11. The family refused permission, but the Canucks gave it to him anyway. The Makis were livid when Messier wore No. 11 at his introductory press conference.

The Canucks got their man in Messier, but he failed to be the savior they were hoping for. The Rangers were awful without Messier's leadership, speed, and offense. The Canucks were no better. Both teams missed the playoffs in 1997-98, Messier for only the second time in his career. Messier scored only 60 points, his worst full season since 1984-85, when he scored 54 points in only fifty-five games.

■ ■ ■

But perhaps there weren't as many tears over the separation of Gretzky and Messier as one what have imagined. By the time Messier left for Vancouver, his relationship with Gretzky was strained. The families were rumored to be feuding. Rangers coaches, players, and even Neil Smith felt Messier was having trouble sharing the spotlight with Gretzky.

The rumor mill worked overtime with speculation that Messier was mad at Gretzky for not going to bat for him during his contract quarrel with the Rangers, and that Gretzky was insulted that Messier had been insulted by being offered the same money as he was making.

Both players denied that there was any trouble between them. Simply, Gretzky said, Messier was single, while he had a wife and three kids. Of course they didn't hang out together like they used to, but they were still great friends.

At the 1998 All-Star Game in Vancouver, several newspapers reported that the long relationship between Messier and Gretzky had fallen apart. Messier added fuel to the fire by saying that he had stayed in touch with Leetch and Richter, both of whom visited his Vancouver home during All-Star Weekend, but he hadn't stayed in touch with Gretzky. Nonetheless, Messier was angry over the speculation that he was no longer Gretzky's friend.

"That's ridiculous," Messier said privately. "What is that about? That's just awful."

When asked if he and Messier were still close, Gretzky replied: "Oh yeah. No question about it. It's so ridiculous. People try to create, or want to stir up, some kind of emotion, or a spectacle that's not there. How, after twenty years of playing together, can all of a sudden after one month, somebody say, 'They're not getting along?' That's so ridiculous. The first person he called when he left last summer was Janet and I. He said, 'I want to tell you guys because you came here.' And, no question, I came here for two reasons: I wanted to play for the Rangers and I wanted to play with Mark. It's really disheartening when people try to get in the middle of something that's so off base, so not true."

"The difference is Michael [Richter] and Leetchie are single," Gretzky added. "People sometimes fail to remember I've got a family, I've got kids. I went to the All-Star Game with my son. They were going to dinner Friday night before the skills competition, and I had a Team Canada meeting. They both played for the American squad and had nothing going on, and they went to dinner. Why would I have not gone? I would have gone. We sat beside each other in the locker room. I don't understand why people create this whole thing. People read too much into these things. Don't get me wrong. I wish he were still here. I'm disappointed he's not here. But I'm not mad at him. I probably understand the situation even better than he does, because I did the same thing in Edmonton."

The All-Star Game provided a magical moment between Gretzky and Messier. Messier had turned thirty-seven on the day of the game. Gretzky was a week shy of his thirty-seventh birthday. They combined on what turned out to be the winning goal in North America's 8-7 win over the World All-Stars at GM Place.

In the third period, with North America leading, 7-5, Gretzky made a perfect lead pass to Messier, who already had a step on another former Oilers legend, Jari Kurri. Messier shot a rocket of a backhander under the crossbar behind goalie Nikolai Khabibulin.

Messier pumped his fist in an uncharacteristic celebration as Gretzky skated over to him. They hugged and Gretzky whispered in his ear.

"I told him to check his birth certificate after he scored," Gretzky said. "Maybe he's only twenty-seven."

Later in the game, Messier and Gretzky killed a penalty, then worked a pretty give-and-go to perfection, only to have Khabibulin stop Messier's shot.

"I didn't have to yell for him to pass it," Messier said. "You know, Wayne sees everything out there. There is just some magic sometimes that happens, and it never goes away. For whatever reason, the years we spent together in Edmonton, the style that we played, I don't think that ever really goes away. Sometimes that magic happens between players. I think that we worked at it to make that magic happen over the years. But it felt like it was just yesterday when we were doing it before."

Gretzky and Messier realized they might have shared the ice as teammates for the final time, especially since Messier had already been snubbed by Team Canada general manager Bobby Clarke for a spot on the Olympic team. Messier had dearly wanted to go to Nagano, Japan, and represent Canada and the NHL in the Olympics, but he accepted the snub without complaint.

The Gretzky-Messier reunion hadn't been as sweet for Messier in October, when the Rangers visited GM Place for the first time. Gretzky scored three goals in a 6-3 win for the Rangers. After the game, the Canucks closed their locker room doors for a players-only meeting. Asked whether the team meeting consisted of him talking and his teammates listening, Messier said, "I hope they were listening."

"There's an awful lot of things going on here in Vancouver, and a lot of work to do, and we have to build ourselves up," Messier said. "I was looking at the game as a measuring stick against the team that is quite possibly favored to win the Stanley Cup. I enjoyed my six years in New York, but I have deep responsibilities to this team, and hopefully I can do the things I was able to do in Edmonton and New York. But nothing's going to happen overnight. You don't build a winning program in four hockey games, We have to continue to try to do things the right way and slowly build a foundation. It took a long time in Edmonton and it took a long time in New York. This is like when I went from Edmonton to New York."

Playing against the Rangers was emotional for Messier, but it was nothing compared to the Canucks' visit to the Garden on November 25. By that time, Canucks coach Tom Renney had been fired and replaced by Mike Keenan. Canucks general manager Pat Quinn had also been fired, so Keenan was temporarily handling both jobs.

Messier's return was an emotional night. The love affair between Messier and the fans had not ended. When the Canucks took the ice for the start of the game, he was greeted with loud cheers and several banners. Some read:

"He came. He saw. He won. Thanks Mess."

"Management's MessTake."

"This is the house that Mark built."

"11 . . . Forever our captain."

Rangers management did the right thing by Messier. They put together a video tribute, accompanied by Carole King's song, "Now and Forever," and played it on the big video boards hanging above center ice. When the video was played prior to the opening face-off, there might not have been a dry eye in the Garden. Messier cried. Referee Don Koharski and his two linesmen had to console Messier and make sure he was okay for the opening face-off. He wasn't. His swollen red eyes teared throughout the first shift.

"I couldn't see," Messier admitted afterward. "I didn't think I had any tears left after this summer. It was the toughest decision I've ever had to make."

He was asked if he regretted leaving that part of his career behind.

"No," he said. "I know why I left it behind."

The night was perfect for Messier. He scored a goal against Richter and the Canucks won, 4-2.

■ ■ ■

Messier's first two years in Vancouver were difficult. He was perceived by his teammates as being more loyal to Keenan than he was to them. Linden, who had given up the captainship to Messier, and Gino Odjick, Linden's long-time friend, were traded to the Islanders, prompting Odjick to accuse Messier of trying to run the team.

"He didn't break a sweat for the first ten games and just waited for Tom Renney and Pat Quinn to get fired," said Odjick, who was very popular in Vancouver. "He talks to the ownership all the time and he's responsible for Keenan being here and he's part of trades."

In Vancouver, the fans and the media were no longer certain that Messier was a savior. He was injury prone, slowed by a hyperextended elbow that limited what he could do with the puck. That only exaggerated his shortcomings without the puck.

In his second season with Vancouver, Messier suffered a concussion after colliding with the goalpost, then missed more than a month with a knee injury. He returned and almost immediately suffered a groin pull that cost him a few more games on the sidelines.

Messier played in only fifty-nine games in 1998-99 and scored only 48 points. The Canucks finished with the worst record in the Western

Conference. For the first time in his career, Messier missed the play-offs two years in a row.

Along the way, Keenan was fired by new Canucks general manager Brian Burke and replaced by former Colorado coach Marc Crawford.

Despite all of Messier's troubles and injuries in Vancouver, by the end of his twentieth NHL season he was still hitting major milestones. He played in his 1,400th career game. His 610 career goals tied him for seventh with Bobby Hull. Messier had 1,050 assists, which put him ahead of Marcel Dionne and Gordie Howe for fourth place all-time. And, with 1,660 points, Messier was fourth on that all-time list, trailing only Dionne, Howe, and Gretzky.

■ ■ ■

Then, in April, Gretzky phoned Messier and told him he was retiring. The Rangers, too, had missed the playoffs for the second year in a row, and although Gretzky led the team in scoring, he had missed twelve games because of injuries.

Gretzky's retirement ceremony was held on the final day of the 1998-99 season at Madison Square Garden. Gretzky had been fighting his emotions for days, but he got teary-eyed when he saw Messier before the game.

Messier, too, had been fighting back the tears since Gretzky had broken the news to him. His best friend in hockey was retiring. An era was coming to an end. They had spent twenty years together in hockey, and now one of them was retiring. Messier couldn't help but reflect. For him, it was both a happy and a sad occasion. His friend was retiring on top.

Gretzky stood on the ice for the retirement ceremony and watched as family members, friends, and former teammates wished him well. When Messier stepped onto the ice, the Garden crowd erupted with cheers. Gretzky and Messier were together again, for the last time.

And when NHL commissioner Gary Bettman announced that the entire league would retire Gretzky's No. 99, Gretzky said that his number should not be raised to the Garden's roof until after Messier's No. 11 went up there.

Afterward, Messier tried to not get emotional when asked about his friendship with Gretzky.

"Well, you know, Wayne and I grew up together as 18-year-olds and going through the things we did in Edmonton obviously cemented a bond between us that is next to being brothers," Messier said. "There was so much pressure on him, and he knew he had some friends that he was able to talk to when we were younger, and where he could be himself, he could be Wayne Gretzky inside the dressing room. And I think that because of that, and because of the championships, and because of the things that we were able to do, not only on the ice but off the ice as well, but especially on the ice when the pressure was on and we were able to somehow find a way to win, those friendships are really cemented by those occasions.

"You know, obviously when you're not playing on the same team, it's harder to stay in as much contact with anybody, whether it's Kevin Lowe, who's one of my best friends, or Paul Coffey or whatever, all the guys. But, you know, we've established a friendship and a bond that's next to brotherhood and will be there forever."

Gretzky and Messier. There had never been another player like Gretzky. There had never been another player quite like Messier. There may never be another one like him again.

"It's hard to make it sound like more than a friend patting him on the back," Leetch said. "He's one of those guys you're just really lucky to be his friend and involved with his life. But trying to describe him, it's hard to do him justice to those who haven't met him."